# GET ON BOARD!

INDIGORIVER
PUBLISHING

# GET ON BOARD!

Interviews with the Soul Train Dancers
1971-1975

STEPHEN MCMILLIAN

*Get on Board: Interviews with the Soul Train Dancers 1971-1975*


Library of Congress Control Number: 2025951153
ISBN: 978-1-969935-01-5 (hardcover) 978-1-969935-13-8 (paperback)
978-1-969935-02-2 (ebook)

*Get on Board: Interviews with the Soul Train Dancers 1971-1975* is not affiliated with the current owner of Soul Train, BET Networks, nor is it affiliated with Soul Train Holdings or any of its affiliates.

This work is based on the personal reflections and recollections of the dancers interviewed by the author between 2011and 2019. Some information may have changed since the interviews took place. While every effort has been made to present their accounts accurately, memory is inherently subjective and may be influenced by time and perspective. The author does not claim to provide a definitive or exhaustive record of events but rather a faithful representation of the experiences shared. Interviews have been edited for clarity and brevity.

Editors: Deborah Froese
Cover and Interior Design: Emma Elzinga

Printed in the United States of America

First Edition

3 West Garden Street, Ste. 718
Pensacola, FL 32502
www.indigoriverpublishing.com

Ordering Information:

Quantity sales: Special discounts are available on quantity purchases by corporations, associations, and others. For details, contact the publisher at the address above.

Orders by US trade bookstores and wholesalers: Please contact the publisher at the address above.

With Indigo River Publishing, you can always expect great books, strong voices, and meaningful messages. Most importantly, you'll always find . . . *words worth reading.*

I dedicate this book to my mom, Evelyn McMillian, who is the reason I began watching *Soul Train* in the first place on those Saturday mornings when she turned to Channel 5 at 11 a.m. to watch between my Saturday morning cartoons.

I also dedicate this book in memory of Adolfo "Shabba Doo" Quinones, who helped me to get this book deal.
Dance on for eternity, my friend.

# Contents

# Foreword

By sharing this book with the world, Stephen McMillian is giving us a precious gift. It's a fun, informative, and truly educational gift, long overdue. It provides readers with never-before-shared input about an era and young people who literally changed the world. They gave it a blueprint for a culture's *creative genius*: its style of dance and style of dress.

But reading this book gives you, dear reader, an even deeper insight if you choose to wake up and see it. Through interviews presented by the author—someone who was actually there on that *Soul Train* scene while history was being made—you get new insight on a movement. The movement had begun years before, but it culminated with new opportunities being made available to Black African Americans. Through *Soul Train*—and the awesome dancers who truly made that show what it was—the world witnessed an evolution and continuing revolution that, indeed, was televised! Multi-millions are thankful for that!

At the time of this televised revolution, accomplished by the tireless struggles and successes of the pre-Civil Rights Movement, you saw beautiful, joyous, free young people having a great and enviable time when you turned on your TV on Saturday mornings. These dancers, and *Soul Train* in general, were thankful beneficiaries of a hard-earned struggle to be an integral, successful, visible, and respected part of America's society.

The cameras captured the true stars of *Soul Train*: these young people, with their skillful and unique dress styles and dance creations—which are still imitated to this day, some fifty years later! But this book also captures their voices, thoughts, and opinions, some which have never been shared before. You'll get to marvel and know them in a way you never expected all those years ago. (I do know a little about them; I proudly first gave many of them a voice of recognition as the editor of *Right On! Magazine.)*

— **Flo S. Jenkins**, Author of *Telling Our Stories Ourselves*, Editorial Consultant, Former Editor of *Right On! Magazine*

# Preface

When you think about *Soul Train*, the first thing that comes to people's minds is the dancing, music, and fashion of the era. Often times, we think about the glitz and glamour but hardly the *Soul Train* culture.

The late great Don Cornelius gave us the timeless catch phrase, "Love, Peace and Soul," that will forever be tied with the show and connected the culture to mainstream society. As a child, I watched *Soul Train* with my father every Saturday. Don't get me wrong, *Soul Train* of the eighties was very entertaining, but I fell in love with the program when they showed *The Best of Soul Train* and focused on the episodes of the seventies featuring the Robot Campbell Locking. Even years later, as an adult in my early forties, I'm still a Locker and a Robot. That just shows how much watching *Soul Train* has had an effect on my life. Today, we have television shows like *American Soul* that dramatize in cinematic form the mystical origins of *Soul Train* to introduce a new generation to the *Soul Train* phenomenon. But the new shows are not historically accurate.

This book, however, *is*. In it you will hear from dancers and onlookers alike. So, if you want to hear the truth from the horse's mouth, gaze your peepers into this book and let your mind dance across the pages as if they were a dance floor, and get down to the real happenings going down.

— **Orlando Henry a.k.a. Lando Magic**, Co-Founder and co-owner of FlameOnRadio, www.flameonradio.live

# Introduction

Never in my wildest dreams did I ever think that me, a shy freckled faced kid from the rough inner-city section of Jersey City, New Jersey, would one day become a Soul Train dancer, much less enter show business.

Like many people, I watched *Soul Train* for many years, intrigued by the various dancers and the guest artists that came to the show, as well as the show's features including the Soul Train Scramble Board and the Soul Train Line and, of course, its esteemed host, Don Cornelius.

Although I was a very shy child, I still had a great love for music and entertainment, thanks to my parents, other relatives, and family friends. I had some moments dancing at home with my family and around other relatives, but for the most part, I didn't dance. I just observed others. Over the years, I marveled at Soul Train dancers including Patricia Davis, Jimmy "Scoo B Doo" Foster, The Lockers, Fawn Quniones, James Phillips, Tyrone "the Bone" Proctor, Sharon Hill, Mr. X (the excitable dancer with the giant toothbrush. I truly admired him!), Cheryl Song, Jeffrey Daniels, Jody Watley, Odis Medley (the man with the masks and costume), Thomas Evans, Reggie Thornton, Louie Carr, and many others.

Also, I was—and still am—a huge fan of The Jackson 5, The Jacksons, and Michael Jackson as a solo artist. When the Jacksons performed "Dancing Machine" on various television shows, I was mesmerized, totally in awe of Michael's Robot dancing. I also was a fan of the famed mime couple Shields & Yarnell; Gene Anthony Ray of the movie and television show *Fame*; C3PO from the *Star Wars* movies for his robotic movements; as well as various breakdancers and pop lock dancers.

When I was a toddler, my family and I would attend Arthur Mitchell's famed Dance Theatre of Harlem troupe rehearsals. I enjoyed seeing the dancers' graceful movements and subconsciously took notes.

After graduating from Morgan State University, I broke out of my shell and started going to clubs and dance parties in the New York City area. When the music hit me, I would go out on the dance floor and let everything I had absorbed over the years come out. I gained a little notoriety over those years. When I would be traveling to work, passersby would ask, "Weren't you at the dance party last Saturday?" or "Didn't I see you at the club last weekend?"

For a late bloomer like me, that was humbling. With newly found confidence, I decided to find out how to become a dancer on *Soul Train*. I called Don Cornelius Productions in Los Angeles and asked about the procedure. I was told to send a photo and letter to the show's dance coordinator, Eric Casem. I did this about three times and heard nothing back. So, after the third time, I called and asked to speak to Eric directly. As fate would have it, he just happened to be in the office at the time. We spoke and connected, and the rest is history.

I will never forget a conversation I had with Fred "Rerun" Berry from The Lockers and *What's Happening*! TV program. In the late nineties, he had moved to New York to open an acting school called Rerun's Acting School. I was one of his students. Knowing that he used to dance on *Soul Train*, I asked for advice about being a dancer on the show. He simply told me "Dance your ass off!"

Noted.

By the time I became a dancer on the show, it was taped at Paramount Studios, Stage 30. Because I still lived in New Jersey at that time, I flew back and forth once a month from New Jersey to Los

Angeles for six years. They taped four shows back-to-back one weekend out of every month. When word got around that I traveled across country every month to dance on the show, I was dubbed *Soul Train's* most dedicated dancer. When the show had a taping the weekend after the 9/11 terrorist attacks, I was concerned but still flew out to Los Angeles. All the dancers chanted my name in unison for still coming to the show despite the height of terrorism fears. I was so gratified.

I came on when comedian Mystro Clark was the host, followed by Emmy Award winning actor Shemar Moore, and then Dorian Gregory, the program's final host. This was at the height of what was called the "neo soul" era, and I saw some great artists come to the show such as Musiq Soulchild, Alicia Keys, Jill Scott, Angie Stone, and Anthony Hamilton. I also saw new and upcoming rappers such as Ludacris and Nelly & the St. Lunatics, as well as legendary rappers like Naughty By Nature, Queen Latifah, and P. Diddy and iconic legends like The Temptations, The Isley Brothers, Jeffrey Osborne, and Freddie Jackson.

I basically did freestyle dancing along with my main moves, locking and roboting. I remember both Nelly & the St. Lunatics and Diddy really liked my Robot dancing. When I was back in Jersey, walking through my neighborhood, I was totally surprised by little boys who had seen me on the show and enthusiastically asked me to do the Robot. I would always oblige. I was happy that my family and friends enjoyed seeing me on *Soul Train*. My maternal grandparents watched the show, and my grandmother kept a photo of me on the show in her purse and would show it to her neighbors and refer to me as her "Soul Train boy."

Like all of the dancers, I too had my share of the fried chicken after the long tapings, although when the show had its thousandth episode, the dancers weren't served chicken any longer. Instead, we were treated to an exquisite lunch at Paramount Studios' commissary that weekend. From that time on, a craft food service was set up for the dancers and crew outside Stage 30 with a variety of sandwiches, hot meals, pastries, and fruit—and no more chicken! I guess it was like the old saying,

"From grits to groceries!"

It was also wonderful to be able to attend the annual Soul Train Music Awards and the great after parties.

I am truly thankful to God for making it possible for me to be a part of what is the longest-running syndicated music program in television history. Moreover, this freckled faced kid from New Jersey is forever thankful to be a part of a group of soulful brothers and sisters who, like me, got a chance to shine every week before millions of viewers.

# The Soul Train Gang

When you think of the 1970s, many things come to mind such as the end of the Vietnam War, Watergate, gas shortages and the oil crisis, "Tricky Dick," The Jackson 5, eight-tracks, large Afros, platform shoes, polyester leisure suits, and great soul, funk, and disco music. There was also the so-called "blaxploitation" movie craze that included classic films like *Shaft*, *Superfly*, *Coffy*, and *The Mack*, as well as TV shows like *Good Times*, *The Jeffersons*, and *What's Happening!* And let's not forget the acclaimed Emmy-winning miniseries *Roots* and a funky locomotive called *Soul Train*.

The brainchild of Don Cornelius, *Soul Train* began as a local weekday television show in Chicago on UHF channel 26, debuting on August 17, 1970, and ending in June 1976. It moved to Los Angeles in 1971. By October of that year, it aired across several US television markets in national syndication. By 1972 and onward, it aired in many other major markets in the U.S..

Special recognition must be given to the dancers who appeared in the first national episode, dancers such as Jan Hunter, Rodney Moss, Steven Lott, Phyllis Bradley, Lynn Jackson, and Anthony Crandle. Jan Hunter and Rodney Moss were largely responsible for getting many students from their school, Los Angeles High School, to appear on the first national episode that aired on October 2, 1971.From the start, millions of viewers tuned in every Saturday to see not only the recording artists but also the dancers. Because *Soul Train* was a dance show, many viewers watched the program primarily for its dancers who were initially called the Soul Train Gang. In 1975, when Cornelius and his business and producing partner, Dick Griffey, formed a musical group on their Soul Train Records label called the Soul Train Gang, the television program's dancers were simply called the Soul Train Dancers from that time on. Viewers across the country marveled at the dances the Soul Train Gang displayed weekly and would go to clubs and parties executing what they saw them do on television.

*Soul Train*'s early dancers were, and still are, the roots of the show and influenced the dancers that came afterward. The kinetic and exciting dance moves the Soul Train Gang created and brought to the program—such as the Breakdown, Locking, and the Robot—are still revered. They influence younger generations to this very day, many of whom were not even born when *Soul Train* originally aired. But thanks to YouTube and reruns of the program some years ago, many younger dancers have been watching... and learning.

It is very important to chronicle and preserve history accurately. Far too often, history is either lost, stolen, or misconstrued. For instance, the moonwalk, made world famous by Michael Jackson, was reportedly first displayed by famed vaudevillian performer and tap dancer Bill Bailey in the early 1940s. There is footage of Bailey doing this move, which was initially known as the Backslide. There is also footage from the late 1930s of young Black men doing dance routines that would years later be known as breakdancing. On that same note, many younger people in the US and overseas are doing the dances done by the Soul Train Gang in the seventies with no knowledge about the history of those dances or the dancers who originated them.

The wild and excitable dancing of the Soul Train Gang was born from the struggle of the sixties civil rights era: water hosings, police brutality, the assassinations of Medgar Evers, Malcolm X, and Dr. Martin Luther King Jr. Dance released the pent-up anger and frustration that youths on the show, many of whom grew up and resided in the inner-city sections of Los Angeles, had either experienced, seen, or heard. But the dancing was also about brotherhood and friendship, as evidenced by the handshakes and slaps of five executed during locking routines.

In the late sixties and early seventies, Black pride was on the rise. From the Godfather of Soul's powerful anthems such as "Say It Loud (I'm Black and I'm Proud)," "Soul Power," and "Get Up, Get Up, Get Into It, Get Involved," to the Black Panther revolution and the new Black hair care products, Afro Sheen and Ultra Sheen, the Soul Train Gang indeed showcased Black pride, Black beauty, and Black power through their dance moves, fashions, and large and short Afros, and cornrowed hairdos. Furthermore, they exemplified the slogan, "Black is Beautiful" and showcased that indeed "we are here, we are important, and we matter."

The Soul Train Gang became famous nationwide, appearing in major news and magazine publications, primarily in the new Black teen/young adult magazine *Right On!* which was first published in October 1971, the same month that *Soul Train* first aired nationally. From the magazine's February 1974 issue through the latter part of the seventies, the Soul Train Gang graced its covers almost every month. The magazine had feature articles about various dancers, along with many color photos taken during photo sessions at Griffith Park in Los Angeles and other local areas. It also had monthly fan letters addressed to the dancers. One popular regular, Joe Chism, ultimately had a regular monthly column in *Right On!* titled "That's the T!"

The dancers also appeared in TV specials and movies. They received thunderous ovations during the Soul Train road tours from August 1973 to early 1974, opening for acts such as The Whispers, the Sylvers, The Moments, and Eddie Kendricks. As one dancer told me, they received ovations similar to the ones audiences gave at The Jackson 5 concerts. And much like The Jackson 5, members of the Soul Train Gang were heroes to Black youths across the country.

Many recording artists of that time, including James Brown and The Jackson 5, were mesmerized by the Soul Train Gang's dance steps. They wanted to meet the dancers and learn steps from them. In fact, several of the dancers actually worked with Brown, The Jackson 5, and other legendary artists such as Diana Ross and Aretha Franklin, and they performed in places such as Las Vegas, New York City, and even overseas in Japan.

The Soul Train Gang and the show itself were so famous that *American Bandstand* creator and host Dick Clark created a very short-lived Black dance show entitled *Soul Unlimited* to rival *Soul Train*. Many of *Soul Train*'s dancers danced on both *Soul Unlimited* and *American Bandstand*. Don Cornelius didn't like that, but in hindsight, his dancers' appearances on those programs helped make *Soul Train* even more popular, especially when one of their popular couples, Tyrone Proctor and Sharon Hill, won a dance contest on *American Bandstand*.

Although several of the early and later dancers went on to fame in the entertainment industry, a large number of them remain unsung. They were known simply as dancers from *Soul Train*. After they stopped dancing on the show, they were either forgotten or unknown—until now.

As a writer and entertainment journalist, I wrote and contributed many articles to various print and online publications. Among them was SoulTrain.com, which was the official website of the show from 1999 to 2016.

Over the years, I interviewed many celebrities and covered many events, including movie premieres, concerts, and awards shows. Because I formerly danced on *Soul Train* and grew up admiring several dancers from the show, I got to know many of the dancers and wanted to find a way to give these earlier dancers the exposure they deserve. Sure, many of them were profiled in *Right On!* Magazine, but that was years ago, and people do forget. I wanted to do something to remind people of the history and legacy of those dancers. Hence, I began interviewing various dancers from the seventies and eighties every month.

There have been several great books written about the history of *Soul Train* as a show, but never one solely about its dancers and their contributions to the entertainment world. This book helps remedy that.

Some of the dancers I interviewed were not well known on the show and never became famous. But the bottom line is, their stories and legacies are just as important as those of popular regulars. As I mentioned earlier, these and the other early dancers are *Soul Train*'s roots. They are the forerunners to the dancers that came after them, including myself, and they deserve to be given their props.

Let's also not forget about *Soul Train*'s local dancers from Chicago. They are actually the first roots of the show's dancers, and they came before all of the Los Angeles Soul Train Dancers. From the time the local show first aired on August 17, 1970 to when it ended in June 1976, the local Chicago Soul Train Gang received acclaim and generated excitement throughout the Chicago area. They are indeedthe true original Soul Train Gang.

*Get On Board Volume 1: The Soul Train Gang*, consists of dancers who performed on *Soul Train* from 1971 to 1975 when they were called the Soul Train Gang. The years they appeared on the show are listed in parentheses next to their names.

You will not only learn their stories about dancing on *Soul Train*; you will also learn about their other accomplishments outside the show, their personal challenges, and what they are doing currently. Their stories are entertaining, inspirational, and insightful.

Now get on board and fasten your seatbelt for a fascinating ride as you journey along with the Soul Train Gang!

BACK IN THE DAY

CURRENT PHOTO

# Crescendo Ward

## (1974 – 1976, Chicago show; early 1980s, national show)

*Soul Train* began in Chicago in the early 1970s. The show and its dancers gained notoriety a few years later on the nationally syndicated program. Wayne "Crescendo" Ward was one of *Soul Train*'s best from Chicago. He became part of a dance troupe known as The Puppets and went on to do big things in the entertainment industry as an entrepreneur, dancer, choreographer, producer, writer, and actor. In fact, *Soul Train* literally saved his life. Here is his story.

SM: What was your passion growing up as a kid in Chicago?

CW: Dancing. I used to do The Twist and the jerk as a kid.

SM: Who or what inspired you to dance?

CW: My mother was a dancer as well as an opera singer. I would imitate anything I saw. I really admired Fred Astaire, Gene Kelly, and The Lockers.

SM: When did you hear about this new show called *Soul Train* in Chicago?

CW: I was still a kid when it first aired. After school, there were three things I watched: *Soul Train*, *Speed Racer*, and *The Three Stooges*. You had to be a certain age to get on *Soul Train*, like sixteen or seventeen.

Don Cornelius was the host at that time.

SM: How did you get on *Soul Train*?

CW: Well, I used to enter the talent shows at Austin High School, and I would win. Some people who had been on *Soul Train* told me you had to stand in this long line at the Chicago Board of Trade building, and you had to have a partner. My best friend, Janice, liked to dance as well. So, we decided we were going to go on *Soul Train,* and because she was so fine, we were put in front of the line!

SM: What do you recall about that first day at *Soul Train*?

CW: First of all, I was surprised to see the size of the studio. My living room was bigger than *Soul Train*'s set! I said, "This is it?" [laughs] Also, I met these guys that were like the kings of *Soul Train*. They were Melvin Shrunpert, Anthony Fairchild, Carlton Knight, and Sammy Feltz, and they called themselves the Soul Train Dancers. They were the best dancers on *Soul Train* and, just like me, they patterned themselves after The Lockers. We would later form a dance group, The Puppets. The first day Janice and I went on the show, we were placed in the back of the crowd. When a song came on, and I asked one of the other dancers to give me some room, I did a split. The station manager said, "Hey, bring that guy up front!" That's how I began dancing out in front.

SM: Did you meet the host Clinton Ghent on that first day?

CW: Yes, I met Clinton. He said I was a pretty good dancer, and I told him I would come back. I was one of their best dancers and became one of the regulars, so I didn't have to stand in that long line anymore.

SM: Do you remember the artists that came to perform on the show while you were a dancer?

CW: There were The Chi-Lites, The Impressions, Blue Magic, mostly local Chicago talent. The Chi-Lites did it quite a few times because they were a Chicago group.

SM: How did it feel to see yourself dancing on the show?

CW: Since the shows weren't taped, I never saw myself on *Soul Train.* By the time I got home, the shows had already aired.

SM: In the documentary, *Hippest Trip in America*, you talked about how you nearly got beat up after a day of dancing on *Soul Train.*

CW: Well, I was taking my girlfriend home to the Cabrini Green Projects. When we got off the L-Train, we heard gunshots, and the closer we got to Cabrini Green, the louder the gunshots were. But then the shooting stopped, so we continued to her building, and she went inside. As I left, four guys walked in my direction and said, "What's up? Represent!"

So, I kissed my finger and put up the peace sign and said, "No love," which meant you had no affiliation with any gang.

So, they were like, "Where are you from?" and started patting my pockets. They took my money and my gold chain and said, "Get your punk ass out of here!"

But then one of them recognized me and said, "Wait a minute, I know this mutha f***a. That's that *Soul Train* mutha f***a!" [laughs] "He can dance!"

He asked me to cut a move, and I did a James Brown split. Then they gave me back all of my money. What was so funny was that he told the others to give me *more* money and informed me to take a cab home since it was a bad neighborhood!

SM: Wow! *Soul Train* definitely saved your life that day!

CW: Yes, it did! When I got home, my mom was looking out the window, and she saw me getting out of a taxi. I didn't tell her what happened because she would have told me that I wasn't going to Cabrini Green anymore.

SM: Tell me about how you became a part of the dance group that would later be known as The Puppets.

CW: The guys I mentioned earlier were eyeing me and saying things like, "He thinks he can dance." They weren't calling themselves The Puppets yet, just the Soul Train Dancers. They would be doing a show, and I would just show up. At one show, they introduced me as another great dancer from *Soul Train* and called me "Chicken Wayne" because I was so limber in my movements. Then I did a backward flip and a split and a lot of other moves in a short amount of space. So, they put me in their group because they couldn't do gymnastics like me.

SM: So, what happened after you became a part of the group?

CW: Clinton told us we should branch out and start doing more shows and get paid. So, we started putting on our own events for cash and performed on *Soul Train* as well as opening up for Rufus; Earth, Wind & Fire; The Spinners; The Pointer Sisters; and all the other groups that played in Chicago. The Puppets were the opening act for all those groups. All of this came from *Soul Train*.

SM: Did you ever dance on the national version of *Soul Train*?

CW: Yes. I danced on the national version of *Soul Train* in my twenties just to have the satisfaction of saying I danced on the LA version. But by this time, I was a choreographer, and I even choreographed a major Diana Ross special in the early 1980s. I also staged The Pointer Sisters act, and I danced with them during one of their performances. By that time, there were other major projects I was involved with.

SM: What were those projects?

CW: One of them was a lip-synch show called *Puttin' On The Hits*. I was also involved with another show called *FTV*. I was a regular on that show, along with Khandi Alexander, who later played on *CSI*. I was also the talent coordinator for the dance section of *Star Search*.

SM: Tell us about your company, Wardance Entertainment.

CW: I formed my company, Wardance Entertainment, to produce live events. My celebrity judges included legendary street dancers like Don

Campbell and Boogaloo Sam. I was shooting these events on Betamax technology to preserve them and began editing people's reels and pilots for TV shows. So, my company branched out, and we are now a multifaceted entertainment company specializing in live events, live web streaming, film and TV production, writing, and facilitating anything in entertainment. The latest thing we are doing is producing crowdfunding videos for kickstarter.com.

SM: Did you ever meet or interact with Don Cornelius?

CW: Yes. I met him at the taping of the *Hippest Trip in America* documentary and at an Oscar screening party for people who couldn't go to the Oscars. I would always see Don and his son Tony at these parties.

SM: What would you like to say in Don Cornelius's memory?

CW: He left an impact not just on the urban community but on entertainmen.

SM: Do you have a word of wisdom you want to share?

CW: Don't follow any rules you had nothing to do with making up. If you have a passion for something, do it your way.

BACK IN THE DAY

CURRENT PHOTO

# Jan Robinson Hunter

(1971–1972)

Just call Jan Robinson Hunter the "First Lady of *Soul Train*." She appeared on the very first national episode. Upon hearing about the show, she spread the word to several people at her school, Los Angeles High School. She was largely responsible for many of the dancers appearing on its first episode. She is also an actress and taught drama. One of her students was the late legendary Oscar-nominated filmmaker, John Singleton.

SM: While people might say they are an original Soul Train dancer, you can truly make that statement since you danced on the very first episode that aired nationally. How did you hear about the show?

JH: Pam Brown, who was selected to be the show's dance coordinator, had a brother named Ron Brown, who was a high school football player. He came to a cheerleader's meeting and told me his sister Pam needed dancers for a show that was like a Black version of *American Bandstand*. He asked if I'd be interested in doing it. It sounded like fun, and no strings were attached, so I said sure. He also asked me to get some of my other friends to come to the show, so Anthony Crandle, Steven Lott, Phyllis Jackson, and others came with me. One of them was Rodney Moss, and I asked him to be my dance partner for the show.

SM: So, you and Rodney were very instrumental in getting a number of dancers for that first episode?

JH: Right! So, when I was asked to dance on *Soul Train*, Rodney got together a group of guys who could dance, and I got a group of girls who could dance, and we were given a date and time to come to Queen Ann Park to audition.

SM: What was the audition process like?

JH: Don Cornelius and Pam Brown were there. They told us they were going to take a look at how we danced and our styles. They put on some music, and we danced, and when the music stopped, they started making their selections. Me and my friends passed the audition and were told we were going to appear on the first national episode of *Soul Train*. They gave us the date and time to show up as well as some parameters of what to wear.

SM: What do you remember about that first weekend taping of *Soul Train*?

JH: Two shows were filmed that Saturday, and another two were filmed on Sunday, so we pretty much danced all day and all afternoon for the entire weekend. There was a popular Black-owned fried chicken restaurant called Golden Bird, and they had the best fried chicken you could get. The *Soul Train* staff fed us the Golden Bird chicken and orange soda water during breaks. This was our only pay and all of the dancers were tickled to death!

SM: I was told that in the early days, the dancers, most of whom were minors, taped into the late-night hours and sometimes into the early morning.

JH: We would come in at about 10:00 a.m. and wrap up taping at about 5:00 or 6:00 p.m. They were long shootings, but I don't ever remember us being kept late.

SM: You also appeared in some of the Ultra Sheen commercials that were sponsors for *Soul Train*. How did that come about?

JH: I was approached by Tomas Kuhn who helped produce *Soul Train*. He asked if I would be interested in doing some commercials for Johnson hair care products. At that time, I was already modeling for Sears & Roebuck and did a shampoo commercial and another one for perming your hair. So, in addition to dancing on the show, the production staff set up schedules for me to tape the Ultra Sheen commercials. I got paid a lot of money to do these commercials and was also given lots of boxes of their products. I also got my Screen Actors Guild (SAG) and American Federation of Television and Radio Artists (AFTRA) cards while I was doing these commercials. It worked out really well. I got residuals for doing these commercials for about fifteen years, which helped put me through college, buy me a car, and get me an apartment. This was all a blessing!

SM: Among the acts on that first episode were Gladys Knight & the Pips, the Honey Cone, and Eddie Kendricks. What do you remember about them on that taping?

JH: Gladys and the Pips were very friendly, and between their performances, they chatted with us. They were like your auntie and uncles. The Honey Cone were really sweet and nice girls. They didn't come on set acting like stars; they wanted us to feel comfortable with them being there, and they were very sociable and polite. However, Eddie Kendricks didn't speak to any of us. For one of the Ultra Sheen commercials, I was told to say that Eddie Kendricks was my favorite artist, which wasn't true. Marvin Gaye was my favorite artist. But I was told to say Eddie because he was going to be one of the artists on the pilot episode.

SM: The early seventies was a golden time for soul music. What memories do you have of other artists that performed on the show?

JH: Curtis Mayfield was so kind and so tiny! I remember that during down time between performances, he would just sit around and smile, and you could tell he was a good person with a good heart and spirit. Bill Withers was a very quiet guy but very polite and a gentleman. He didn't interact with the dancers but just took direction from the stage manager and director. When Al Green first came to the show, he was virtually unknown. But I remember him with his hat cocked to the side wearing those hot pants!

SM: [laughs] When he was performing "Tired of Being Alone," you were dancing behind him and looking at him with this wide-eyed expression of disbelief.

JH: [laughs] We thought he was dressed a bit outrageously. We were all kind of giggling about that because he was so over the top!

SM: As you said earlier, Don Cornelius was at the dance audition, but what are your recollections of him on set for that first weekend's taping?

JH: No one knew who Don Cornelius was. We thought he was corny and dressed like he was trying to be a pimp. He was very arrogant, and he postured a lot. We heard he was from Chicago, so we just thought his style of dress was a Chicago look. But we were Los Angeles kids, and we thought that long sky-blue coat and green boots were corny! [laughs]

SM: Did you experience any jealousy while being on the show?

JH: I really didn't. If there was any ugliness, it was behind my back because no one ever acted that way to my face. In those early days, we were on set dancing and just happy to be there.

SM: One of the fun things about the early years of *Soul Train* was its weekly dance contests. That first season, the winners of each weekly episode competed in a dance contest at the end of the season. What do you recall about this?

JH: Rodney Moss and I were featured on the first episode, showing off our dance steps in the creative dance segment, but the winner of the very first dance contest was my best friend, Crissy Thomas, and her boyfriend, John Clark. Rodney and I won on the second episode.

SM: In *Soul Train*'s first few seasons, all the dancers in the studio had a chance to go down the Soul Train Line. In later years, only certain dancers would be selected. The early Soul Train Lines appeared to be more fun and less political.

JH: To be honest, when the Soul Train Lines were filmed during my time on the show, everyone got the opportunity to come down the line. It was much later on when the producers began working with editing, and they only chose certain people. The show had its favorites as it became more famous, and certain girls got featured because they were popular—and for "other things" too. *Soul Train* just got a little trashy as they had girls shaking their body parts as if they were pole dancers. The show did not begin like that.

SM: What could have potentially been a horrible situation allegedly took place after the end-of-season dance contest on *Soul Train*, right?

JH: Right. I had on a long red dress and was waiting backstage alone when a certain Black entertainment producer saw me standing by myself and put both of his hands on my shoulders and pushed me up against the wall. He tried to put his mouth over my mouth. With both of my hands, I pushed him away and asked him, "What are you doing? I'm only sixteen years old!" I turned to the right and made my way down the hallway, and I was going to find a friend of mine to tell him what that producer had tried to do.

SM: There was a tragic incident that took place only moments later, right?

JH: Yes. I ran out of the Palladium and saw this big crowd. When I stuck my head into the crowd, I saw my good friend Bobby lying on the ground. He had been beaten across the street from the Palladium by a gang. He and his brother Chucky wore leather coats that evening, and these gang members beat up Bobby and kept beating him until they killed him. It was even on the news. I didn't tell my mom nor my dad what that entertainment producer tried to do to me. My dad is an ex-military man, and he didn't play when it came to his daughter.

SM: So, you didn't tell anyone what happened to you that night?

JH: I told my friend Chrissy, but I basically kept it to myself all these years.

SM: So, when that Black entertainment producer passed away, what were your feelings?

JH: When he had died, many people called, saying things like, "You must feel terrible." But I didn't want to slander his name or incriminate him, so my only comment was "Yeah, I heard about that," and I just kept it moving. But it was real and a terrible memory.

SM: What did you do after you moved on from *Soul Train*?

JH: I went away to college and got my degree in theatre. I continued performing, and I was accepted into the Ensemble Company in Houston, Texas. I became a professional actress while I was working on my degree in theatre. I enrolled in the California Educators of Theatre Association (CETA), and they were hiring artists in residence. So, I graduated with my degree and then got a job teaching drama to children in River Oaks, Houston. I was doing plays and teaching drama at the same time.

SM: Did you ever return to California?

JH: I returned to California in 1985 and continued acting and got a job at Crenshaw High School as a drama teacher. At Crenshaw, one of my students was John Singleton, who went on to UCLA. When he came back and said he wanted to make a film called *Boyz in the Hood*, he asked if he could use some of my students. Certain scenes were shot at Crenshaw High School, and I played a teacher in one scene passing out the SAT test.

Tyron Turner was also one of my students. He had a lot of talent but no discipline. One day, I got a call to send a couple of my students to an audition, so I sent him. So, a week goes by, and he comes to class with a VHS tape. I popped the tape into a video cassette recorder (VCR), and

Janet Jackson's "Rhythm Nation" came on the screen, and that was the start of his career taking off. Tyron ended up doing *Belly, Menace to Society*, and quite a few other films. He is now a protégé of Jamie Foxx, and we're still close to this day. And John has done all these wonderful things in the movie industry. I am so proud of him.

SM: We lost John Singleton some years ago. What would you like to say in his memory?

JH: His passing was very heartbreaking and difficult. I remember him being different from the other boys. He avoided gangs but was friends with all kinds of kids. He was a nice kid, very well mannered, and subdued. We had a good relationship.

SM: What are you doing currently?

JH: I'm a retired theatre educator and director at the School of Performing Arts. I actually taught at the School of Performing Arts in Houston where Beyoncé attended.

SM: How would you describe your overall experience with *Soul Train*?

JH: It was an outstanding opportunity and a foundation for me being a performing artist. It catapulted me into a career that I would not have necessarily gone into.

SM: What word of wisdom do you want to share?

JH: You've got to follow your dreams, and you've got to have a dream. You also have to trust your instincts because bad things happen out in the world. It was only by God's grace and mercy that I didn't get caught up in certain things. I'm no better than anyone else, but I do believe a hand of grace was over me. Also, coming from a family who gave me confidence in who I was, this kept me from being taken advantage of as a young girl in the entertainment industry.

CURRENT PHOTO

# Rodney Moss

### (1971–1972, 1973, 1975)

The future of what we would come to know as *Soul Train* may not have happened if a certain phone call to Rodney Moss had not been made and answered. Rodney, a student at Los Angeles High School at the time, helped to make the first national episode of *Soul Train* come together. He, along with Jan Hunter and several others, is one of the original members of the Soul Train Gang from its inception as a national television show.

**S**M: You and Jan Hunter were basically responsible for getting all the dancers on *Soul Train*'s first national episode. What do you recall about that time?

RM: It was the summer of 1971. Jan and I attended Los Angeles High School. I got a call from Ron Brown, who also went to LA High, that his sister Pam Brown needed dancers for a new television dance show. So, Jan and I contacted people from our high school and told them about this new show.

SM: What do you remember about the day you and the other dancers filmed the first pilot episode?

RM: School buses picked us up from Queen Ann Park on a hot summer August day. We got into the studio at 9:00 a.m. and got out about 11:00 p.m. or midnight.

SM: Were the dancers on those first few episodes mainly from Los Angeles High School?

RM: Right. For about the first six months, there were only about thirteen couples dancing. Later on, kids from other area high schools came on the show.

SM: You also danced on *American Bandstand* for some time, right?

RM: Yes. The beginning of *Soul Train* was so important due to the exclusion of some Black dancers on *American Bandstand*. On that show, Black dancers were chosen by how they dressed, while the White dancers just simply went inside the studio.

SM: What was the recognition like for you from being seen on television weekly?

RM: Kids would come up to me at the mall and at basketball games at the Forum asking for autographs and how to get on *Soul Train*.

SM: You mainly danced on the show for its first season, but every now and then, you would come back to the show, right?

RM: Right. I danced in the show for about twenty months. The show's first five episodes were just kids dancing and partying. I didn't like the pop lock era later on—maybe I wasn't open to it—so I moved away from *Soul Train*.

SM: While you were at *Soul Train*, you developed a friendship with Don Cornelius, right?

RM: Yes. Don Cornelius became a friend. When he was flying back and forth from Chicago to Los Angeles to tape the show, he stayed at the Continental Hyatt House on Sunset Boulevard. When Don wanted to buy suits and clothes, he would call me to go to the stores with him. We went to Fred Slatten's, a men's shoe store on Santa Monica Boulevard west of La Cienega Boulevard, and he bought twenty pairs of shoes! I would also take him to my grandmom's house, where she made dishes like fried chicken, macaroni and cheese, and greens.

SM: Speaking of footwear, do you remember Don wearing some tall greenish boots with some designs on them, along with a sky-blue hot pants suit on *Soul Train*'s first episode?

RM: Yes, those boots were from Fred Slatten's store. We would take our shoes there to get things painted on them.

SM: Who were some of your favorite artists that you enjoyed watching perform while you were on *Soul Train*?

RM: Sly and the Family Stone, The Jackson 5, and The Fifth Dimension. Also, The Delfonics, The Dramatics, and Blue Magic. *Soul Train* was a new vehicle for our Black artists. Certain mainstream television shows excluded Black artists and Blacks working behind the scenes. If I was running a show, the cameramen, stage managers, and engineers would all be Black. I am not anti-White, but I am pro-Black.

SM: When you and the other dancers from Los Angeles High School filmed those first four national episodes, none of you knew that this show was going to last so many years or that it would become iconic. You were all just eager kids wanting to dance and be seen on television. What do you have to say about that?

RM: Exactly. At that particular time, we had no idea we would be making history or that we were going to be on the longest-running syndicated show in television history.

SM: What would you like to say in memory of Don Cornelius?

RM: What Don Cornelius did was unprecedented. He only had about six hundred dollars in his bank account, but he took a chance. He was a trailblazer. I had a personal relationship with him, and he was very kind to me.

SM: What word of wisdom do you want to share?

RM: If I had to sit on a mountaintop and impart a lesson, it would be that life is the classroom. Therefore, everyone who comes into your life is there to teach you a lesson.

BACK IN THE DAY

CURRENT PHOTO

# Patricia Davis

(1971–1975)

Patricia Davis is one of the original members of the Soul Train Gang who danced on the show from its third episode and became its first popular regular. A dance icon as well as a fashion icon, she was noted for her dynamic, unique dancing and, later, for her stylish 1940s outfits. Legendary Diana Ross nicknamed her "Madame Butterfly" because of the flowers and butterfly pieces she wore in her hair.

Patricia could execute locking, splits, neck rolls, the Robot, and other dance moves with great precision. She was featured in numerous issues of *Right On!* magazine, had her own monthly column in *Rock & Soul* magazine, and made an appearance on the TV show *The Dating Game.* She also appeared in movies, on TV specials on major networks, and was voted Soul Train's original All-Time Diva at the first annual Soul Train Gang Reunion in 1997. She was an Ambassador Representative Soul Train Dancer aboard the 2020 Soul Train Cruise. Indeed, her popularity, during and after her time as a Soul Train dancer, is unprecedented.

SM: First off, let me ask, where are you originally from?

PD: I was born in Fort Worth, Texas. My family and I left Fort Worth when I was five, and we moved to Los Angeles.

SM: What inspired you to want to be in show business or to have a career in dance?

PD: I really didn't think about a career in show business at the time. I was too young. I just loved to dance and wanted to dance. It was all about dancing for me.

SM: When did your interest in dance begin?

PD: It began in Texas. I always just loved dancing when I was a little girl. My Aunt Mildred had a café in Fort Worth, and her customers always wanted to see me dance, so someone would play a tune on the jukebox. When I started to dance, people would give me ten cents, and I would use the money to buy candy. [laughs] After me and my family moved to Los Angeles, there was a store we went to called Minnie's. One day, me and my friend Katie were there and saw another little girl dancing. The customers gave her money for her dancing talent.

My friend Katie told me that I could outdance that girl, but at the time, I was too shy to show I could dance. So, the next day, Katie told the owner of the store, whose name was Minnie, that I could dance. Minnie asked if I could dance, and I said yes. Katie, acting as if she was my manager [laughs], told Minnie that I would dance if she gave me some Kit Kats. So, I danced, and the store's patrons watched and were amazed. I got not only candy but also money. When my dad came to Minnie's to pick me up, I was sweaty and had a bag of candy and money. He had no idea that I was sweaty from all the dancing I was doing in the store. [laughs]

SM: How did you become a Soul Train dancer?

PD: One day at a block party, Mrs. Alcott, an African dancer, got about six kids in the neighborhood, and we did an African dance routine. Another woman in the neighborhood at the block party knew Pam Brown, who was the dance coordinator of *Soul Train* at the time. She asked my mother if she could give our number to Pam. Pam had told her she was interested in having this little girl who could really dance to come to *Soul Train*. Pam called her, and I went to audition for the show. I passed the audition and became a Soul Train dancer. However, there was an age limit to being a dancer on the show, and I was younger, so I lied. [laughs]

SM: What were your impressions when you first went on the set of *Soul Train*?

PD: People really dressed their best. Afros, suits, hot pants, everyone moving to the music. We all had fun. There was competition, but it was all in fun. During breaks, we told jokes and laughed, and we practiced dance routines.

SM: What are your early memories of Don Cornelius?

PD: Don dressed in all these leather outfits. Me and the other dancers thought he was the hottest thing alive.

SM: Several of the dancers danced on Dick Clark's *American Bandstand* as well as *Soul Unlimited* at the same time they danced on *Soul Train*. Were there any repercussions from dancing on both shows?

PD: Don didn't like it. He would say, "I saw you dancing on *American Bandstand*," but we weren't banned from *Soul Train*. Many of us danced on Bandstand, including me, Joe Chism, Damita Jo Freeman, Tyrone Proctor, and Sharon Hill. In fact, Tyrone and Sharon won a dance contest on Bandstand.

SM: The Soul Train Gang would hang out and dance at several clubs in Los Angeles, right?

PD: Oh yes! There was the Citadel, Maverick's Flat, and some others. My mom, who was very strict, would let me go to these clubs because there were no drugs there, no smoking allowed, no consumption of alcohol, and no guys trying to pick girls up. Those clubs were strictly environments for dancing. It was all about dancing and having a good time. No fighting, no guns, no violence. Young people these days have lost that sense of innocence.

SM: You were very influential on the show in dance, hairstyles, and fashions. You became famous for the flowers and butterfly decorations that adorned your hair. What was the inspiration for that?

PD: That came about when Diana Ross did the movie *Lady Sings the Blues.* Diana wore flowers in her hair as Billie Holiday did. I loved that, so I would come to the *Soul Train* tapings wearing flowers in my hair. Then soon, some of the other girls started wearing flowers in their hair. Then, I started wearing butterfly ornaments in my hair, and Diana gave me the nickname "Madame Butterfly" because of it. I wasn't trying to start any trends. I was just being me. I loved wearing flowers and butterflies in my hair, and it just caught on.

SM: Viewers couldn't wait to see what you were going to wear on the show. For example, you were also a trendsetter with the 1940s fashions you wore on *Soul Train* in its third season. How did that come about?

PD: At the time, The Pointer Sisters were popular. They were into wearing fashions from the 1940s, and I loved their style. So, I went to secondhand stores, bought old skirts and dresses from that era, and wore my grandmother's shoes. Again, I just loved the 1940s fashions and was not trying to start any trends. I was just being me. I wore the clothes, but I didn't let the clothes wear me.

SM: There was also the time you dressed like a little girl with your hair in pigtails while you were pretending to drink a baby bottle. You were so adorable!

PD: The inspiration for dressing like a little girl and holding that baby bottle came from my creativity and having a fun good time and not caring what anyone was saying or if they were laughing. There's a little kid inside of all of us, and it's what keeps us young and keeps us moving and enjoying our lives. I just allowed that little girl inside of me to come out and be who she is with my pigtails, baby bottle, and the little tears in my eyes that were made out of rhinestones.

SM: You and several of the other dancers became friends with a lot of the guest stars that came to the show, right?

PD: Yes, James Brown, for example! He was such a great, down-to-earth man. He would even eat fried chicken with the Soul Train Gang after tapings. I remember one time he brought one of his daughters to the show, and he told her to "go to Auntie Pat, and she can show you how to dance."

SM: You even wiped the sweat off Marvin Gaye's forehead when he sang "Let's Get It On" on *Soul Train*. Did you keep that tissue as a souvenir? [laughs]

PD: [laughs] That was fun! Back then, we were able to speak to and interact with the guest stars.

SM: Do you have any personal favorite memory of an artist that performed on *Soul Train*?

PD: Yes, when Tina Turner performed on the show.

SM: You and several of the dancers were also good friends with Michael Jackson and the Jackson family and visited their home a number of times, right?

PD: Yes. They invited me and Gary Keyes to their dressing room because they loved our dancing on the show. After that, they invited Gary, me, and some of the other dancers to their house. We would be in their living room teaching them dances like the Robot, locking steps and certain neck movements. We would even go to the movies with them, but they had to wear disguises so that no one would recognize them.

SM: Michael has said in interviews that he was sad and shy during his adolescence. Did you witness any of that during the times you spent with him?

PD: Yes, I got a sense of his shyness. He just wanted to dance and perform. But when he came off the stage, he was introverted. It was hard to get away from the camera and the stage. I was the same way. On the set of *Soul Train*, when the cameras were off, I stepped away from them because I was very shy. But Michael could also be a prankster. Once, when another dancer and I were at his house, he asked her, "Do you want some potato chips?" She said, "Yeah, I like potato chips!" So, Michael gave her the bag of chips. She reached into the bag, and there was a snake in it! [laughs]

SM: [laughs] So, you also got to see Michael's playful side?

PD: Yes. I even had a nickname for him. Dodo Bird! [laughs] One time, at a party for Al Green at his brother Tito's house, me, Michael, Little Joe Chism and Al Green tried to teach David Bowie how to do the Robot. It was so funny!

SM: The death of Michael Jackson several years ago was shocking and a huge loss. Since he was a friend of yours, I know that it must have been especially painful.

PD: Oh yes. Michael's death was very sad.

SM: The popularity of *Soul Train* opened up many doors for the *Soul Train* Gang, one being that several of you were able to go out on the road as part of The Soul Train Road Tour.

PD: Yes! The dancers who went on the tour included me, Freddie Maxie, Connie Blackino, Lynn Pickens, James Foster, Gary Keyes, Jimmy "Scoo B Doo" Foster, Don Campbell, and Tyrone Proctor. We would open the shows and do our dance routines before the groups that were part of the tour, such as The Whispers and the Sylvers, came out to perform.

SM: What was it like being a part of that tour?

PD: It was so much fun. We traveled on a bus all around the US with the Sylvers, The Whispers, and other artists. We performed at places like the Apollo in New York City and other big venues. We had such a wonderful time, and we have so many stories of the things that happened while we were on tour. Later, we even opened concerts for James Brown.

SM: You were so popular on *Soul Train* that you got tons of fan mail and appeared in many issues of *Right On!* magazine and, for a time, even had your own monthly column in *Rock & Soul* magazine. How did that come about?

PD: A lady by the name of Lisa called me one day and asked if it was possible that I could do a column for the magazine answering fan mail and answering fans' questions. It was a lot of fun doing that.

SM: Being one of *Soul Train*'s most popular regulars even had you on The *Dating Game.*

PD: I don't remember how that happened, but it was quite fun being on the show and was really an experience. The guy that I picked played football. Did I go out on the date with him? No. [laughs] He was so fresh! He called me every day, sometimes two or three times a day, asking, "When are we going on our date?" I don't remember how I got out of it, but I didn't go on the date with that guy. But it was a fun journey!

SM: Being a popular regular being seen on TV can bring about unwanted attention and even jealousy. Did you ever experience any jealousy while you were on *Soul Train* from any of the other dancers?

PD: Yes. People often thought I was stuck up, but I was just very shy. There was one situation on the show with this loud older girl who would always pick at me. At one taping, my flower fell out of my hair. She picked it up and put it in her mouth. She started dancing around with it and even stole my dance partner. I asked for my flower back, but the girl said, "No." I wasn't looking for any trouble, so I went to sit on the bleachers with my parents, who attended that day's taping. My back was turned, and she came up to me and poked me in the back and said, "You want your flower back?" I didn't answer. She kind of pushed me or punched me in the back again even harder and asked, "I said did you want your flower back?" I turned around and swung a punch at her and she called me a bitch. Somehow, we wound up on the floor and had a fight, but I won and didn't get one scratch on me! After that ass whooping, neither she nor anyone else ever bothered me again.

SM: Wow! Don Cornelius wasn't on the set at the time the fight happened, but when he returned later and found out about it, what did he say?

PD: He just wanted to know who won the fight. [laughs]

SM: You were also responsible for bringing the first non-Black dancer to the show, right?

PD: Right. I brought on Deney Terio, and we went down the Soul Train Line together.

SM: The Soul Train Gang was so famous that celebrities like Diana Ross wanted several of you to be a part of their act. How did that come about?

PD: Diana had picked me, Little Joe Chism, Damita Jo Freeman, Eddie Cole, and Wanda Fuller to be a part of her show in Caesar's Palace in Las Vegas.

SM: What was that experience like working with and being with Diana?

PD: Diana was my idol. I remember one time I bought some slippers of various colors. Diana saw the slippers and admired them. She asked where I got them. I told her from Woolworth's, so she gave me the money to go to Woolworth's and buy those "cheap shoes." [laughs]

I remember another time she invited us to her home in Lake Tahoe for a barbecue. While we were there, we decided to ride a boat out in the water by her house, and we rode the waves. She was so angry at us, and she yelled at us to "get your asses out of there," and she scolded us. [laughs]

SM: Several of you also performed with Aretha Franklin as well, right?

PD: Right. Aretha's brother, Cecil, called me personally. He told me that Aretha wanted me to be in her shows at Carnegie Hall and Radio

City Music Hall in New York. That was such a wonderful experience. We even got to hang out at Aretha's home in New York.

SM: The R&B group Blue Magic was also on the same bill as Aretha and the Soul Train Gang on those shows. That was one dynamic show!

PD: It was! I also remember one of the members of Blue Magic tried talking to me! [laughs]

SM: You and some of the other dancers, Perry Brown, Bert Woods (a choreographer), James "Scoo B Doo" Foster, Eddie Cole, Wanda Fuller, and Damita Jo Freeman had formed a dance group called Something Special while all of you were still dancing on *Soul Train*. (Freeman later left the group to pursue other avenues of show business.) You got a chance to travel on the road with some big-name stars. How did this happen?

PD: We had a manager, Daniel Ben Aviv, who knew the manager of Tom Jones, and so we traveled and performed as part of Tom Jones's act in New York and other places.

SM: It was during this time that you and the other members of Something Special left *Soul Train*. Was it hard for you to leave *Soul Train*?

PD: No, not really because we were traveling so much by that time. I told Don Cornelius we were traveling a lot, and Dick Griffey even told him also. So, Don understood. In fact, Dick wanted me to be in the group he was forming called Shalamar, but I had commitments with Something Special. So, that's when Jody Watley became a part of that group.

SM: Tell me about your days of being a part of Something Special?

PD: We traveled all over the world! We had the opportunity to perform with Tom Jones, Natalie Cole, Rufus & Chaka Khan, The Pointer Sisters, and others. We sang and did various dance routines.

SM: During that time, you also had the opportunity to appear in a movie called *Disco 9000*. How did that come about?

PD: I got a call that the producers of the film wanted me to do a scene in which I would jump out of a cake and do a dance routine to Johnnie Taylor's "Disco Lady." So, I agreed, and I did the routine. It was a lot of fun doing that.

SM: Why did Something Special break up?

PD: One of the members of the group had an alcohol problem and was missing shows. Also, some of the members were fighting a lot. So, Something Special disbanded after that.

SM: When did you decide to move to Austria?

PD: In the early eighties, a lady named Catherine Miller called me and said there was a promoter in Austria who wanted a male breakdancer who could sing and asked if I knew anybody who fit those criteria. I said yes and gave her Eddie's number. About five hours later, Catherine called again and asked if I was interested in doing choreography for the background dancers of a singer named Bilgarie. I was very interested and said yes, but she told me I would have to leave the next day. So, that was the beginning of it.

SM: You and Eddie were even singing duet at one time, right?

PD: Yes. We were a duet who called ourselves Essence. We were a duo for a long, long time.

SM: What have you done professionally and personally since that time?

PD: On June 12, 2007, I married Karl Bachmayer, a doctor who is a wonderful and great husband. I also sing with a gospel group, I still dance, and I teach locking dance classes. I also released some CDs. My first CD was *Mamarena,* and my second CD was *Choose Your Future.* I had a single out called "I Wanna" that features me and Chris T, and it can be downloaded via iTunes.

SM: You have a special message to younger women you would like to share, right?

PD: Absolutely. Women need to get back to pure beauty and class. We as women need to get back to that and get away from T&A. Be beautiful and sexy but have class with it. A lot of women have lost respect for themselves.

SM: Do you have one fond, unique, special memory about *Soul Train*?

PD: I remember that some of us got some special outfits from a Soul Train line of clothing. I was given a red skirt and a red top, which I loved, and I was given a lot of products from Ultra Sheen. That smell of Ultra Sheen reminds me of a moment of happiness when my mother was alive. It gives me a special feeling.

SM: In 1997, Joe Chism put together the very first Soul Train Gang reunion. What was that like for you?

PD: I saw brothers and sisters. When I saw them, I remembered how we danced together, fought together and laughed together. Who can do that other than brothers and sisters?

SM: In 2020, you, along with eighties Soul Train dancer Derek Fleming, were part of the Soul Train Cruise, representing the Soul Train Dancers and teaching dance classes. I was on that cruise and was so happy to hang and dance with the two of you! Tell me about your experience.

PD: It was really very nice, and I was just so happy. You never know if people still remember you. I live in another country, and I figured nobody remembered me. But they did, and it was such a blessing.

SM: Indeed! Many people wanted your autograph and took photos with you. People who watched *Soul Train* in its early days still remember you.

PD: It's funny, but every time I go back home to Los Angeles, people will stop me and say, "Are you that girl from *Soul Train*?" After I was married, and me and my husband were in Los Angeles, people would ask me that question, and my husband would say, "What are they asking you?" I told him I used to dance on *Soul Train*. I didn't even tell him before we were married. He was like, "Who did I marry?" [laughs]

SM: We lost several dancers from the show over the years, many of whom were your close friends such as Don Campbell, Little Joe Chism, Shabba Doo, Tyrone Proctor and Eddie Cole. What would you like to say in memory of each?

PD: Don Campbell left a great legacy with the background of locking, and up until this day, that dance still lingers on. I see people in Europe starting to do it, and they think it's something new, but it's not. When you see those young kids locking, the spirit of Don Campbell is living on. He had this certain personality and way of moving that was dominant and fun and couldn't be broken. Little Joe and I were pretty close. He was such a jovial person, always positive and smiling, even when it was a hard time. That was his personality. He always had that beautiful smile and gracefully flowed down the Soul Train Line as if nothing was in his way. I really loved Tyrone Proctor. He made a lot of jokes and would sometimes say something out of the blue, and you would wonder, "Should I laugh or what?"

Shabba Doo was a strong personality. He didn't take no mess. When something went down, he was going to speak about it. He's a person I learned a lot from because sometimes you have to speak up in life, no matter what. Eddie and I have known each other for years through Soul Train, Something Special and Essence. We were like family. He taught me how to pray really hard. When I went to see him a day before he died, he couldn't talk since he was very sick, but his eyes were saying he was ready to go, and I prayed over him. The next day he left in God's peace. He fought until he was ready to go. All of these guys left me with something that will help me be better in the future as the years go by. The older I get, the more I say, "Thank you, God, for sending those people into my life."

SM: What would you like to say in memory of Don Cornelius?

PD: He was like a father figure. He molded us in the same way as if we were his own family. He did what he was supposed to do.

SM: Do you have any advice or word of wisdom you want to share?

PD: Down the road of life there's hate, there's lots of jealousy, and then there's love and dreams you must follow. There is a God. Believe Him, not man. Hold your head high, be strong, and stand against trouble-makers. Nothing can hurt you.

CURRENT PHOTO

BACK IN THE DAY

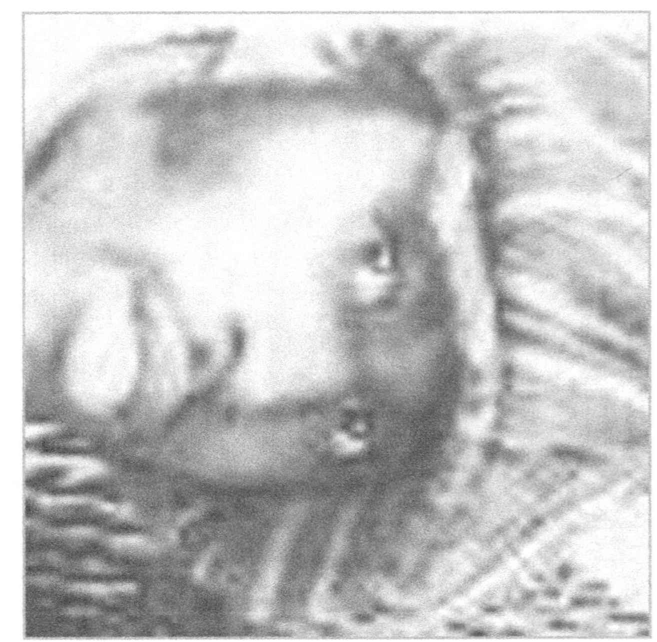

# Don Campbell

(The creator and inventor of "locking," 1971–1973)

Before the Moonwalk, before breakdancing, there was a dance move that helped serve as the basis and roots of street dancing as well as freestyle, hip-hop dancing, and the breakdance revolution. The dance move was called the Campbell Lock, or "locking" as it became commonly known. Locking started out as a dance step before *Soul Train* came into existence, but in the fifty-plus years since its birth, it has become a national movement and a phenomenon all around the world. To this day, there are kids, teens, and adults in many countries who have learned and are still learning how to do this amazing dance step.

Over the years, many people have falsely laid claim to devising this movement, but there is only one creator, originator, inventor, master, and innovator of locking. He is the one and only Don "Campbel Lock" Campbell.

SM: Don, I am privileged and honored to have you do this interview. Was dancing something you always wanted to do? Was that your passion growing up?

DC: When I was growing up, I wanted to do something positive with my life and to be a positive influence on someone. I never got involved with gangs and stuff like that. I just wasn't that type of kid. I avoided the streets. I lived around the gang element, but I would avoid problems. I was at home all the time, and I loved to draw as a child.

SM: So, drawing was your first love?

DC: Yes. I was the kind of kid who could have fun on his own by picking up a pencil and drawing. I would do lots of sketches. I loved to sketch toy army soldiers. I would also ask my mom and brothers to model for me, and I would even look in the mirror and start sketching my face and hand, doing self-portraits. I was so good that I went to the famous art schools, Otis Art Institute and Chouinard's. Those are top-ranked art schools in Los Angeles.

SM: So, you basically were sort of an introvert and became immersed in drawing?

DC: That's right. I wanted to be an artist. My mom always thought I was going to be a famous artist. Everything was going that way until I went to Trade Tech College in downtown Los Angeles for commercial arts. During lunch period, I would carry my sketch pad around, and I'd sketch people for five or ten bucks. As far as dancing goes, I didn't dance until I attended college.

SM: So, how did the locking phenomenon begin?

DC: I give credit to a guy named Sam Williams. I first met him at Trade Tech in the cafeteria. He and his friends would be sitting by the jukebox, jamming and partying. One day, when I was drawing, Sam walked over to see what I was drawing and said I was pretty good. He then invited me to come over and sit with him and his friends. So, I started sitting with them and watching what they were doing. I had never been around people who could dance. Sam and his friends, Sweet T, and Doozer Ray, a dancer that Don Campell met in school who never became famous, are real hip people, lively and so smooth. At that time, the big dance craze was the funky chicken. Sam was the baddest funky chicken in the world! [laughs] He would have everyone jumping. I had seen him on a local TV show in Los Angeles called *Boss City* doing the funky chicken. He was real bad! He tried to show me some of his moves, but I wasn't very good. He would say, "You're all right, you're all right." As he was teaching me, I would just lock my hands and tighten up my shoulders.

SM: So, what you just described is a part of the basics of locking.

DC: Locking is not really freezing. It's like you lock, stop, and then continue. So, this was what I did around Sam and his friends. Sam would say, "Do that again, do The Lock, lock your hands! That's cool! That's a bad move!"

SM: When did you start locking in clubs?

DC: It was at a club in downtown Los Angeles where I went to watch Sam, his buddy Sweet T, and their girlfriends dance. Another girl was with them who was mad that her partner hadn't arrived yet. Sam saw me and encouraged me to go on the dance floor. He said, "Campbell, just get on up and dance." The music came on, and eventually, twenty couples were pulled off the floor. When I knew I was still on the floor with only five couples left, I was the happiest man in the world! Sam and his partner won first place, and Sweet T and his partner won second. Even though I didn't win that time, I was just glad to remain on the floor after those twenty couples were pulled off before me. If it weren't for Sam, I would never have gotten up on the dance floor. So, right after that, I would ask Sam and Sweet T when and where the next dance contest was going to be.

SM: Maverick's Flat was another club in Los Angeles where you won dance contests.

DC: Yes. It was located close by Fox Hills, where a lot of rich Black people lived. This was where The Commodores, Chaka Khan, Richard Pryor, and a lot of others performed when they were starting out. But I was just there to participate in the dance contests.

SM: So, dancing at these clubs and in these dance contests was a way for you to break out of your shyness?

DC: Absolutely. Remember, I was a quiet kid. But when Sam Williams invited me out, I got more confident. After a while, people were wondering what kind of dance I was doing. I was never popular before that. But once I became popular, everyone knew me. All the girls who could dance always wanted to dance with me.

SM: Hence, you became very well known around Los Angeles and all the clubs.

DC: I started getting so popular, other people couldn't win dance contests. I won so many dance contests at the Climax that the owner of the club paid me fifty bucks to stay out of one contest so that other people could win. I loved competing. If the dance contest started at noon and I got there at ten, I was on the floor until a quarter to three. I had confidence. During those dance contests, I would say, "Bring it!"

SM: Did you ever practice doing your locking routines?

DC: No, because I was dancing all the time. I just took this little dance move and kept extending it. I never had to practice because I was always on the spot at the clubs. I was the kind of dancer who danced wherever the crowd was. I would jump on the floor, in the air, on tables, on stages, and smack the floor and do splits. I was spontaneous combustion!

SM: I interviewed your good friend Jimmy "Scoo B Doo" Foster, another legendary Soul Train dancer, and he told me that when he saw what you were doing at the club with all of these upper body movements, he was really intrigued by it.

DC: I first met Scoo B in 1970. He was the first person to lock after I started doing it. He began to combine his own dance steps such as the Scoo B Doo, the Scoo-Bot, and the Scoo B Kick with locking. When he came out of seclusion years later, I went on the internet and told people about him and began hooking him up. So, he started getting work, and now, like me, he is teaching dance classes all around the world.

SM: When did you first realize you were starting to become famous?

DC: I was at Mavericks Flat, and two or three people came dressed like me with knickers, striped socks, apple caps, and crisscrossed suspenders. They would go on before me, and they danced like me and dressed like me. But after a while, I didn't care, because when it was my turn, I came up with something new and topped what they did. I did some things most people wouldn't try, like sliding under tables, jumping in the air, locking, and splitting. I would do whatever was necessary to win.

SM: So, you started the trend of wearing the type of outfits and styles that all The Lockers would eventually wear?

DC: Actually, Sam Williams was an influence on me with his dress style. Sam wore an apple cap and suspenders, but he didn't crisscross his suspenders like I did. So, I dressed similar, but I crisscrossed my suspenders. He also wore marshmallow-cork-type shoes, which came in different colors. I would buy long striped socks as well as knee pads to protect my knees when I was dancing. When you're young, you can take a lot of pain, but I had to change things when I got older.

SM: How did you become a Soul Train dancer?

DC: An audition was held for this new show called *Soul Train* at Denker Park. The show's coordinator was Pam Brown, and she had heard about my popularity at the clubs. So, I asked my partner Damita Jo Freeman to come down to *Soul Train* with me. The show had a dance contest every week, and if you won, you got to stay on and compete in the finals. Damita and I won the contest our first weekend on the show.

SM: You became so popular with your dancing you even had a record named after your dance, the "Campbell Lock." How did that come about?

DC: Before The Lockers dance group was formed, a record producer saw my dance and thought it was a phenomenon like The Twist. Also, back during that time, I sang. So, I worked with this producer, and he was the first person I hooked up with to promote me as a singer/dancer. So, he got the music together, and I sang on the record. He tried to get it on Motown or Stax but got it on a small independent record label instead. I didn't hear from him for two or three months, but my record started getting a lot of airplay on KGFJ radio station in Los Angeles, and it became very popular locally.

SM: So, the record didn't get pushed any wider nationally?

DC: No. While the producer was gone, Toni Basil came into my life and became my manager. When he came back, he was mad that Toni was my manager, but she was only helping to promote my dancing. Unfortunately, I never made a dime off the record. Some years later, when I formed my dance group, The Campbell Lockers, I received a legal letter which claimed that record producer owned the name Campbell Lockers, so from that time on the dance group was called The Lockers.

SM: When did you first meet Toni Basil?

DC: I met her at the Citadel club. Most people think she was originally a part of The Lockers, but she didn't dance in the group when it first started. She was my manager then. To this day, Toni and I are the best of friends. I owe Toni everything. From day one, she would stand up for me all the time. She knew the connections and promoted me. She would take me to a lot of movie stars' houses, and I would have my boom box, and she would sit the boom box down, turn the music on, and I started locking it up. This is how I started getting work.

SM: Getting back to your days of dancing on *Soul Train*, what was that experience like for you since you were already well renowned in clubs in LA.?

DC: When I first came on *Soul Train*, it was still beginning, and the big star artists like James Brown didn't come on, so the dancers were heavily featured. The cameras covered the people who would really get down. So, when the camera was focused on me, I would do all I could do, doing all the things I was doing in the clubs. It was good to watch yourself on TV every week. Going down the Soul Train Line was the biggest thing.

SM: You were initially a part of the Soul Train road tours, which included The Whispers, the Sylvers, The Moments, and others. What was that experience like for you?

DC: When we went to North Carolina for our first show on the road, half of the kids in the audience were dressed like me. That was another sign that I knew I was getting popular. It also meant the world for me to travel with entertainers. They would talk to me and tell me about life. Walter and Scotty from The Whispers were real cool. They would just talk to me straight up and also tell me things about the entertainment business.

SM: There was a story that you were kicked off *Soul Train*. Is that true?

DC: This is what happened. At the time, *Soul Train* didn't have White dancers on the show, so Toni Basil wanted to come on the show. She wanted to be the first White girl to dance on *Soul Train,* so I told her to come with me. Later, when there was a break during the show, Don Cornelius saw Toni and started talking to her. Toni told Don that *Soul Train* was just as good as *American Bandstand* and that the only difference was that locking wasn't done on Bandstand. Toni was just trying to promote me, but Don took offense to that. The next thing I knew, at the next taping, I came to the front entrance of the gate like always, but the guard stopped me. He said I was not allowed to come in anymore. Don took offense that Toni was trying to get me a paid job on the show due to my locking becoming popular. After I was kicked off, Don made it a rule that there was to be no more locking done on the show. Some of the only ones who he would let do it included Scoo B Doo, Damita, and a few others.

SM: Was this when you formed The Lockers dance group?

DC: Yes. After I got kicked off the show, Toni told me to get some dancers to form a dance group. I went back down to the Climax and the other clubs to find all the baddest guys that did my style of dance. I saw Fluky Luke, Campbell Lock Jr., Shabba Doo, Fred "Penguin" Berry, and Slim the Robot, and asked them all to join me in my dance group, The Campbell Lock Dancers. In hindsight, if I hadn't gotten kicked off *Soul Train*, I would have never had a dance group.

SM: All of The Lockers were dynamic, but Fred Berry was a real standout.

DC: Fred and I were real good friends. We hit it off right off the bat. We met at Maverick's Flat. He was a quiet kid who didn't really dance. He started getting into dancing after seeing me dance.

SM: How do you feel that a dance group you named after your dance became such a phenomenon around the world?

DC: We were the first ones to cut the color line with street dancers. I asked Toni to join the group since she knew the steps and then Shabba Doo, who was Hispanic, came in. They couldn't call us just a soul group anymore. In the seventies, it was hard to get on the big TV shows, but then we did *Dinah Shore, Carol Burnett, Midnight Special*, and TV specials like *The Roberta Flack Special, The Grammy Awards*, and *The Doris Day Special*. We even did *Johnny Carson* twice.

SM: It must have been an honor when The Lockers went back to perform on *Soul Train* as paid professionals.

DC: Don Cornelius brought us back to his show twice. When Don saw me and the group on all these TV shows and going to Vegas and around the world, he called Toni up and booked us on *Soul Train*. When I went back on the show, remembering the day all of those dancers were laughing at me when I got kicked off, I was feeling so good! The greatest day I went on *Soul Train* was the day they brought me back. We even had our own dressing room. On the door was *The Campbell Lock Dancers*. I had tears in my eyes. We were finally getting paid. Each one of us got paid about six hundred dollars. That was the first time I ever got paid on *Soul Train*, aside from the dance contest. I was so excited.

The first time we went back, we were The Campbell Lockers, and the second time, we were just called The Fabulous Lockers. When we were doing a lot of TV shows and traveling the world, there were other dancers on *Soul Train* who quit and formed their own dance groups, like Something Special and The Dancing Machine.

SM: The Lockers also had the privilege of performing at the MGM Grand Hotel, right?

DC: Ours was the first dance act to perform at the MGM Grand Hotel when it opened. We were the opening act for Roger Miller and Pat Cooper.

SM: The Lockers even performed with Frank Sinatra.

DC: Yes, at Carnegie Hall and the Chicago Stadium. He was really nice to us. Toni told Frank's manager about us, and he invited us to Frank's room at the end of his concert. He knew Toni Basil and her dad, and that's how The Lockers got the job at MGM.

SM: Why did The Lockers break up?

DC: It was around the time we appeared on The *Dick Van Dyke* Variety Show. One day, three of The Lockers came up to me and said they wanted another member to be the leader of the group. Toni Basil also left around this time to focus on her own career.

SM: What did you do professionally after The Lockers broke up?

DC: I became a Chippendale dancer. The first time I danced at the club, I wore boxing trunks and rolled them up! I was shy about it at first. But after a while, I got used to it and started wearing bikini briefs. Eventually, it was so much fun. I even developed characters for my stage act.

SM: When and why did you quit being a Chippendale dancer?

DC: I decided to leave Chippendales after six months because even though the tips were great, the pay wasn't. I had a family to support.

SM: Being that you are one of the all-time greatest dancers in entertainment history, I know you and the other Lockers met and knew Michael Jackson, but did you ever have a chance to work with him?

DC: I worked with him when he was doing the "2Bad" video. This was a video like "Thriller," and he wanted some of The Lockers to be in it. He hired me, Shabba Doo, and Fluky Luke. The set was on an airplane hangar in San Fernando Valley, which was built like a haunted house. Michael wanted us to come out of a chimney like ghosts or spooks. We had top hats on and our Locker-style outfits. One day, Michael shook my hand and bowed down in front of me and told me that he had tapes of all of my performances, everything I've done. He was praising me like I was the star! He also greeted and shook the other Lockers' hands, and then he walked onto the set.

SM: That must have been very gratifying to you that the King of Pop told you that your dancing had an influence on him.

DC: I didn't even know he was really interested in me personally. That was the luckiest thing in the world to meet him and shake his hand. And Mrs. Jackson was one of the nicest people I ever met. My daughter was with me, and she still remembers that.

SM: I remember at the first Soul Train Gang Reunion in 1997; you received an award for being the creator and inventor of the Lock. How did you feel receiving an award from your peers from *Soul Train*? That must have been an honor.

DC: It was a humbling experience for me. It was wonderful.

SM: Tell us when you met your wife, who, it goes without saying, is your rock.

DC: I met my wife, Mary Ann, at a club called Pier 7 in San Fernando Valley in 1972. I asked her if she would dance with me. She's Italian and she could dance like a sister! We won the dance contest and exchanged numbers, and the rest is history. We've been together since 1973.

SM: You've been teaching dance classes for a number of years. What is the basic setup of your classes?

DC: During my classes, I show the basics of the move. Locking is based on the creativity of the individual. Once you learn The Lock dance that I do, you put yourself into it. Once you get the dance down, everything else will flow out of you. That's why certain dancers that do my dance are popular—like Scoo B Doo who would incorporate locking by kicking his legs high. Fluky Luke was double jointed and limber, so when he would do The Lock, he would always combine his own style with it. Slim the Robot would add roboting to his locking. That's what makes the dance work, adding your own flavor to it. That's what it takes. To me, the foundation is you just have to learn The Lock and how I did it. Without The Lock, all of the other kinds of moves done with it won't work.

SM: Locking is now world-renowned, and you teach locking classes around the world.

DC: Dancing has made me able to go all around the world to places like China, Japan, Moscow, and St. Petersburg, Russia. I am booked to go to Taiwan in April. When I was in St. Petersburg, Russia, I got to take my oldest son, Dennis, with me. My son was going to teach the dance classes, and I was mostly going to tell the history and teach the basics of locking. We were at the basketball training center, and I was upstairs sitting next to the guy who brought me to St. Petersburg. He started to cry and said that fifteen years earlier, people couldn't dance the way they wanted in Russia. And here I was, teaching Russian kids to dance the way they wanted to. I felt so humbled to be told that I was teaching kids to be free with their dancing. It wasn't a color thing over there; you were just respected as an artist. I was treated like a king the whole time I was there. This same gentleman carried my bags when

I got off the plane. When I got to the hotel, I found out he actually owned the hotel!

SM: This is a testament to what you and your style of dancing mean to multitudes of people.

DC: It was a humbling experience going to places like that. When I went to Brazil, I enjoyed the kids and the people. Those kids could dance their booties off! I have also seen kids locking in China and Japan. There are great dancers all over the world.

SM: What would you like to say in memory of Don Cornelius?

DC: He was the first one to put me on the big stage that got the world to see what Campbell Locking was. It started me on my path to success. I will forever be in his gratitude, and I thank him for having me on his show. I loved dancing on *Soul Train*. It was a wonderful ride.

SM: What words of wisdom do you want to share?

DC: To the rest of the Soul Train Gang, love, peace, and soul!

*This interview was conducted in 2013, seven years before Campbell passed away. I can't thank him enough for allowing me to interview him. To his family: thanks for your approval of the interview to be included in my book. My deepest condolences. May he rest in peace, and may his legacy live on.*

# Jimmy "Scoo B Doo" Foster

(1971–1974)

Scoo B, Scoo B Doo, where are you? For years, many have wondered whatever became of Jimmy "Scoo B Doo" Foster, legendary *Soul Train* dancer and one of the major pioneers of the locking dance movement. His dance style was a force to be reckoned with. Rumors surfaced that he was homeless and had died many years ago. But to the contrary, Scoo B is alive and well. He is teaching dance classes all across the US and abroad—and he can still throw down on the dance floor. He is teaching all of the signature moves he created: the Scoo B Doo, the Scoo-Bot, the Stop and Go, the Scoo B Hop, the Scoo B Kick, the Scoo B Walk and a new one, The Pause. Jimmy Scoo B Doo Foster is back!

SM: First off, where are you originally from?

JF: I was born in Sacramento, CA, but was raised in Los Angeles.

SM: What was childhood like for you?

JF: Up until I was seven years old, my childhood was great. But from seven to fourteen, I experienced some really traumatic times.

SM: What helped give you the ambition to get into dancing?

JF: When I was fifteen and a student at Fremont High School, I went to a noon-hour dance party with my friends Randolph and Rudolph.

BACK IN THE DAY

CURRENT PHOTO

After that party, I went to the house parties they attended and just continued to observe the dancing until I experienced bullying at some of those house parties.

SM: So, what happened after that in terms of your inspiration for dancing?

JF: When I was sixteen, Rudolph and Randolph told me about a club called Maverick's Flat. On that very first night, I saw Don Campbell. As I watched Don, I was intrigued by his style of dancing, so I started practicing every day. I practiced by myself in the beginning. I created dance steps within locking.

SM: So, seeing Don Campbell Locking at Maverick's Flat gave you that zest for dancing, correct?

JF: Absolutely! He is the creator of locking with the upper body movements. The moves for locking came about by doing a lot of things accidentally, like when he pointed at people who laughed at him because he didn't know how to dance. That pointing became part of the moves. But I created the dance steps within locking, so I began practicing and creating the steps, the first of which was the Scoo B Doo. All of the steps I made up were in my feet. I combined locking with my style of dancing.

SM: So, after watching and observing Don, when did you guys eventually meet?

JF: One night, while at Maverick's Flat, Don needed a ride home. He came up to me and asked, "Are you from anywhere around here?" I said, "Yeah." He asked, "Can I get a ride home?" After that, we started practicing dance steps together, and he snuck me into various dance clubs. We became real buddies.

SM: How did you get the nickname Scoo B Doo? An old issue of *Right On!* magazine quoted you as saying its origin came because Scooby Doo was your favorite cartoon character.

JF: That's not true. Here is the real story behind my nickname: Don Campbell knew Scooby Doo was a popular cartoon, but I had no knowledge of that cartoon. One day he just started saying, "Scooby Doo! Scooby Doo! Scooby Doo!" and gave me that nickname. After that, the nickname craze of all street dancers began. It just went wild!

SM: There was another dancer with your same nickname that caused confusion, right?

JF: Yeah! So, my brother suggested that I do something to distinguish our nicknames, so people knew exactly who I was. So, I added my first name, Jimmy, to Scoo B Doo.

SM: So, you, Don Campbell, and the rest of The Lockers became a tight bunch?

JF: Yes. Shabba Doo and Campbell Lock Jr. were my roommates. Damita Jo Freeman gave Greg the nickname "Campbell Lock Jr." because he was trying to look and dance like Don Campbell. I love Greg, Shabba Doo, and Fluky Luke. They were my closest friends, and I would die for them.

SM: Speaking of Damita Jo Freeman, you two were one of the most popular couples on *Soul Train* in its early days. How did you two meet?

JF: I met Damita through Don Campbell at Maverick's Flat. She, Don, and a group of people all used to dance and hang together. She even named my dance the Scoo B Doo and we are real close friends to this day.

SM: How did you become a Soul Train dancer?

JF: Pam Brown asked Damita to bring friends to Denker Park in Los Angeles. So, she brought me, Little Joe Chism—and others—and we showcased our dancing skills and did the Soul Train Line.

SM: Describe what it was like the first time you went to *Soul Train.*

JF: I was really amazed by what I saw. I was so in awe of all of the lighting, the cameras, and how organized everything was.

SM: What artists that performed on *Soul Train* stand out in your mind?

JF: Well, there were The Jackson 5, Aretha Franklin, and Al Green. But James Brown really stands out. He told me that he watched me every Saturday. Whenever he performed at the Los Angeles Forum, we would perform with him.

SM: You have a very special memory of your first meeting with Michael Jackson.

JF: Yes; Greg Pope, Don Campbell, Fred "Rerun" Berry, and I were at a movie theatre, and we saw Michael. We approached him and said, "Hi, how are you?" Michael answered, "I know who you are Scoo B Doo!" The Jackson 5 and James Brown were two of the main artists really interested in the Soul Train Gang.

SM: Aside from the guest stars and the dancing segments, what other memories stand out from your days of dancing on *Soul Train*?

JF: The late tapings and only getting a box of chicken afterward. [laughs]

SM: You and Damita won a dance contest on *Soul Train* in which the Godfather of Soul, James Brown, was one of the judges. To be declared winners by the hardest working man in show business and a dance legend who paved the way for Michael Jackson and others must've been an honor.

JF: It was incredible! This dance contest was only for the members of the Soul Train Gang. Nothing can really describe what that was like. Damita and I felt like we were both making history.

SM: Indeed, you both were! You, among other members of the Soul Train Gang, toured as part of the Soul Train Road Tour. What was that experience like?

JF: It was exciting! We toured with the Sylvers, The Whispers, and other artists. We traveled on a bus going from city to city.

SM: Being that you and Don Campbell were friends, and you created the dance steps within locking, how come you weren't part of The Lockers dance group?

JF: Don and I didn't agree on particulars that had to do with the dance scene, so it was decided that I wasn't going to be part of the group.

SM: How did you feel about that?

JF: I was very upset. But around 1974, Damita called me and said she was forming a new dance group called Something Special with members of the Soul Train Gang and that they were going to tour with Tom Jones. She invited me to be part of the group. I was with Something Special from 1974 to 1979, and we toured in the US and overseas.

SM: Around this time, you left *Soul Train*, correct?

JF: Yes. Something Special's manager, Daniel Ben Aviv, wanted me and the other dancers to leave the show because he felt we should be getting paid for our talent.

SM: You also worked with Diana Ross on her 1981 TV special. What was it like working with her?

JF: She really respected the dancers who worked alongside her. She knew me from dancing on *Soul Train*. It was wonderful working with her.

SM: What did you do after Something Special disbanded?

JF: Don Campbell was dancing and doing random stripping at a club in Los Angeles called Chippendale's. He asked me if I wanted to become a dancer there to make some extra money, so I did. I danced there until 1984.

SM: What happened in your career afterward?

JF: After leaving Chippendale's in 1984, I had little gigs as a male exotic dancer, but that's not what I really wanted to do. I became depressed. My depression reached its peak in 1985 after I went to a library and looked through many old issues of *Right On!* All of the photos of me and Pat Davis were cut out! Seeing my photos go missing made me feel like a nobody, and I went into a deep depression. I stayed out of the dance scene and didn't lock anymore.

SM: This was when the rumor that you died had started, correct?

JF: Yes. Around 1986, I did die emotionally and spiritually. I gave up on life. I was homeless and had odd jobs here and there. I was living in and out of hotels and hanging out on Skid Row for seven years. It was an extremely difficult time for me.

SM: So, you were not involved with dancing or locking at all during that time, correct?

JF: Right. However, from 1985 to 1992, I studied the roots of locking again and how it all began. I began to go over in my mind how locking came to be.

SM: During this period of soul searching, did you have a spiritual center to keep you anchored?

JF: Absolutely. My grandmother. She taught me to always believe that everything was going to be all right. The hardest time of my life was from age seven to fourteen, and somehow, God brought me out of that. I got my life back together with the Lord in 2003.

SM: A very special person came into your life in 2006, right?

JF: Yes. It happened when I was at the Fitzgerald Casino in Las Vegas. I was on the balcony praying to God to please bring someone into my life to help me. The next week, my future wife, Gina, passed by the same place. I was downstairs, and she saw me and spoke to me. God brought Gina and me together, and we got married in 2007.

SM: Did Gina know that you were a former Soul Train dancer?

JF: [laughs] No. I didn't even tell her initially that I used to dance on *Soul Train*. In fact, when Gina and I went to dances, I wouldn't dance. Later on, when she found out more about me, she was surprised that I kept that information from her! [laughs]

SM: 2010 began the reemergence of Scoo B Doo and people found out you were not dead after all. Explain how all of this came about.

JF: In January 2010, Gina typed my nickname into the internet search engines and came up with all kinds of things about me and my influence on dance. While we were looking, we found out my very close and dear friend Greg Pope had passed away. I was really hurt by his death, so Gina sent a message stating, "My name is Jimmy Scoo B Doo Foster, and I want to express my condolences over the passing of Greg Pope." Skeeter Higgins replied. We reunited, and he posted photos of him and me on the website, along with a story that I was very much alive.

SM: The VH1 documentary *Soul Train: The Hippest Trip in America* also played a part in your reemergence, right?

JF: Yes! When I was watching that documentary, I was so gratified by all of the footage shown of me and that Don Cornelius mentioned my name. It really boosted my self-confidence and helped me to realize my contributions to dance and locking.

SM: As a result, you have been teaching numerous dance shops in Las Vegas, correct?

JF: Yes. I teach all the dance steps that I created within locking, the Scoo B Doo, the Scoo-Bot and others. I also formed the Elite Locking Camp, where I teach dancers all about the movement, history, and dance steps of locking.

SM: What would you like to say in memory of Don Cornelius?

JF: It was a privilege to know him. He was the greatest MC that ever lived. I was surprised to hear him say in the 2010 documentary *Hippest Trip in America* that if it weren't for certain dancers like Don Campbell, Fred "Rerun" Berry, Damita Jo Freeman, Pat Davis, and me, Scoo B Doo, his show wouldn't be what it was. I never knew he felt that way about us until that documentary.

SM: In the last few years we lost a number of dancers, all of whom were legendary pioneers: Don Campbell, Shabba Doo, and Tyrone Proctor, all of whom were not only legendary pioneers in dance but were also three of your closest friends. What do you want to say in their memory?

JF: There's one thing about all of them: each of them loved dancing, and that is the most important thing.

SM: Do you have a special word of wisdom you would like to share?

JF: Yes. This is very important. Besides locking being a dance, it is the first dance I ever did in my life. It made me happy. It made me feel good and free. That's what locking is all about; that's how it was created, out of loving life. People who want to study locking need to stay out of the politics of locking. Locking was born out of love and is about love, friendship, and family. It's all about the love of the dance, not the politics.

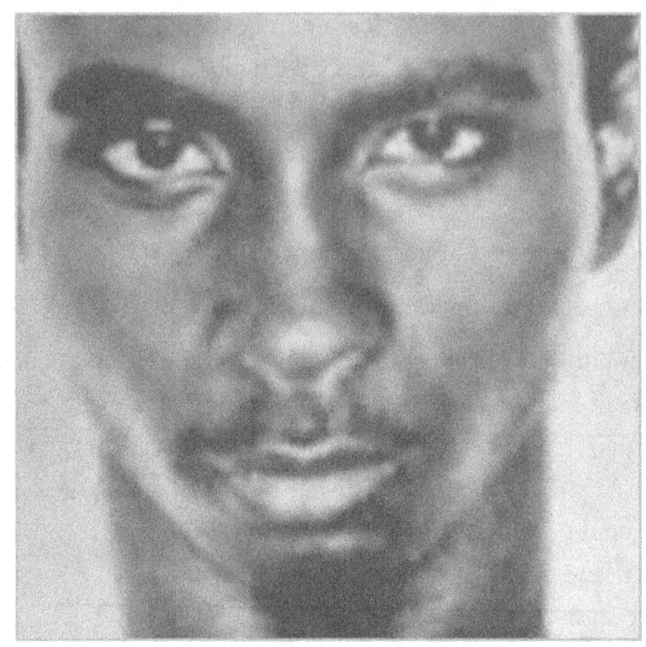

CURRENT PHOTO

# Gary Allen

**(1971–1975)**

You might have seen a 1970s clip from *Soul Train* showing a guy going down the Soul Train Line with some extremely tall platform shoes. That was none other than Gary Allen, who is not only a dancer but an actor, fashion designer, and singer. He showcased early on his great fashion sense and had a style of his own and applied that to whatever he does.

**S**M: What was your passion growing up?

GA: Acting and dancing were my first two passions. I had a real love for fashion, and at one point in the 1960s, my beautiful mom was a model. It was inspiring because the designer would give her a garment, and she would return with a fabulous new look. So, yes, my mom inspired my love for fashion, and that love increases my will to survive.

SM: What do you recall about your first time going to *Soul Train*?

GA: My initial memories of my very first tapings of *Soul Train* are vague. I do remember it was an early Saturday morning in Hollywood on Sunset and Bronson. We would arrive with a change of clothes since we taped four shows one weekend out of every month and got the two-piece chicken dinner from KFC.

SM: Do you recall when you won one of the weekly dance contests that got you and your partner into the finals?

GA: I remember winning the dance contest, but I never received the hair care products. [laughs]

SM: Do you remember the dance that you and your partner did?

GA: My dance partner, Cheryl Enouex, and I won the dance contest with a dance I called The Lean. The Lean was popularized by this great club dancer named Andrew Frank. Andrew was like the king of dance, and no one could outdance him. You should also know that Andrew danced on stage with the fabulous Diana Ross when she sang "Love Hangover" at the Universal Amphitheatre.

SM: What did it feel like to you to be on a show that became a sensation across the country?

GA: I remember feeling how lucky and cool it was to be on *Soul Train*. I was on the show with the *Soul Train* superstars of the time, such as Damita Jo Freeman, Little Joe Chism, Pat Davis, Tyrone Proctor, Vicki Abercrombie, and Niles Gay, as well as Randy Gardner, Allan Crowder, and Thyais Walsh, who were a part of the Pasadena Crew.

SM: When did you stop dancing on *Soul Train*?

GA: 1975 was my last year on *Soul Train*. Being selective about what songs I would dance to, I didn't go down the Soul Train Line every time I was on the show but would just hang out in the seating area with the others who didn't dance. I wasn't hard to miss. I wore the tallest platform shoes on the show. I remember one particular time Don Cornelius said, "Wait a minute. Where's Gary Allen? Make Gary Allen go down the line." So, I had to go down the Soul Train Line and was the first one to start that line.

SM: I've seen some Soul Train Lines where you were wearing those very tall platform boots. They were humongous! Did you ever fall while wearing them? [laughs]

GA: [laughs] No, I never fell wearing those platforms. They were like mini stilts. I bought my first platforms from Brass Boots in Beverly Hills, then another pair of boots where I had the platforms added. I also bought another pair of White platforms on Kings Road in London while on a trip to Europe with my classmates after graduating from a year's course in fashion merchandising.

SM: Did you ever interact with Don Cornelius?

GA: Yes. My favorite Don Cornelius story is when he helped me get an audition for a co-starring role in a blaxploitation film titled *Black Shampoo*. I was cast as a character named Artie in the film, and it was my very first co-starring role right out of high school. Years later, he found out that my sister was Stephanie Mills's manager, so we had a stronger connection.

SM: What have you done in the years since leaving *Soul Train*?

GA: I built up my portfolio as a male model even though there was no work in the modeling industry for Black men at that time. But I had a dream, and I pursued it with everything that God blessed me with. I knew Black men were modeling in Paris and London, so I created a career by seeking work and working with photographers. I had a killer portfolio and worked freelance with young European fashion photographers doing editorial work that was avant-garde and high fashion.

SM: Tell me more about you getting into the fashion and design world.

GA: I started designing when I was in high school. In 1972, when I was a senior at Dorsey High School, I would walk home from school down a street called Santa Barbara Avenue, which is now Martin Luther King Boulevard, and a man named Hal Murray, who was opening a modeling agency, noticed me. He told me he was starting an all-male Black troupe. He asked me if I would like to audition for it, and I did. That was my first time on a runway. I was a part of the agency for a year or two. Hal was giving fashion shows like "Paris is Burning" and "Men Are Diamonds, Diamonds are Forever." Hal Murray was truly my mentor.

SM: Did any opportunities arise for you from being at Hal Murray's agency?

GA: Yes! A gentleman named David Alexander discovered me at Hal Murray's "Men Are Diamonds" fashion show in 1973 or 1974. He taught me how to do fashion work in Hollywood and introduced me to other models. He also gave me a list of working photographers in Hollywood. I worked with so many people, like Gene Paglioso and Sam Emerson, who would later be Michael Jackson's photographer. I owe a lot of my achievements to David. He was a mentor, and he was responsible for my career.

SM: What happened in your career afterward?

GA: I moved to New York in 1976 or 1977. Later, in the mid-eighties, when I was in New York, I had an exclusive contract to be Billy Idol's designer of his wardrobe and stage clothes. He was great to work with.

SM: You opened up your own business at one point, right?

GA: Right. When I came back from London, I started working as a stylist for Swanky Modes as their West Coast representative, styling shoots with photographers. In 1979, with just seventy-five dollars, I opened my own design business called For Divas Only and it went public in 1982. I created a technique all by hand, weaving macrame all in knots.

SM: You are also a recording artist. Tell me about this.

GA: I was the lead singer of a group called Neighbor's Voices. The group's musicians worked at my company during the day and rehearsed at night. I later left the band and went solo. I recorded a four-track extended-play record (EP) titled In White America, which is a compilation of songs I co-wrote and co-produced. Its sound was kind of new wave. I then put music aside for a while to focus back on fashion designing.

SM: Are you currently working on anything else outside of fashion and music?

GA: My mother wrote a children's story, and I'm turning it into an audiobook. It's called *Lucky the Mouse,* and it's about an orphaned homeless mouse looking for a home.

SM: Describe your overall experience on *Soul Train.*

GA: *Soul Train* was the zenith of my career, a Venus of inspiration.

SM: What would you like to say in memory of Don Cornelius?

GA: I thank Don so much for his support.

SM: What word of wisdom do you want to share?

GA: I've taken it upon myself to turn negative energy into art. That is my life scope.

BACK IN THE DAY

CURRENT PHOTO

# Yolanda Touissant

(1972–1976)

Known as Little Joe Chism's regular dance partner in the 1970s, Yolanda Toussaint was a vibrant and terrific dancer as well as a "fashionista." She always had a bright smile and attracted viewers to her warm "girl next door" aura. Here is the story of her days as a popular regular on *Soul Train.*

**S**M: What were your aspirations when you were growing up in Los Angeles?

YT: To be a teacher. Dancing was just a hobby.

SM: How did you become a Soul Train dancer?

YT: I was at a club called Mavericks Flat. Pam Brown, *Soul Train*'s dance coordinator, saw me and invited me to go on the show. At the time, I didn't have a partner, so I didn't go. But a few months later, I met Little Joe Chism at Mavericks Flat, and we became friends. He was already dancing on *Soul Train*, so he invited me to come to the show, and we became dance partners.

SM: What were your impressions when you first went on *Soul Train*?

YT: It was a lot of fun! I was literally in awe of all the lights, the cameras, and all the action.

SM: Did you ever do the Scramble Board?

YT: Yes. Little Joe and I did the Scramble Board. We won a year's supply of Ultra Sheen and Afro Sheen products.

SM: What do you remember most about Don Cornelius?

YT: I was very proud of him. I didn't know that he owned the show until sometime later. We didn't really have a lot of Black people who were entrepreneurs at that time, so I was very impressed by that.

SM: You and Little Joe were contestants in a Soul Train dance contest, which was judged by Don Cornelius and James Brown. What was that experience like?

YT: I was very nervous! [laughs] But we just did our routine and had a good time.

SM: Did you and Little Joe practice routines for the Soul Train Line? Your routines were really together.

YT: No, we didn't rehearse. We basically just free-styled down the line. We showcased the latest dances and the latest fashions.

SM: You've seen a lot of famous stars perform up close on *Soul Train*. What stars stand out from your memories?

YT: The Jackson 5, James Brown, Smokey Robinson, Al Green, Chaka Khan, and the Supremes, which was Little Joe's favorite group. He was truly in love with them. Aretha Franklin was incredible! She sang her numbers live, and her soulful voice echoed through the soundstage. Her raw talent left quite an impression on me.

SM: Were you able to interact with and meet any of these celebrities personally?

YT: Yes. For example, when The Jackson 5 were on the show, Damita Jo Freeman and Little Joe came up to me and said that we were going downstairs to meet them. We met them all in their dressing room and took photos with them before they went upstairs to perform.

SM: Do you have one very special "OMG" moment from *Soul Train*?

YT: Yes, when Marvin Gaye came to the show! He was singing "Let's Get It On" and was pulling different girls out of the crowd to sing to him. All of a sudden, he pulled me out of the crowd and sang to me, and afterward, I gave him a little kiss on the cheek.

SM: Did you ever get recognized in public as a result of dancing on *Soul Train*?

YT: Little Joe and I were recognized by people we didn't even know. We became instant stars. One time, we were in Hollywood, and all of these fans ran up to us and wanted our autographs.

SM: Any other special memories from *Soul Train*?

YT: The Soul Train Christmas parties held every year were always so nice. We got to rub elbows with a lot of the entertainers that attended the parties.

SM: Was it difficult to leave *Soul Train* after five years of being on the show?

YT: I felt I was outgrowing it. I was working for the IRS and transferred to Northern California. One time, after moving to Northern California, I got off the train, and a woman looked at me and said, "Don't you dance on *Soul Train*?" [laughs] I was so blessed to have been on *Soul Train.*

SM: What have you been doing in the years since leaving *Soul Train*?

YT: I got married, and I have two sons and a daughter. I also make jewelry as a hobby.

SM: In 1997, Little Joe helped put together the very first Soul Train Gang reunion. What was that experience like?

YT: It was so wonderful and long overdue and very well organized. I just wish it was sooner and more of the dancers could have attended.

SM: Sadly, we lost Little Joe a year later. What would you like to say in memory of Little Joe Chism?

YT: His death was very devastating. He helped me get on *Soul Train*. He was very sociable and likable and always had something nice to say. If he were alive, he would have a million friends on Facebook.

SM: We lost a number of other dancers in recent years such as Tyrone Proctor, Shabba Doo, and Don Campbell. Anything you would like to say in their memory?

YT: I love and miss them all! I also want to say that Don Campbell was one of the pioneers of street dance. He was very much loved, and he was a gentle giant.

SM: How would you describe your overall experience on *Soul Train*?

YT: It was a very wonderful experience being on *Soul Train*. If it weren't for Don Cornelius, I wouldn't have my Soul Train brothers and sisters.

SM: What would you like to say in memory of Don Cornelius?

YT: Don is greatly missed, and it was so sad he was unable to see the love that people had for him and his show after his passing.

SM: Do you have a word of wisdom that you want to share?

YT: I like to live by the golden rule: Treat people the way you want to be treated. Live the life you want to live and make the most of it. For instance, after Michael Jackson died, a friend of mine and I made a vow that we were going to go to all the concerts by the artists we wanted to see perform. So, live life to the fullest, and above all, keep God first!

# Connie Blackino

(1972–1975)

Los Angeles native Connie Blackino is one of the original dancers of the early seventies Soul Train Gang. Her natural style and rhythm were a great treat for the eyes, and her excellent dancing prowess even got her into the finals of a Soul Train dance contest judged by both Don Cornelius and the Godfather of Soul, James Brown. Her story is a triumph of the spirit and in this exclusive interview, she shares her powerful testimony.

**S**M: My first question is, way before *Soul Train*, did you always love dancing?

CB: Yes, I started dancing when I was six. I took tap and ballet lessons up until I was ten.

SM: How did you become a Soul Train dancer?

CB: I went to Denker Park, where Pam Brown was the park's recreation director. She had an audition and different records were played. Everyone was trying to outdance the other, and she picked certain ones to be on the show.

SM: What are your memories of when you first went on the set of *Soul Train*?

CB: I remember the excitement and the disbelief that we were dancing on television! When *Soul Train* came about, it was an unexpected

BACK IN THE DAY

CURRENT PHOTO

and good thing. It was like a dream that you were actually dancing on television. Now that I look back, we had no idea we were becoming a part of history.

SM: Indeed. None of the early dancers had a clue about the ride they were about to embark on. My next question is—and I always ask dancers this—did you get your share of the chicken and soda during breaks?

CB: I did! [laughs]

SM: Who were some of your favorite artists that performed on *Soul Train* during the time you were a dancer on the show? Who stands out in your memory?

CB: Stevie Wonder was one of the most impacting artists to me because he was a part of that era, and as time has gone on, he is someone who is still here.

SM: Do you remember when all of the dancers stood around him as he sang a tribute to *Soul Train* while playing his piano?

CB: Yes! I remember that day because I couldn't get to the front where Stevie was. We were all trying to squeeze in to get near to Stevie, and several made it up front—like Vicki Abercrombie and Thyais Walsh..

SM: I spoke to some of the dancers about dealing with jealousy once they became well-recognized. Did you ever deal with jealousy during your time on the show?

CB: Yes. It wasn't malicious jealousy. Quite naturally, everybody wanted to have their time to shine. Some would always shine more than others. Certain dancers like Patricia Davis and Damita Jo Freeman were the shining stars. Damita could get down, but Pat had signature moves and came up with stuff that no one else was doing, and some couldn't stand her for that.

SM: You got down yourself. You could hold your own on the dance floor. I've seen footage of you. You were doing your thing!

CB: Well, thank you! Dance was my first love, and singing was my second love.

SM: There were so many dances back in the seventies, like the Breakdown and the Funky Chicken. Did you have any favorite dances?

CB: I don't think I really did. I studied tap and ballet until I was ten, and then I stopped. There was a time I was losing my rhythm. I had two cousins who could dance really well, and they took me to the skating rink where people would skate and dance, and they could really get down. They helped me get with the groove of dancing. Also, Wanda Fuller, another Soul Train dancer, was my best friend and a great choreographer. We used to do talent shows and things like that. My cousins and Wanda were natural dancers. I just developed a love for dance. So, I was able to incorporate the little bit of training I got as a young child. I wasn't a natural dancer, but I learned to get with the groove of it.

SM: Do you remember those long, endless *Soul Train* tapings?

CB: That was all fun! We used to bring a couple of outfits to change into, and all of us girls would be primping in the bathroom, trying to look better than the others.

SM: Did you ever do the Scramble Board?

CB: Yes. I got the Johnson Products. I also received a plaque that said, "Reach for the stars because you may fall upon a mountain." I lost the plaque, but it is a motto I will always remember.

SM: Did you have any favorite dance partners on *Soul Train*?

CB: Lamont Peterson, Eddie Cole, and Tyrone Proctor. I have my loving memories of dancing with those three guys on the show.

SM: There was a dance contest on the show judged by James Brown and Don Cornelius. You, Lamont, Patricia Davis, Gary Keyes, Damita Jo Freeman, and Jimmy Scoo B Doo Foster competed against one another in the finals. You and Lamont gave the others a run for their money.

CB: Oh, yes! I had forgotten about that after I went through some really hard times in my life. One day, my son called me and said I needed to Google my name. So, I did. I came across that clip from the dance contest. It brought tears to my eyes. I needed to be reminded of where I began. That's how far removed I had become from all my dilemmas in life. I don't know how many people Don has touched, but that was a big uplift for me to remember. This is how important Don Cornelius was to me in my life, and I regretted that I never got to see him again.

SM: That's really great because all of you were personally chosen by Don and James Brown to be the finalists in that dance contest.

CB: Yes. They are true legends.

SM: You visited the Jackson family's home with some of the other dancers before, right?

CB: Yes. I went with Pat Davis and Sharon Hill. We would all just be hanging out at their home. Many years later, I was told that Michael Jackson had a crush on me. I wish I'd known that back then! [laughs]

SM: You and several other *Soul Train* dancers were a part of the Soul Train road tours. When I interviewed fellow dancer Freddie Maxie, she told me that you and she were almost not part of the tour, and at the last minute, Don Cornelius wanted a couple from New Orleans to be a part of the tour.

CB: I do remember there was some kind of controversy over the final team that was going on the tour. That was also when I began my downfall in life. I was young and began to fall off the wagon. I was pregnant. No one knew. When I first agreed to do the tour and started in the process of rehearsing for the tour, I found out that I was pregnant. I still went on that first trip to New York City. When I got back to Los Angeles, I knew I wasn't going to be able to continue because a month later, the news came out that I was pregnant.

SM: Despite all of that, Pam Brown really put in a good word for you and Freddie and insisted that you two were going on the tour. As it turned out, the couple from New Orleans was unable to be a part of the tour. Do you remember the overall excitement of being a part of that tour, traveling with the Sylvers, The Whispers, Eddie Kendricks, and other artists?

CB: It was a real exciting time for us all. This was at the time Don Campbell and Freddie, who was also a part of the tour, were getting recognition for locking. But for me personally, it was a bittersweet time because I knew that I wasn't going to be able to fight the battle to continue. This is how I fell off the scene. I went home and had to tell my mom I was pregnant.

SM: You still danced on *Soul Train* afterward for a while, right?

CB: Yes. I came back to dance on the show for a little while, but it was a real lonely time for me. The sad part came when I had my baby and went back to the show. Pat, Eddie, Wanda, and Scoo B started working with Diana Ross and Tom Jones. Don Campbell had developed The Lockers dance troupe. It was a real bittersweet time for me, because just when I needed to be available to be in the mix, I had a baby. Everyone else went forward. All of the people I had been exchanging with up to that time had started out on their journeys and were living their passion. After I had danced on the show for a little while longer, I started working in music.

SM: Tell us about your journey after leaving *Soul Train*.

CB: After I left *Soul Train*, I worked and then went to school a while. When I was about nineteen, I started working in a lot of different bands. I traveled back east and to Canada. I got with a group called 24 Karat Gold. They got some radio airplay but never got really big. Then I came home for a while. My mom would take care of my son while I was on the road. When I started to fall in life, I was in my mid-twenties, and a lot of bad things happened. My mother died around that time. I fell into a bad place, and for years, I forgot about anything artistic I had done. I just fell into a bad place. That's why when I saw that clip on YouTube, it brought me back to a place where I said to myself, "That's right, I used to sing, I used to dance." It reminds me of the scripture that says when you train a child in the way he should go, he will not depart from it. Seeing that clip was at a very important time in my climb back to life.

SM: What are you doing currently?

CB: I am working on a project called *Blood Excursion,* which was formerly called *Convicted*. It's a gospel message but not gospel music. It's a testimony, and the songs that are a part of the project are all new school flavor. The songs focus on the fall of life, the prayers of life, God's love that carries you, surrendering to God, becoming His warrior, and being a testimony of life. So, the project is a testimony of my life. It's my journey, and I am doing it as a testimony. I wasn't supposed to be here, but God left me here for a reason. I'm at this stage of my life where you should always tell your testimony because you never know who it's going to help. Tell the story the way it really happened or as close as it can get. If you don't tell the truth, it's not a testimony.

SM: Very true. Your daughter is in show business as a singer, right?

CB: Yes, Eulalia was raised by her grandmother from four to fifteen. When she came back into my life, I remembered how I used to sing and dance. At fifteen, she worked with Sade, and when she was sixteen, she worked with Macy Gray. I took her into the studio to help her develop the project she put out called *Internal Lullabies*. She worked at The House of Blues here in Hollywood. She's a sultry singer like Sade. She's my real project today. All the things I have done through *Soul Train* and on my own journey when I was young have been a real good catalyst for her to have a platform to begin from.

SM: What do you want to say in memory of Don Cornelius?

CB: I hate that I never got to see Don again to say thank you. The man had a very deep true soul. I would challenge everyone who was a part of the Soul Train era in the seventies, eighties, and nineties, and part of Don's personal journey to not let time pass and forget what his journey has done for many people. When people say "*Soul Train*," don't think of the worldly part of him but think of that man's dear sweet soul.

SM: Do you have a word of wisdom you want to share?

CB: Whatever your goals are in life, be careful of your choices. Remember your choices because choices always have consequences. The consequences can be good things or bad things. Sometimes, you can make a choice that you can never get back from, so always remember to make good choices. If you don't know the answer, be still in God until you do.

# Leo "Fluky Luke" Williamson

(1972–1975)

Monroe, Louisiana, native Leo "Fluky Luke" Williamson was a member of the legendary Lockers dance troupe that changed the face of dance and helped give birth to the breakdance/hip-hop phenomenon. His style of locking and roboting was always a visual treat. The King of Pop even wanted to learn his moves. He was destined for stardom at a young age, and when it was time for his star to shine, he was prepared. Here is his story.

SM: Watching footage of you as part of The Lockers, it just seemed like dancing was in your soul. Was dancing always your aspiration?

LW: As a kid, I really wanted to work as an actor in a sitcom. I later took acting classes at Cosumnes River College. When I was about fourteen, I wanted to dance. I had a cousin named Althea Mumford who could tap dance. She would be in these dance productions, and she got me involved. Sammy Davis Jr. came to one of these productions, and I was able to meet him and shake his hand.

SM: That's quite an honor! Were you involved with any other dance or musical productions as a kid?

LW: I was part of the Young Americans when I was thirteen. My cousin, Nora Grant, helped me become a part of it. We would mix

BACK IN THE DAY

CURRENT PHOTO

choreography with singing.

SM: Although you were born in Louisiana, you grew up in Los Angeles. As a teen, you attended Crenshaw High School. Right?

LW: Right. I had a lot of friends who went there who eventually became famous, such as Rams football player Wendell Tyler, the baseball player Ellis Valentine, and Marques Johnson, who played basketball with the Milwaukee Bucks.

SM: How did your journey with *Soul Train* begin?

LW: Well, it first began when I met Shabba Doo in Chicago. I later got to know his mother, his sister Fawn, and younger sister Gina when he and his family moved to Orange County in California. He invited me to come out with him to go to this dance show called *Soul Train*, which he danced on while he lived in Chicago. It was so cold in Chicago! [laughs] When we got to the tiny stage set, the red light was on, which meant the show was in the process of being filmed. Shabba Doo and I were told not to come in until the red light was off and Don Cornelius finished up his hosting duties. Afterward, Shabba Doo introduced me to Don, and we went to this after party where Don got a check to take his show to Los Angeles.

SM: Incredible! So, you were there to witness when Don got the green light to take *Soul Train* nationally?

LW: Yes. The party was wonderful! The music played there was great! After the party, Shabba Doo and I rode with Don, and he showed us where he lived. I had a really great time out in Chicago.

SM: Did this lead you to become a dancer on the show when it moved to Los Angeles?

LW: No. One Saturday afternoon a year later, I went over to my girlfriend's house to help me with my homework. The TV was on, and *Soul Train* came on. I was excited by what I saw. I was like, "What is this? Who are all these people dancing on the show?" They were splitting and kicking, they were just getting down! Three weeks later, I ran into dancer Patricia Davis at my school. I recognized her from *Soul Train*, and we got to know each other. She's the one who got me on the show.

SM: What do you recall about your first time being on *Soul Train*?

LW: Man, my heart was thumping so fast from all the many beautiful African American women there! [laughs] Don Cornelius even remembered me from when I went to visit his local show in Chicago. There were people from Crenshaw High School, Dorsey High, and Beverly Hills High. Everyone was having a slamming good time!

SM: You had also won a dance contest on the show, right?

LW: Yes. The first time my partner and I came in third place, but the second time we did the contest, we came in first.

SM: What are your favorite memories of the guest stars that came to *Soul Train*?

LW: James Brown! The Lockers even got a chance to do some concerts with him. I also have fond memories of when The Temptations came to the show, as well as Smokey Robinson, who took me up to his house and we talked about music.

SM: You also had a great encounter with Michael Jackson while on *Soul Train*.

LW: Yes. When The Jackson 5 came to the show, Michael came over to me during a break and asked me my name. He realized that I locked differently from everyone else and wanted me to teach him some moves. We practiced at the studio in his home in Encino. I wanted to lock off "ABC," so when he put on the record, he watched as I showed him the moves, and he picked up on them until he had them down pat. I remember him introducing me to his brother Randy and his mother. Jermaine happened to walk into the studio, and he was a little annoyed at Michael because he was supposed to be using the studio at the time. [laughs]

SM: What an honor to have taught the future King of Pop locking. Do you have any other memories with the Jackson family?

LW: The Jacksons once had a party for Michael at The Citadel in Los Angeles. The Lockers, many of the Soul Train dancers, and other celebrities were there. We had a great time. I remember Jermaine gave me a ride because I had no ride back home.

SM: How did you become a part of The Lockers?

LW: Toni Basil came to a basketball game at my high school. After winning the basketball championship, me and other dancers did a victory dance to the Edwin Starr song, "War," and we tore it up! Toni came over to me afterward and admired the way I danced. She asked for the name of the dance I was doing. I called it The Crazy Leg. She then introduced me to her friend Don Campbell and wanted me to be a part of their dance group called The Lockers. So, she called my dad and asked his permission for me to join. They later met, and he gave the okay for me to join. Then I met the other members of the group: Greg "Campbell Lock," Jr., Bill "Slim the Robot" Williams, and Fred "Penguin" Berry. Shabba Doo didn't join until a little while later.

SM: How did you get the nickname "Fluky Luke?"

LW: My friend had the name Fluky Luke Jr. My nickname was Leo-Lock. So, when I became a part of The Lockers, Toni Basil said I needed to have a better character name. She threw out a couple of names and said, "What about Fluky Luke?" It was just a coincidence that my best friend's nickname was Fluky Luke Jr. He had a relative who was a professional cartoonist with the nickname Fluky Luke. So, we had to ask permission to use that name as my stage name for The Lockers. I got the okay to use it, and that's how the nickname stuck, which I had copyrighted.

SM: Who taught you how to lock?

LW: Fred Berry showed me the first parts of locking, and Greg showed me other locking steps. Greg introduced me to Jimmy "Scoo B Doo"

Foster, and we were all roommates for a while. Scoo B and I had jobs at 2010 Coffee Shop on Wilshire Boulevard.

SM: Do you remember the first or one of the first professional gigs that The Lockers did?

LW: Yes, for a Roberta Flack TV special. It was the first time we were filmed professionally as The Lockers. We had an agent at the time. The special was live, so there were no rehearsals on set. It was pretty much all improv. I remember the producers and cameramen being angry because they couldn't keep up with the dances we were doing.

SM: What was the experience like working with Roberta Flack?

LW: Roberta was a very nice person, very soft-spoken. She even calmed things down when some of the Lockers and the other dancers on the special had an argument. She also invited us to her house.

SM: Another big break came when you guys did the *Carol Burnett* show.

LW: Absolutely! Carol Burnett and her producers were really easy to work with. They let us do the dance moves we wanted to do on camera, and the cameramen kept up with us.

SM: For a little while, even though The Lockers were professional and had an agent, you guys still danced on *Soul Train*. When did you guys decide to stop dancing on the show?

LW: We stopped dancing on *Soul Train* because we were in the unions (SAG and AFTRA). We were paid performers, and since we were not paid as Soul Train dancers, we eventually left.

SM: The Lockers did go back to perform on *Soul Train* as professional performers twice, and you were paid. What was it like for you guys to go back on the show that gave you guys your very first TV exposure?

LW: It was great! I never expected Don to invite us to perform on his show. It was an honor.

SM: The Lockers have had so many great opportunities to work with a lot of great people on stage and TV. Tell me about some of The Lockers' other career highlights.

LW: We toured with Frank Sinatra, who was such a cool person. We did a Doris Day TV special. She was astounded by all of the moves we did, and she was a joy to work with. We performed on the *Grammy Awards* behind Aretha Franklin, which was cool and pretty unique. We also did the *Tonight Show, Wolfman Jack, Merv Griffin, Mike Douglas*, and *Dinah Shore*. Don Campbell would get mad if our nicknames were mispronounced. We were also on Dick Van Dyke's variety show. He was a very cool and smooth comedian, and he told us he wanted to dance like us. So, we did a skit in which he wore a Lockers outfit and hat, and we taught him locking moves.

SM: The Lockers even had the pleasure of meeting other legends and future legends during TV show tapings and tours. Who were some of those people, and what are your memories of those meetings?

LW: We met Lucille Ball, who was real nice to us. We also met John Travolta, Robin Williams, Bing Crosby, Milton Berle, and I even met Sammy Davis Jr. again during a rehearsal for a network special he and The Lockers were on. He drove me up to his home, and I met his wife, Altovise. I told him how much I loved his rendition of the song "The Wicked Old Witch is Dead."

SM: Some of The Lockers were in the classic movie *Wattstax*. How did that opportunity come about?

LW: A producer of the film saw Greg Pope—a.k.a. "Campbell Lock Jr."—at a club and wanted him to do a routine in his film, which was a concert held at the Los Angeles Memorial Coliseum. Greg got me and some of the other Lockers to do some routines. Some of it made it in the final cut of the film.

SM: What was it like to perform on *American Bandstand*?

LW: It was fun. We also wanted to dance during other segments of the show, but Dick Clark told us that we were only paid to do our performance. We wouldn't get paid to dance during the dance segments of the show since we were in the union. We understood, and he let us dance during other parts of the show—and we cut the floor up!

SM: What was the experience of doing the seventies hit TV show *What's Happening*?

LW: All of us were excited. We met all the lead actors on the show. Ernest Thomas taught us about the importance of being on time and coming back fast when break time was up. We really appreciated that.

SM: You were married to Fawn Quinones for a time, correct?

LW: Yes. We married in 1974, and we had a son, but due to irreconcilable differences, we divorced in 1977. Our divorce was finalized in 1979. I remarried in 2008 to Elizabeth Gomez.

SM: Why did The Lockers break up?

LW: Basically, after our contract fizzled, no agent would take us on. We were viewed as a novelty act, and at that time in 1977, agencies didn't have the need for novelty acts.

SM: Shabba Doo was able to get you on the variety show, *NBC's Big Show*, right?

LW: Yes. It was taped at Gower Studio. He got me, Ana Sanchez, Patricia Davis, and others to perform in many dance numbers on the show. The show didn't last long, however.

SM: Being that you were no longer dancing or in the entertainment industry, what were things like for you afterward?

LW: It was a difficult time for me. I wanted an office job, but no one would hire me. I eventually got some jobs here and there, such as a job in a federal program and a job in the automobile club. I filed for unemployment in 1983 or 1984 and later got security guard work, which lasted until 1988. Then, I did temporary job assignments until I landed a job at Walmart in Burlington, New Jersey, for ten years.

SM: You, along with Don Campbell, Shabba Doo, Greg "Campbell Lock Jr.," and other notable dancers were a part of Michael Jackson's

"Ghosts" video in 1996. What was that experience like working with and being reacquainted with Michael?

LW: It was fun! I happened to meet up with Shabba Doo, and he helped me become a part of the project. We wore a lot of heavy makeup and outfits to resemble ghosts and zombies while doing our locking steps! [laughs] Michael never forgot us.

SM: You now have a new style of dance and rap, right?

LW: Yes. It's called "leocougarcop," a combination of dance and rap that I have been working on.

SM: Any other personal achievements you want to share?

LW: I graduated from the Ultimate Medical Academy with a degree as a medical assistant.

SM: Congratulations to you, bro! In one word, what was your overall experience with The Lockers?

LW: Fantastico!!

SM: You still teach locking, correct?

LW: Yes! I teach all kinds of dance classes such as hip-hop, tap, ballet, jazz, and "lockercizing" classes.

SM: What word of wisdom do you want to share?

LW: For anyone who wants to dance or go in the entertainment industry, educate yourself, learn about the business, and become more business-oriented.

BACK IN THE DAY

CURRENT PHOTO

# Sherry "Sage"Newman

(1972–1974)

> Sherry "Sage" Newman didn't try to be a popular regular or fit into any cliques on the show. She was just happy to be on the show to dance, have fun, and see the recording artists. Years later, she devoted her life to helping others live better and enriching lives. Even with glaucoma, she has not let that stop her from doing anything she wants to do, not even becoming an author. Here is her story.

**S**M: How did you become a Soul Train dancer?

SN: My mother, Pat Newman, was very active in the community. She knew a lot of people, such as Maxine Waters. She had her own show on KGFJ radio called *Pat's Points* that aired Sundays. Through her connections, she met Pam Brown, who was the dance coordinator for *Soul Train*, and she introduced me to her, so that's how I got on the show.

SM: When you first walked on the set of the show, what were your impressions?

SN: I remember thinking how small the place was! But it was still very exciting.

SM: What are your memories of some of your favorite artists that appeared on the show?

SN: I remember when Aretha Franklin was on and Al Green. When I asked him what his zodiac sign was, and he wouldn't answer, I was so mad! When The Jackson 5 came on, I was mainly focused on Jermaine [laughs]! One memory that stands out is when the Delfonics came on. I was able to kiss one of their members. That was a good kiss!

SM: What was it like for you going down that Soul Train Line?

SN: I remember one time I went down with my partner, Gary Allen. Right before we went down the line, my top busted! I was able to get it fixed, but when I went down the line with him, I was very cautious.

SM: I call the early to mid-seventies the golden era of *Soul Train.*

SN: We were very proud of ourselves! In the beginning, there was a fun sweetness to the show. There were different kinds of dancers, even one with a big toothbrush. But as the years went on, it became very scripted.

SM: What was the camaraderie like among the dancers?

SN: I saw some cattiness, and there were cliques. Damita Jo Freeman was never cliquish but always very nice. I remember a group of dancers from Pasadena who were referred to as the Pasadena Crew. After I left *Soul Train,* I moved to Hollywood and worked at the House of Pancakes. The Pasadena Crew would come there before going to the tapings. I also remember Cheryl Song from school. She wore pigtails and big glasses. When she became a cheerleader, she came out of her shell, and by the time she got on *Soul Train*, she showed everyone up!

SM: What were your impressions of Don Cornelius?

SN: I respected Don. He was never inappropriate with any of us. Don was nice, but I kept my distance and stayed in the background. We were happy when he cut his Afro down! [laughs]

SM: What are your memories of the "gum lady," Pam Brown?

SN: She kept peace on the set and kept all the dancers in line. She was Don's assistant, and she would check people if they dressed or acted inappropriately.

SM: What do you remember about the clubs in Los Angeles?

SN: After the *Soul Train* tapings, we went to clubs like Maverick's Flat and the Total Experience. We had so much fun. Those were the days!

SM: Some of the dancers said the early days of *Soul Train* had very long tapings. Do you recall that?

SN: Yes! We usually started at 10:00 a.m. and would wrap about 1:00 a.m. Being that we taped on Saturdays and Sundays, if the Saturday taping ran very late, we were expected to be at the studio bright and early on Sunday morning. During breaks, we got two pieces of chicken and orange soda.

SM: What was it like doing the Scramble Board?

SN: I only got one bottle of Afro Sheen, not a one-year supply as I was promised. I also only got one *Essence* magazine instead of a year's subscription.

SM: You have gone through some challenges over the years. One was being diagnosed with glaucoma. Tell me about this.

SN: When I was in my mid-thirties, I went to get fitted for glasses and contact lenses but I was never told that I needed to go to an ophthalmologist. I was diagnosed with glaucoma at age thirty-nine. Everyone needs to get their eyes checked, especially their eye pressure.

SM: I can imagine it must have been very challenging for you.

SN: Yes, but many people call glaucoma a disability, but I call it a "different ability." Anytime you put "dis" in front of a word it's negative, like dislike or discontinue. So for me, glaucoma is a different ability and a challenge, which is basically a determination to overcome a difficult situation. I am also a survivor of domestic violence, and I currently have a wonderful new partner in my life.

SM: Congratulations! Despite all the challenges you faced, you have done a lot of wonderful things in the years since and you're still evolving.

SN: Right. I am the CEO Valley Light Industries, where I am an advocate working with people who have special needs. I also started working with children and took them in. I am the proud foster parent to thirty kids over eleven years, many of whom were troubled and abused girls. Additionally, I worked with and counseled women who came out of prison and I am the author of the book *Valory Light Goes to School* about a little girl with Down Syndrome who meets other children like her in school. I am also working on other books, including my memoir, and I have a patent for a new product called Butchie Boots, which are like GPS trackers placed in the compartment of children's footwear so that parents will always know where their children are. This can save children from abduction and other crimes.

SM: What do you want to say in memory of Don Cornelius whom we lost tragically?

SN: I was so disheartened by his death. I have nothing but respect for the man. He was always professional.

SM: What word of wisdom do you want to share?

SN: In life, you grow. We are not the same people. When I nurture young girls, I look at myself and see that I have survived.

# Erwin Bernard Thompson

(1972–1975)

There were many great dancers on *Soul Train*. But one of the best dance couples in the history of *Soul Train* was Erwin Bernard Thompson and Diana Price, who happened to be the first married couple who ever danced on the program. Their routines and moves were always perfectly coordinated and timed, and they were a treat to watch. They were even featured in an exclusive interview in *Right On*! Magazine. Here is the story behind half the couple known as *Soul Train*'s dancing duo.

SM: Where are you originally from?

ET: From right here in Los Angeles.

SM: Did you love to dance when you were a child?

ET: As a child, I loved dancing even though I was too young to know what dancing was. [laughs] Everyone knew I could dance. I was at every dance hop when I was a teenager. Prior to that, from first to sixth grade, May Day dances would be held, and kids from all the schools in the area would attend them.

SM: How did you get on *Soul Train*?

ET: I was at a club called the Citadel, which, along with the Climax and Maverick's Flat, was one of the biggest clubs in Los Angeles. Pam

BACK IN THE DAY

CURRENT PHOTO

Brown was there that night. She saw me dancing and invited me to come to a taping. This was around the time when the national version of *Soul Train* was just getting off the ground.

SM: Before you went on, had you seen the show?

ET: I think I saw one or two episodes before I was invited to the show.

SM: What are your memories of that first taping?

ET: The first time I went to *Soul Train* was with Pat Davis. I met her at the Citadel the same night I met Pam Brown. She needed a partner for the show that weekend, so we danced together. It was such a fun day.

SM: What were your impressions of Don Cornelius after seeing him in person for the first time?

ET: I was very impressed. I was so happy for him and for the show promoting good, clean fun for Black teens and helping to give them exposure. I was elated that this was an all-Black thing. It was an exciting time for Black people, a time of brotherhood. Those were times I will never forget.

SM: Did you get recognized after being on *Soul Train* that first time?

ET: Yes. After the airing of my first time on the show, I went to the store on Broadway for my mom, and people recognized me and applauded!

SM: Don doesn't always get the credit he deserves for giving young people the opportunity to be exposed on nationwide television.

ET: That is true. I remember one time he made it possible for me and other dancers from the show to go to a grammar school to meet and greet fans. We weren't on his payroll, but we helped him out, and we all had a stake in letting many people know about *Soul Train*. He appreciated that.

SM: This was when you got to know fellow *Soul Train* dancer Tyrone Proctor, right?

ET: Yes. One of the times, after we had finished distributing fliers about

*Soul Train*, he didn't have a way to get back to Hollywood, so I gave him a ride. When I saw him some years ago at a Soul Train Gang reunion, he told me he would never forget what I did for him that day.

SM: Were you involved in the entertainment industry before you went to *Soul Train*?

ET: Yes. Prior to *Soul Train*, Eddie Cole, a girl named Valencia and I had formed a dance group called The Natural Three. We got an agent and were booked to dance at colleges and schools.

SM: Why didn't The Natural Three continue?

ET: The group just phased out, so we jumped on the Soul Train bandwagon.

SM: After that first weekend appearing on *Soul Train*, did you become a regular?

ET: No, not yet. I still had to audition in order for my name to be on a list for the regular dancers. Me, Eddie Cole, Wanda Fuller, and Diana Thompson went to Denker Park in Los Angeles, where they held auditions. We all got picked and became regulars.

SM: Did you and your future dance partner and wife Diana meet at this audition?

ET: We actually first met at the Citadel. We just clicked. We both loved to dance, and we started conversing, began dating, and got married in June 1973.

SM: I have to say that you and Diana are, in my opinion, one of the tightest dance couples in *Soul Train*'s history. Your moves were always together, and you were always in sync. You both epitomized what the joy and rhythm of dance was all about. In fact, *Essence* magazine used to run an ad for *Soul Train* every month in the seventies featuring a drawing of a couple dancing and I really believe that couple was modeled after you and Diana.

ET: Wow! Thanks! [laughs]

SM: I'm sure it took a lot of rehearsals for you two to get your moves down pat.

ET: Diana and I rehearsed every day when I got home from work. She had rhythm, but I had to teach her and help her with the steps, but she eventually picked up on the beat. Her main drive was school, and her energies were focused on that.

SM: Did you and Diana ever dance on *American Bandstand*?

ET: Yes. We went on Bandstand and had a lot of fun.

SM: Did you two ever appear on *Soul Unlimited*, which was produced by Dick Clark?

ET: Yes. Don Cornelius was mad about that program. He had his show, which was only a few years old, and this new show was taking most of his dancers.

SM: Did Don ban any of the dancers who danced on *Soul Unlimited* from dancing on *Soul Train* again?

ET: Well, he didn't actually come out and say that you would be banned from *Soul Train*, but we picked up on his demeanor. But I enjoyed going to *Soul Unlimited* also. Dick Clark also did a lot in giving young people television exposure.

SM: Do you have any OMG moments from *Soul Train*?

ET: Yes! Several. I remember one time when Michael Jackson was on the show; during a break in taping, he stood on the stage dangling his microphone, which had a very long cord. Without him knowing, the microphone hit me on the head by accident! [laughs] Another moment was when Gladys Knight and the Pips were on the show. I was standing close by the stage, and during a break in taping, Gladys came to the side of the stage. She reached out to me and said, "Hi. How are you?" We had an instant connection, and she was just the nicest person.

When Diana Ross came to the show to do an interview with Don, she signed her autograph for me during a break. She signed it "Bernardo."

[laughs] I still have the autograph. She was so nice. Smokey Robinson was another great and wonderful person. He and I took a picture together.

SM: When the Godfather of Soul James Brown came on *Soul Train* with the J.B.'s, that had to be one of the most memorable experiences of seeing an artist on the show.

ET: It was definitely an experience to see how his production was made and put together! With James Brown, we never had to wait on set and watch him and his band set up. When the dancers had lunch, his band set up all their instruments, so by the time we got back on the set, they were ready to perform.

SM: It must have been a memorable experience to see new artists come on *Soul Train,* such as when the late, great Minnie Riperton first came to the show.

ET: She sang with class. It was like listening to a bird. She had no strain whatsoever in her voice. Artistry was definitely at its highest during that time.

SM: You and Diana eventually divorced. Could you explain what led to you two no longer being together?

ET: Diana and I just grew apart. I put in a forty-hour work week, along with spending time with Diana and rehearsing our routines. I wanted to go in a different direction, so I stopped dancing on *Soul Train*, but she was still going to the show since she had gotten "the camera bug." I had to break away and get out of the dance scene for a while and find some "me" time. Something had to give.

SM: What did you do after that situation?

ET: I got a new job and started making a decent living and taking classes. I still danced at clubs, but I needed to concentrate on me.

SM: You have since remarried, right?

ET: Yes. In 1992, I remarried. Between the both of us, we have three adult children, seven grandchildren, and one great-grandson.

SM: Congratulations! Have your kids and grandkids seen any footage of you dancing on *Soul Train* with that big Afro?

ET: Yes. They get a trip out of seeing that footage. They always compliment their pop and grandpa! [laughs]

SM: Considering your background in dance, do you ever see yourself teaching dance or being involved in the entertainment industry again?

ET: In 2006, I was looking to work in some capacity with *Soul Train* when I found out it was canceled! But I would love to teach dance. Since I am a former *Soul Train* dancer, I wouldn't mind going on *Dancing with the Stars.*

SM: What do you want to say in memory of Don Cornelius?

ET: I'd like to take this opportunity to acknowledge Mr. Don Cornelius for opening doors and providing a sense of a dream come true for many. Being a part of history is certainly something to be proud of, and I really appreciate that. To the dancers on the show whom I've come to know all of these years, love and respect to you all, and thank you for being a special part of my life!

SM: What word of wisdom do you want to share?

ET: I would encourage everybody, no matter how young or old, to still follow your dreams, walk the straight and narrow pathway until your mission is accomplished, bypassing all distractions.

SM: By the way, you had the most together Afro back in the day! You must have used a lot of Afro Sheen to hold it up. Right on brother! [laughs]

ET: Thanks! [Laughs] I look at old pictures of myself now and I ask myself, what was I thinking? [Laughs] When we would go to the movies I would make some people mad because my natural would be blocking their view so I would move! [laughs]

BACK IN THE DAY

CURRENT PHOTO

# Thyais Walsh

(1972–1976)

Thyais Walsh, that "pretty girl with the model looks and pretty smile," was one of the most often seen faces on *Soul Train* in the early to mid-seventies. She was one of several dancers who comprised the "Pasadena Crew," a group of stylishly dressed dancers from Pasadena, California who came to *Soul Train* to, as Don Cornelius would say, "style a while" and dance and have a good time. Walsh is also an accomplished actress and model, having graced many magazine covers, including *Essence*, as well as appearing on many television shows and commercials, including an Ultra Sheen commercial. She knew what she wanted from a young age, and she went on to pursue it with passion.

SM: What were your aspirations as a child?

TW: Actually, to be a singer and then a model.

SM: Did you grow up in Pasadena?

TW: I was born in Birmingham, Alabama, and raised in Baltimore, Maryland. I moved to Los Angeles when I was in middle school.

SM: I was told Pasadena was where many affluent African Americans have lived over the years.

TW: There were celebrities who lived in Pasadena because they didn't want to live in Los Angeles.

SM: How did you become a dancer on *Soul Train*?

TW: I was in my first year of high school, and they were looking for more dancers. We auditioned at Denker Park with Pam Brown. Allen Crowder was my dance partner, and the other couple was Renee Crowder and Larry Jennings. Allen and Larry were up-and-coming designers, so they would just design all of our clothes, which we wore on *Soul Train*. Before we did *Soul Train*, we started this group called Black Rose Odyssey where we put on fashion shows and Allen and Larry made our clothes. When *Soul Train* came along, we would be dressed to the nines.

SM: What were your impressions of the first day you stepped onto the *Soul Train* set?

TW: We were getting ready to have fun and to meet people. Being able to see the entertainers close up and to go dancing and to be on television was a big thing! We loved to dance! But back in the day, it took forever to tape those shows.

SM: Being a former dancer on the show, I know that there was a lot of waiting around between dance numbers and artists' performances. How did you deal with all of that?

TW: We would sneak out and then come back! Sometimes, there were parties or events that took place on the same weekends *Soul Train* was shot. Once we got to meet and know some of the entertainers that came to *Soul Train* like Labelle and The Jackson 5, they would invite us to their parties, and we'd get to know them. So, we would leave and go to one of the parties we had been invited to, and then we'd come back to the studio and tape and dance for the rest of the night. We would eat the fried chicken that was given to the dancers, but sometimes we'd sneak out and get our own food.

SM: Aside from the Pasadena Crew, who were some of your other friends on the show?

TW: Little Joe Chism, Damita Jo Freeman, Pat Davis, Tyrone Proctor, everybody!

SM: So, it was really a family-type atmosphere.

TW: Absolutely! It was like a family reunion every month we taped the show. We would see each other in other places during the month, but we all knew we were going to get together and have a good time one weekend every month.

SM: Were you ever recognized in public during your time dancing on *Soul Train*?

TW: Oh, yeah! Especially after the Stevie Wonder episode where a close-up was done on me during his performance. There was a show with Johnny Mathis, and he called me out to sit with him because he liked the way I had my hair. I had my hair braided with bells on the ends of my hair. That was a really cool moment.

SM: Did you ever deal with jealousy on the set or off the set as a *Soul Train* dancer?

TW: No, I didn't, not that I know of. If someone was jealous, I didn't pay attention to it.

SM: What were your impressions of Don Cornelius? Some dancers I spoke to found him to be intimidating.

TW: No, I don't think he was intimidating. He was doing his job. Our group really didn't pay that much attention to him. We were having fun and trying to get on the risers and dealing with Pam Brown and Chuck Johnson (dance coordinators for the show).

SM: Were they very selective in the process of putting dancers on risers?

TW: Yes. If you were dancing, they were really fair about who they would let on the risers. They rotated the dancers so that everybody had a chance to be on the risers.

SM: What performers did you enjoy watching perform on *Soul Train*?

TW: Labelle! They came on with those unique outfits, and we all ended up being Labelle fans. We would get all dressed up to see their concerts when they came to town. I also enjoyed Roberta Flack, Stevie Wonder, Al Green, and Teddy Pendergrass, with Harold Melvin & the Blue Notes. James Brown was fabulous! I just enjoyed everybody because to me their performances were like private concerts. You had a chance to meet them and go backstage and talk to them. I ended up becoming friends with Jermaine and Jackie Jackson, as well as Patti Labelle, Nona Hendryx, and Sarah Dash. I still know them and talk to them to this day.

SM: Did you ever dance on *American Bandstand*?

TW: Yes. It was different, but it was fun. It was more of a fine-tuned machine compared to *Soul Train* in terms of production and timing, and how it was done because it had been done for so long.

SM: When did your modeling career begin?

TW: I left *Soul Train* and started modeling in New York with Ford Modeling Agency at the age of seventeen during the summer and holidays. I was one of the few Black girls with Ford. Eileen Ford really believed in me. I think I was one of the first people from *Soul Train* to book a commercial for Ultra Sheen that aired during *Soul Train*.

SM: What was the experience like filming that commercial? Was it a long taping?

TW: Yes! It was an all-day shoot.

SM: Did you do magazine covers or other commercials?

TW: At seventeen years old, I was the youngest girl on the cover of *Essence*. I did cigarette ads, hair ads, beer ads, and a ton of catalogs. I was one of the top ten Black models in the country at one point. I also modeled in Europe and Paris, and I was on many major Black magazine covers. I had about nine commercials running at one point. I've also done *Law & Order* and had guest spots on *Different Strokes*, *T.J.*

*Hooker* and other shows.

SM: Many young women who pursued modeling careers dealt with a lot of shadiness behind the scenes. Was it all positive for you as a model, or did you have to deal with underhanded things that went on in the modeling industry?

TW: Back in the day, there wasn't a lot of work for Black girls. There was the light-skinned and dark-skinned kind of thing. Being that I was middle-complexioned didn't make it easy. Eileen Ford of the Ford Modeling Agency believed in me and gave me a chance. Billie Blair watched me when I was doing the junior modeling shows. I was just blessed. I was a New York model, and Los Angeles models are totally different from New York models. In New York, we were all in it, trying to help each other.

SM: What advice would you give to girls who want to go into the modeling profession?

TW: First of all, the business has changed a lot, so everybody thinks they can model. When I was starting out, you got paid pretty decently for what you were doing and got an agent. The business has changed so much, and a lot of girls are being exploited. Back then, you had to go with a legitimate agency, do a lot of catalogs and test pictures. If aspiring models are attending school or college, they should go to the photography department and ask one of the photographers to test them and see what their look is like. At colleges, there are always photography departments. That's how I did it. I went to the photography department when I needed pictures and decided I wanted to model. I had a lot of great people who encouraged me and pushed me and talked my mother into letting me go to New York to pursue my modeling career.

SM: What are you doing currently in your professional career?

TW: I just moved back to Los Angeles some years ago. For over fifteen years, I was doing regional theatre in New York and studying theatre as well so I could be a great actress and not just a pretty girl. I wanted to hone and study my craft. I am currently writing and acting and getting back to doing commercials.

SM: What would you like to say in memory of Don Cornelius?

TW: What Don did with *Soul Train* was brilliant. He created something for Black artists to get exposure, like Arsenio Hall did. You didn't see a lot of Black artists on *American Bandstand* like you saw on *Soul Train.* Don also gave Black high school kids something to do one weekend out of every month to boost their self-esteem and feel good about themselves. They had a chance to feel good about themselves for one weekend dancing and being seen on television.

SM: What word of wisdom do you want to share?

TW: Follow your dreams and trust God. Believe in yourself and have faith no matter how hard it gets, and work at it. Study your craft. People nowadays think success is going to happen overnight, or it should happen overnight, or that somebody owes them something. It's work. It's show business. It's a business. It's about how you are marketing yourself as well as how you are representing yourself both on and off camera. Up-and-coming artists have to be very well educated and have command of the English language, and they also need to know how to act in all situations. You have to be a chameleon in this world.

# Victoria Abercrombie Walker

(1972–1977)

Victoria Abercrombie Walker, or "Vicki," is one of *Soul Train*'s all-time "fashionistas," well known for her great fashions and styles she wore during her time on the show. She is also known for her own individual dance style that stood out among the other dancers. One of *Soul Train*'s popular regulars, she has always believed in being an original, not a carbon copy of others, and she carries this same belief to this very day.

SM: Where are you originally from?

VW: I was born in Texas but raised in Los Angeles.

SM: What were your aspirations when you were growing up?

VW: I wanted to be in show business. People always said I was going to be famous or something special. In high school, I was voted most popular in my class and was also voted Prom Queen, and I was a majorette in eleventh grade. I liked dancing, but I was more into fashion.

SM: How did your journey with *Soul Train* begin?

VW: I was invited to go on tryouts for *Soul Train* at Denker Park in Los Angeles. I passed the audition, and I went to the taping.

SM: What do you remember about that first time at *Soul Train*?

CURRENT PHOTO

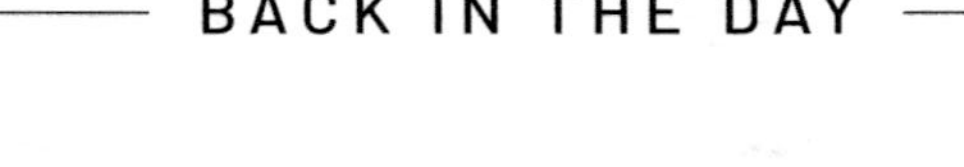

BACK IN THE DAY

VW: It was such a long day! I was exhausted at the end of the day, but I had a desire to come back again the next day.

SM: Who are some of your favorite artists that performed on *Soul Train*?

VW: The Jackson 5, the Sylvers, Stevie Wonder, Marvin Gaye, Labelle, Barry White, Chaka Khan, James Brown, and The Pointer Sisters.

SM: The Pointer Sisters were definitely trendsetters at that time. They influenced the looks of some of the other girls on the show like Pat Davis and Fawn Quinones. Were you influenced by The Pointer Sisters?

VW: I loved The Pointer Sisters! I loved their 1940-ish style outfits with the floral dresses and the platform heels. They were very unique.

SM: What do you remember about Stevie Wonder's first appearance on *Soul Train*?

VW: It touched my heart. He couldn't see, but I was in awe of the things he could do. We can see, and we can't do half of the things he can do. I was so amazed by the *Soul Train* song he created for the dancers. I was overwhelmed by it.

SM: Michael Jackson was on *Soul Train* several times as part of The Jackson 5 and by himself. What stood out to you about him other than his incredible talent?

VW: He seemed kind of shy, but he was more talkative back then. I became friends with the Jackson family, and I even attended the wedding reception of his brother Jermaine and Hazel Gordy.

SM: What were your impressions of Labelle when they came to *Soul Train*?

VW: They were a way-out group! [laughs] But they were entertaining, and they delivered!

SM: I saw that classic clip where you and the other girls were all under a spell when Marvin Gaye sang "Let's Get It On." What was Marvin Gaye like?

VW: He was very approachable and a very down-to-earth, smooth kind of man. It was a total surprise that he was going to be a guest on the show. None of us knew!

SM: Chaka Khan and her band Rufus appeared a number of times while you danced on the show. What are your memories of her?

VW: When I think of Chaka, she makes you just want to dance! She was a party girl and whenever she and Rufus came to the show, she enabled the dancers to party!

SM: You were also on the show when Sly and the Family Stone came and literally turned out the *Soul Train*. What was it like seeing them perform?

VW: One phrase sums them up: they were dynamite!

SM: How do you feel that you were so up close to all of those legendary artists?

VW: It was a once-in-a-lifetime experience. I was in the presence of different artists, many of whom are no longer here, and I am so grateful for that experience.

SM: Did you have your share of the cold fried chicken and warm sodas given to the dancers?

VW: [laughs] I ate the chicken when I first started going to the show, but after a while, I couldn't take it, so I would go out for lunch during breaks.

SM: Did you have any best buddies while you were on *Soul Train*?

VW: Yes! Sharon Hill was and still is my best friend. I am her daughter's godmother. But I had love for everybody on the show. We were all one big happy family.

SM: Did you ever experience any jealousy while you were on the show?

VW: No. I didn't experience any jealousy. It was more like a family on *Soul Train*. There would be a lot of gossip, and sometimes there was some jealousy when certain people got to dance on the risers, but I never personally experienced any jealousy.

SM: You didn't really get caught up in the other styles of dances that the other dancers were doing that were popular at the time.

VW: No, I didn't. I didn't pop lock or do any of those other dances. I had my own way of dancing.

SM: What did you call your style of dancing?

VW: My dance style was called Victoria's Secret. I felt pop-locking was more for guys. I couldn't see myself doing that. Whatever I do, I bring taste to it. Even today, I do my own little thing when I dance, and it's called Victoria's Secret. I'm going to be me. I don't care what anyone else does; I'm going to bring me.

SM: I love that word of wisdom! What was it like working with Pam Brown, who was the coordinator of the dancers of that time? Did you ever fall victim to her "chewing gum ritual?" [laughs]

VW: Yes! [laughs] I loved to chew gum, and Pam used to catch me all the time and would tell me to spit my gum out! I loved Pam! She was loving and kind.

SM: You and several of the other dancers appeared in the movie *Five On The Blackhand Side* in the wedding scene. How did that come about?

VW: The producer, Brock Peters, contacted Pam and said he wanted to use *Soul Train* dancers for a certain scene in the film. It was a lot of fun doing that movie.

SM: In an old issue of *Right On!* magazine, you mentioned you had a problem with stalkers as a result of being a popular *Soul Train* regular. What was that like?

VW: Creepy! It's unbelievable how I would get strange letters and phone calls from people in the middle of the night. I know how celebrities feel! You try to accommodate everyone, but there are just days you don't want to be bothered.

SM: Speaking of *Right On!* magazine, you were featured in several issues. How did that come about?

VW: Flo Jenkins, the editor of *Right On!* called me and wanted me to do a photo shoot for the magazine. The issue in which me and fellow dancer Tyrone Swan were on the cover was one of *Right On!*'s top-selling issues.

SM: What was that experience like doing a photo shoot?

VW: I was nervous at first, but then an ease came over me, and I just did me.

SM: Did you ever dance on *American Bandstand*?

VW: I went occasionally. I wasn't a regular. I went for a change of pace. Dick Clark interacted more with the dancers and sat down with us.

SM: What are your memories of Don Cornelius?

VW: I got along with him. He was like a father, and we were his children. But overall, he isolated himself. He definitely drew a line. He didn't allow people to get too close to him. He had a closed spirit. We knew Don, but then again, we really didn't know him.

SM: You and a lot of the other Soul Train dancers danced on a short-lived show called *Soul Unlimited*. What do you remember about that? How did Don feel about it?

VW: Don didn't like it, but what could he do? We weren't paid and didn't sign contracts with *Soul Train*, so we were free to dance on other programs.

SM: What were some of the disadvantages of being on *Soul Train*?

VW: The dancers made Don millions, but we didn't get anything. The only time we got paid was when we were hired to do something outside of *Soul Train*. The dancers didn't have a salary. That kind of discouraged me, and that's why I stopped coming to the show. On Mondays I was tired and had to go to school after the late tapings. We were stagnated.

SM: What did you do after leaving *Soul Train*?

VW: I went to California State University. I also did some modeling and eventually went into the workforce.

SM: What are your impressions of the later years of *Soul Train*?

VW: I discontinued watching it. It wasn't the same.

SM: You currently run your own business called Something Special. How did that come about?

VW: Something Special is a decorating business. I was influenced by my grandmother, who was a caterer, and I would assist her. God blessed my hands to be creative. Basically, I take something and make it special. I decorate for events, weddings, birthday parties, graduations, champagne parties, and any event that needs that special touch.

SM: What was your overall experience with *Soul Train* like?

VW: I'm grateful for the friendships us dancers had with each other. The bond we have never would have happened if it weren't for Don Cornelius creating *Soul Train*. Coming together one weekend out of the month will always be dear to me. Don's death also helped many of us reconnect.

SM: What would you like to say in memory of Don Cornelius?

VW: He brought entertainment to the world, which enabled everyone to be a part of the celebration because his show was one big celebration.

SM: Do you have a word of wisdom you want to share?

VW: Be you. Never allow anyone or anything to change you. Live the life God has for you.

CURRENT PHOTO

# Sharon Hill-Wood

(1972–1978, 1980, 1981)

Sharon Hill-Wood was one of the prettiest and best dancers to grace *Soul Train*. Her dance routines with her regular dance partner, Tyrone "The Bone" Proctor, won each of them many fans across the country, and they became one of the show's most popular dance couples. They even won a dance contest on *American Bandstand*. She also met her future husband, Mark Wood of the R&B/funk group Lakeside on *Soul Train*. Here is her story.

**S**M: Coming from Galveston, Texas, what were your ambitions growing up?

SW: I was geared toward a career in dancing and music. I just wanted to dance.

SM: How did your journey with *Soul Train* begin?

SW: My older sister always invited me to California. While I was staying with her, a neighbor named Cedric invited me to a skating rink in Los Angeles. After I skated, I went to the ladies' room and met Pat Davis. We spoke, and she invited me to *Soul Train*, taking me on as a guest. I am so thankful to Pat. If it weren't for her, I might never have been a Soul Train dancer.

SM: What do you remember about the first time you were on the *Soul Train* set?

SW: Seeing all of the dancers and the *Soul Train* sign was just like a dream.

SM: When did you first meet your future dance partner on the show Tyrone Proctor?

SW: Well, Pat told me that I had to have a partner on the show. She saw a new dancer named Tyrone rehearsing his dance moves and asked him if he would be my partner. So, we got together and were asked to do a routine for the weekly dance contest. Tyrone and I did the "PA Slaughter," which got us into the Los Angeles finals of the *Soul Train* dance contest. Tyrone and I became real close friends, like two peas in a pod. We remained close friends until his passing.

SM: What were your impressions of Don Cornelius?

SW: Don would sit with his legs crossed and a cigarette in this tall producer's chair. He would watch everything on the set like a hawk. Many dancers would amuse him, especially Mr. X and Don Campbell. He would tell the coordinator, Pam Brown, to put certain dancers on the risers or at the beginning of the Soul Train Line. He also would not permit certain types of clothing to be worn by the girls. Although he was quiet, he would throw out some jokes before introducing the acts. Pam Brown was basically his voice on the set to the dancers.

SM: What were some of your favorite memories of recording artists that came to the show?

SW: Labelle for one. Patti Labelle had such a sweetness about her. The whole group was so coordinated with their outfits. Everyone was excited when The Jackson 5 would perform on the show. All the dancers made sure they were on the set whenever The Jackson 5 appeared. The Whispers were just amazing! When Marvin Gaye was on, all the girls pushed up on him, but I stayed in the background! [laughs] Lakeside was so funky. Chaka Khan—I loved her voice! Barry White and so many other great bands and artists came on, and they really appreciated the dancers. It was like the dancers were given free mini concerts. You could always tell when the dancers really liked the artists. We'd be yelling and screaming, and Little Joe would blow his whistle!

SM: You mentioned The Jackson 5. You and several of the other dancers were friends with them and the whole family. The dancers went to the movies with them. Some of you threw a party for them when they made their debut in Las Vegas in 1974 and would visit their home, hang out with them, and dance, right?

SW: Right! Mrs. Jackson was always kind. Michael was really shy. I remember one time we were visiting, and when we were about to leave at 9:00 p.m., he was hiding behind a hedge. His security guard, Bill Bray, told him he couldn't stay outside because of the effect the cool weather could have on his voice. He went inside, and I remember him looking at us from a window, waving and looking sad.

SM: A number of the Soul Train dancers were also invited to the lavish Jermaine Jackson/Hazel Gordy wedding. I found out that after the reception, there was this big after party at Gwen Gordy's mansion, and you, Pat Davis, Diana Ross, and Lola Falana got down together showcasing your great dance moves!

SW: Yes! It was really exciting to be in the presence of celebrities you looked up to. I remember earlier that day we had just come off the road from a concert and we had to rush to get ready for the wedding! [laughs]

SM: You also had an encounter with Mick Jagger, right?

SW: Right. I met him at the Los Angeles Forum, and he invited several of the dancers on stage to dance. Then he invited us to a party at Diana Ross's house.

SW: In the summer of 1973, you, Tyrone, Pat Davis, Connie Blackino, Gary Keyes, Don Campbell, Jimmy "Scoo B Doo" Foster, Freddie Maxie, and Edith Pickens were chosen to perform as part of the Soul Train road tours. That must have been quite an honor for all of you.

SW: We didn't expect to be so popular! Everywhere we went, the audiences were so happy and excited to see us. They reacted to us like we were stars, like they were seeing The Jackson 5! They would even be screaming for us! It was like a dream.

SM: One of the Soul Train road tours' first stops was at the legendary Apollo Theatre in New York. What was that experience like?

SW: You have no idea what that was like! We were told that if the audience didn't like us, they would throw things at us. We were so nervous, but we worked hard, rehearsed, and realized we just had to do what we do and do our best. When we went out on stage, the kids screamed as we danced. They didn't throw anything at us. The audience received us very well, and they wanted to reach out and touch us.

SM: News and magazine clippings noted that the Soul Train Gang was a smash on the road tours everywhere they went, and the audiences would go into pandemonium when all of you would dance on stage.

SW: Absolutely! One time at the Apollo, however, I almost got pulled off the stage by my wrists by some overzealous fans. I started to lose my balance and nearly fell into the audience, but some of the dancers were able to pull me out of the grip of the fans in the nick of time!

SM: All of you had to execute some pretty intricate routines. Were there any steps that were difficult for you to do?

SW: I remember when it was time to do a handstand and flip routine with Tyrone, I had a problem doing it. I had to mentally go into myself and say that I could do this, so when it was time to execute the routine, I did it. Pat could do all of her movements with such grace and ease. Her splits were something to watch! Don Campbell would add a lot of creative things to his locking dance. His own style was amazing.

SM: Do you have any other special memories about the road tours?

SW: In Chicago, we met Muhammad Ali. He stayed at the same hotel that we did. He playfully acted like he was punching us. [laughs] When we toured with Joe Simon, he and his wife invited us to their home for dinner. It was like a huge feast to us. My parents were sitting up front during our show with Joe Simon. My dad told me my mom cried happy tears when she saw me perform. She was so proud of me.

SM: You and the other dancers that were part of the Soul Train road tours, and subsequently many other Soul Train dancers, graced the covers and inside pages of *Right On!* Magazine. You and the dancers that toured on the *Soul Train* tours must have taken over a thousand photos for the *Right On!* photo shoots done at Griffith Park in Los Angeles.

SW: We were so young at heart! We were just having so much fun during those photo shoots.

SM: There was a great camaraderie among the Soul Train Gang of your era.

SW: Yes. Me, Pat Davis, and James Phillips hung out a lot. He was so funny! I remember when Marvin Gaye was on the show, and he was trying to mimic him! [laughs] All us dancers would go to the clubs and party until we passed out!

SM: Since you were on the show for a number of years, what is your favorite *Soul Train* theme song?

SW: "T.S.O.P." by MFSB. It was so funky!

SM: You and Tyrone had an opportunity to visit the local Chicago version of *Soul Train*. How did that come about?

SW: We happened to be on a tour with The Whispers, and when they made a tour stop in Chicago, Don wanted to take us to the studio where the local version of *Soul Train* was taped.

SM: What do you recall about being on *Soul Train*'s local version?

SW: It was filmed in a small studio with small *Soul Train* signs. The Chicago Soul Train Dancers were so happy to see us and asked us lots of questions. Reginald Thornton, who later danced on the national version of *Soul Train*, was also there, and he was excited to see us. Tyrone and I were happy to interact with our fellow dancers in Chicago.

SM: Being that you and Tyrone were one of *Soul Train*'s most popular couples, it must have been an exciting experience for you two to win the *American Bandstand* dance contest in its 1974 to 1975 season.

SW: There is an interesting backstory to this. I was sitting at a bus stop, and I prayed to God to help me get a car. Later that same month, Damita Jo Freeman told me that Dick Clark had asked for two dancers, a Black couple, for a dance contest on *American Bandstand*, and she suggested me and Tyrone. We participated in the dance contest for six weeks. During that time frame, Tyrone and I would rehearse and rehearse. We tried to be more creative than ever before. We would go to clubs and tell the people that we were in the *American Bandstand* dance contest, and then we would do a dance routine and give them the information on where to send postcards to vote for us.

SM: Were you and Tyrone confident you were going to win the contest?

SW: We didn't think we were going to win. We were the only Black couple in the contest. I remember one White couple wore red, white, and blue costumes similar to the Uncle Sam character that were especially made for them. But we got 60,000 out of 100,000 votes, and ultimately, we won the finals that sixth week. I remember everyone in my hometown of Galveston was so excited and proud. I won a Mazda! God answered my prayer request for a car! Fellow Soul Train dancer Mark Moore taught me how to drive in an empty lot. I was blown away by the whole experience of winning *American Bandstand's* dance contest.

SM: A lot of viewers assumed that the Soul Train dancers were rich and lived in upscale, ritzy neighborhoods, but in reality, many of you were high school or college students and had regular jobs. You worked at Burger King during your time as a dancer on the show, right?

SW: Absolutely. I wasn't too good to work anywhere. When there were dry spells, such as when the dancers weren't touring or when the show wasn't taping, I would get a job for about six months until it was time to go back on the road. I was always able to get a job during slow times. People who recognized me from *Soul Train* would see me working at Burger King and would ask, "What are you doing working here?" People wanted to take pictures with me, but my bosses didn't mind at all since it helped to boost their customer base. My bosses were real cool about it.

SM: From 1976 to about 1978, you, Tyrone, and two fairly new Soul Train dancers—Jody Watley and Jeffrey Daniels—were like quadruplets in terms of your dancing. The four of you were so in sync with one another, whether you were roboting or freestyling.

SW: Our chemistry was so good. Jody and Jeffrey were a lot of fun. Tyrone and Jeffrey would be like two six-year-olds when they were together! They could make your day! Jody was pretty quiet, but she could be funny too. We happen to both be Aquarians. The four of us would be at Jody's house and be creative as we danced and rehearsed our special routines for the Soul Train dance segments and Soul Train Lines.

SM: You used your popularity on the show to help new dancers get on *Soul Train*.

SW: Yes, at that time, all the dancers had to have partners, and Tyrone and I would see new people waiting in line to get in, so we would bring them in out of the heat and tell Pam or Chuck that they were our partners. We never excluded anybody. Years later, I ran into one of the guys I brought in, and he never forgot what I had done for him.

SM: You and your husband Mark Wood of the group Lakeside met through *Soul Train*. Tell me about that experience?

SW: Mark had seen me dancing on *Soul Train* and then he and his group first performed on the show in 1977. Mark asked Chuck Johnson to get my phone number. I told Chuck no. He asked me five times and five times I said no. Finally, Chuck pleaded with me to call Mark since he was worrying him to death! So, I called him to get him off Chuck's back. I was ready for him to be a singer that was looking for a groupie. But when we talked, he said all of the right things. He talked about family and was not talking about himself. I really liked his personality. So, we eventually met, went out to the movies and to dinner. Our chemistry was so good.

SM: How long have you and Mark been married?

SW: Since 1982. We have two sons and two daughters. Mark and I hardly bump heads. He's got my back. I don't have to have a million dollars to be happy. I'm just happy to have my husband and my children.

SM: *Soul Train* regular Little Joe Chism put together the first Soul Train Gang reunion in 1997. It was a wonderful event, and I was there to witness the emotional reunion of you and Tyrone Proctor. You two hadn't seen each other in many years, right?

SW: Right! Little Joe didn't tell me that Tyrone was going to be at the reunion. I was so happy! We've been so close over the years. He was my left arm, and I was his right arm.

SM: Speaking of Little Joe, we lost him in 1998. He was a dear friend of yours and many of the other dancers. What would you like to say in memory of him?

SW: He had that great big smile. He was a jokester and was always on the inside scoop of everything. He talked to everyone and just made everyone feel good.

SM: You and some of the other dancers participated in a great event some years back celebrating *Soul Train*. Tell me about that.

SW: It was an event held one Labor Day. Me, Perry Brown, Thelma Davis, Damita Jo Freeman, Don Campbell, Jimmy Scoo B Doo, Freddie Maxie, and I were a part of this African Festival celebrating *Soul Train*. Deniece Williams and Lakeside performed. When my name was announced, "It's A Love Thing" by The Whispers came on and I did my thing! Afterward, we did a Soul Train Line. It was incredible! Children and little babies came down the line, even people with walking canes came down the line! It was a joy seeing people locking and doing other routines the Soul Train Gang did years ago.

SM: What are you doing currently?

SW: Now that Mark and I have raised our kids, I have started going back to acting and commercial classes and I am also doing a lot of writing. I put those ambitions on hold in the past, because I wanted to be able to raise my kids. I am very happy and thankful, and I have no regrets about anything.

SM: What would you like to say in Don Cornelius's memory?

SW: He gave an opportunity for young Black dancers and paved a way for us. We loved Don and loved dancing on *Soul Train* for the Black community. We danced until our feet burned until the wee hours of the morning, but we loved it, and never asked for a dime. You had to be there to feel the energy and the love

SM: Your longtime friend and dance partner Tyrone Proctor died in 2020. What would you like to say in his memory?

SW: I really miss him. He was like a family member. When we first met, it was like we were destined to be dance partners. His personality always kept me in a good mood. He loved all of the Soul Train dancers, and he was a protector over me, and I felt safe with him. We were so in sync with one another.

SM: Do you have a word of wisdom you want to share?

SW: Find God first and everything will fall into place. Stay grounded with God and stay in His word. He knows your desires and what you want to do. It won't be easy but never give up. You have to be rooted in God first.

BACK IN THE DAY

CURRENT PHOTO

# Thelma Davis Martin

(1972–1981)

Thelma Davis Martin was one of the more familiar faces seen on *Soul Train*. Known for her beautiful short Afro hairstyle, she didn't copy other dancers. She had her own definitive style and originality, which set her apart from the other dancers on the show. During her ten years on the show, Thelma was solely committed to "the dance."

**S**M: Was dancing always your passion?

TM: Yes. Because of my early love of movement and music, my parents always offered my dance theatrics at their many house parties. This was my early prelude to performing for an audience, even though my formal dance training started at around seven years old. I was raised in Pacoima, a suburb of the San Fernando Valley, and I danced locally for various events around the city. Pacoima, being a small community, did not offer the depth of dance experience that I longed for, and I continually traveled back and forth between the Valley and Los Angeles, learning, appreciating, and joining a different kind of dance family. I eventually moved into the greater Los Angeles area, where I embraced the Los Angeles dance culture completely. Dance performing was definitely in my blood from an early age.

SM: How did your journey with *Soul Train* begin?

TM: Because of my involvement with the Los Angeles dance culture, by the time *Soul Train* showed up in Los Angeles, I was already a sought-after dancer performing in contests around the city and in the Orange County area. I received a flier promoting auditions for a new dance show called *Soul Train.* Of course, I went to the auditions at Denker Park. There was a wonderful woman who was over Parks & Recreation for the city named Pam Brown. After I auditioned, she was really excited about me. She said that she had never before seen the way I blended my street dancing with my formal training. My dancing was different and special. Even though the interest and excitement were real, I was disqualified.

SM: Really? Why?

TM: In the beginning years, there was strict criteria that you and your dance partner had to attend the same school, and my first dance partner, Ralph Witherspoon, did not. I left the audition extremely disappointed, especially after the upbeat response I had received regarding my dance style. Later that evening, I received a call from Pam Brown personally and was told the rules had been bent for me as my dance style was so special. The rest is history.

SM: What do you remember about your first time being on *Soul Train*?

TM: It was all very new and exciting. I felt that there was no rhythm or rhyme to the show's format. Don't get me wrong, there was a format, but it was all new and different from what was going on in Chicago and television in general. Don was sort of winging it, taking a step at a time. The whole platform was not written in stone as to how it would go or be taped. They didn't have a set schedule in the early days. Don relied on his friends and associates from the East Coast to fill in as performers.

SM: Your look was also unique and very Afrocentric with the short Afro hairstyle you wore when everyone else wore big Afros at the time. You really stood out.

TM: Well, thank you! I wasn't as popular as some of the other dancers; I was just me, unapologetically Black. We were coming out of the Civil Rights Movement and embarking on the "Say It Loud, I'm Black and I'm Proud" era. Black films, songs, books, poetry, self-awareness, self-esteem, and self-empowerment were all the messages of the time. I never wanted to be like anybody else. I was just going to be who I was. I think I was basically more of a trendsetter than a follower. I did not have aspirations of fame and fortune; with me, it was about the dance, the culture, and staying true to myself.

SM: Indeed. What are some of your favorite memories from being on the show?

TM: I was somehow designated the "Mother of *Soul Train*" or the welcoming committee. Pam started using me to work with the performers to help them out with wardrobe and other duties. You may see me once at the beginning of the show, then you would see me on the riser, and then you wouldn't see me anymore. That's because I was backstage working with the artists. My easygoing nature, my positive attitude, my uplifting spirit, and my basic ability to get along with everyone afforded me opportunities and exposure. It made me the "go to" dancer for help and advice. I loved the responsibility and gave freely of myself.

SM: There were a lot of dances and dance crazes in the seventies. What were your favorite dances while you were on the show?

TM: Every week there was a new dance! [laughs] I don't remember the names of half of them. There was a segment in the early seventies where Don would pick a couple that came up with a new dance, a dance of the week. The dancers would perform on one of the platforms the different dance steps we created in the LA dance clubs like Maverick's Flat. Often, we would make up steps on the spot, and Don would say, "Come up and do it!" Me and my first partner, Ralph Witherspoon, and I did a dance we made up called "The Scrunch," a move from my African dance training.

SM: Did you enjoy dancing on the risers more than on the floor?

TM: I preferred to dance on the floor because there was more movement space. The risers were for specialized steps and were much more difficult to navigate. You had to be a good dancer to be chosen for the risers or have a special look the producers wanted to showcase. Although the cameras would pan to the risers, they would show the floor shots equally.

SM: Who were some of your favorite artists that came to the show?

TM: Gladys Knight & the Pips, The Isley Brothers, Kool & the Gang, Chaka Khan, I could go on and on with this question. The Whispers were always a favorite of mine, and of course, The Jackson 5. I also LOVED Marvin Gaye and Labelle. I got to know and worked closely with these artists.

SM: Speaking of Marvin Gaye, do you remember the day he and Don played that one-on-one basketball game on the set?

TM: Oh, yes! They played the whole day just for the fun of it. The dancers were in the stands rooting and cheering as Marvin performed his numbers the day before. We were rooting for Marvin! [laughs] Don and Marvin used to play basketball at Don's ranch in Encino.

SM: Did you realize back then that you were becoming part of a legacy?

TM: I didn't realize then the impact that whole era with the Soul Train Dancers, the Civil Rights Movement, the Black exploitation films, and the "Say It Loud, I'm Black and I'm Proud" movement was having on the world. As I look back, I am proud of the part I played in history. The culture of Black America, especially West Coast inner-city youth, was on display and had a positive impact on the world.

SM: The Soul Train Dancers are definitely iconic.

TM: Initially, we were called the Soul Train Gang. We had ID cards and were able to go to all of the nightclubs. However, around 1975, our names were changed to the Soul Train Dancers, and some of our privilege was lost. Don's attitude was sort of like, "I made the dancers, the dancers didn't make me." I still feel like people weren't tuning in to the show solely for the entertainment but also for the dancers. Black people got to see a reflection of themselves in a light that was positive, fun, and upbeat.

SM: Did you have any favorite dance partners on the show?

TM: It's hard to say who was my favorite because all of my partners had different styles. I was so versatile in my dance style that many different dancers wanted to dance with me. I was always willing and able to do different routines and steps, always looking to do and try something new. My partners have all transitioned, but I would like to take this time to shout them out: Lil Joe Chism, we put together the very first Soul Train Gang reunion in 1997; Ralph Witherspoon, who I created and showcased the Scrunch dance move with Mr. X, who won five hundred dollars in a James Brown dance contest; Niles Gaye, who had a most unique style; Darryl "Slim" Mitchell, who was commissioned to teach in Japan; James Benjamin, an all-around nice person; Chris Beneby, my Hustle Swing partner—so, so New York! Dewaye Hargrave, just plain fun; Billy Starling, later years; Billy Cobb, and a host of other dancers with whom I was blessed to have the opportunity to grace the risers.

SM: Did you ever have any problems with jealousy while you were a dancer?

TM: I never personally experienced any of that. I was more of a peacemaker. I was like, let's make love and not war. As previously stated, I had an ability to pull people together and ease conflict. I was well-liked and well-received.

SM: Did you ever get recognized in public as a result of being a *Soul Train* dancer?

TM: I still get it. People walk up to me all the time and ask, "Didn't you dance on *Soul Train*?" or "I remember you from *Soul Train*." With the new resurgence of interest in the show and the dancers, I am again being asked quite often about my time dancing on the show. Many of the original seventies Soul Train Gang are still here. That is why interviews and podcasts such as *Locker Legends* and *That Part Right There* are so important in telling the *Soul Train* story accurately. It is vital in preserving the true history as it relates and intersects with our culture.

SM: Did you ever travel or tour as a Soul Train dancer?

TM: I did a lot of promotion work for Johnson Products. Myself, Lil' Joe Chism, and Jeffrey Daniels would be sent to different cities around the country to various stores like Woolworth's that carried Johnson Products. We would do in-store promotions for Afro Sheen and Ultra Sheen and sign autographs. We were also sent out to judge the *Soul Train* dance contests around the country for the finals in Los Angeles. We would go to different cities and judge those dancers that became part of the contests. I have performed all over the world as a *Soul Train* dancer. The Soul Train Gang was also hired as halftime entertainment for The Jackson 5's celebrity basketball games.

SM: You really have seen and experienced a lot as a *Soul Train* dancer.

TM: The early days of *Soul Train* were the hardest days. We didn't have all of the amenities back then. I saw all the transitions and the upgrades during my twelve years on the show, when we went from eating Golden Bird chicken, which was a Black-owned business, to KFC. I've seen all the set changes, even the new tunnel on the set that replaced the old tunnel, which was just a Black hole. *Soul Train* was a place where you could see a reflection of yourself. Don employed almost all African American crew. Some people on the staff were not Black, but Don definitely employed many people of color, from camera people to stage managers.

SM: During *Soul Train*'s heyday in the early seventies, *Soul Train* gave Dick Clark's *American Bandstand* some serious competition. So, along came this show called *Soul Unlimited*, which Dick created to compete with *Soul Train*. Do you remember any of that?

TM: I remember that very well. Some Soul Train dancers were also dancing on Bandstand. Dick would try to coordinate his tapings the same day as *Soul Train*'s tapings. It was almost like Dick was challenging Don. Dick never tapped into Black dance initially. A lot of racism and segregation was still prevalent in the seventies. I never wanted to go on Bandstand. No one was ready to tap into the fact that Black people were photogenic, or that the television screen would like them, or that there was an audience for them. I think Dick put together *Soul Unlimited* as a way to challenge Don.

SM: You and several of the other dancers were part of the classic movie *Five On The Blackhand Side* in the wedding scene. What was it like being a part of that movie?

TM: We had so much fun doing that film. We were in several other movies, too, such as *Disco 9000* and *Youngblood*. We also performed in other television programs such as the *Jerry Lewis Telethon* in Las Vegas and a Diana Ross special, just to name a few. In 1983, I was a featured dancer in Michael Jackson's "Thriller" video. Now, that was an experience like no other! That video was and still is iconic.

SM: What did you do professionally after you left *Soul Train*?

TM: While dancing on the show, I started working in Japan as a choreographer/dancer with a band. I was contracted to work in Japan as a teacher to coordinate openings of various dance and fitness studios all over the country. It seems that while I was there dancing, my talents were being observed and appreciated. Learning that I was a Soul Train dancer was prestigious, so Mrs. Haitsu hired me as her lead coordinating choreographer and dancer. I also modeled, performed in commercials and television shows, promoted clubs, and taught English. My persona as a Soul Train dancer was preserved as I began traveling to and from Japan to Los Angeles and vice versa, teaching dance, choreographing, doing commercials in Japan, and then coming home to do the *Soul Train* tapings, all to keep up my persona. I danced on the show up until the end of 1982 with a few cameos in 1983. Of the original Soul Train Gang, my reign on the show is unparalleled. I am, and will forever be, the longest-running dancer of the original Soul Train dancers.

SM: The dancing on *Soul Train* in the seventies was so free, uninhibited, and creative. How do you feel about the evolution of dance now?

TM: I like some of the stuff that I see. Dance has been taken to new levels. The dancers have stretched the limits of what one can do with dance. Some things I am torn on. Some dance groups are sort of like cookie cutters where everything is the same—the steps and gimmicks that are indicative of Slim the Robot from The Lockers, for example. I see a lot of other dancers besides Black dancers who are taking over the urban dance scene. When I was in Japan, a lot of dancers were starting to emulate what was happening with Black people, so we as a race are definitely trendsetters. I am an original Soul Train dancer who takes pride in the role I played in the show's history.

SM: In the later years of *Soul Train*, the look and feel of the show was different. What did you think of the show from back in the late eighties to its final days?

TM: The format changed so much. It never should have been about certain looks; it should have been about creativity and what the audience wanted to see, not what the coordinator wanted to see. The dance changed into something more sexual. When Don Cornelius and Dick Griffey of Solar Records partnered, it became a whole new world.

SM: You and Little Joe Chism put together the first annual Soul Train Gang reunion. I was so happy to be there, and that was a wonderful event to attend and quite an experience.

TM: When we first started talking about it, it was going to be a small thing like a house party with some of the original dancers. But then I told Joe there were other people that wanted to come as well. I wanted to get people together who haven't seen each other in years, and I wanted it to be a reunion party. Joe contacted most of the people since he knew everybody, while I was the logistics person and handled the decorating and the coordinating of the food. It was so sad when Little Joe passed a year later. Damita Jo Freeman and I were at the hospital when he died. I miss him so much.

SM: Don's death was very shocking to us all. What do you want to say in honor of his memory?

TM: Don was a visionary. He was a great man in terms of recycling Black dollars and doing the right thing in the community and making sure people of color were afforded the same opportunity through his enterprise. He was a ruthless, no-nonsense kind of guy, but he was very protective of the dancers in the early days since he felt a type of ownership over us, not like a father to his children but like we were his possessions. He was never close to the dancers in the beginning; he was very standoffish and aloof. It is a fact, though, that his legacy will live on forever.

SM: Did you want to share the personal losses you experienced?

TM: I lost my best friend, my husband; three weeks after he passed, I lost my mother. Then, my husband's mother passed away a few months later, which was truly unexpected. The last loss was my brother-in-law, the brother of my children's father, who had become quite a fixture in their lives. It was a tumultuous year for me. But my greatest loss was my husband because he was my soul mate and my backbone. One of me and my husband's favorite theme songs was "And the Beat Goes On" by The Whispers.

SM: What are you doing currently?

TM: I'm still a student of dance, taking African dance classes and continuing to service the youth dance community. I am also CEO of my home-based business, Kreative Artistry, a floral design and event planning company, and I'm a consultant with USC's dance department about the history of Soul Train and West Coast street dance. In addition, I serve on the board of the Leimert Park Theatre Consortium, staying active in the community and enjoying retirement from the Los Angeles Unified School District as an elementary school librarian.

SM: What word of wisdom do you want to share with readers?

TM: Share your gifts, but don't give them away. Stay true to yourself, love yourself, and never give up... ever.

# Eddie Champion Cole

(1972–1975)

Eddie Champion Cole was one of *Soul Train*'s most effervescent dancers. He, along with his dance partner Wanda Fuller Robinson, always came up with creative and eye-catching dances, and they became one of the show's most popular couples. Whenever they went down the Soul Train Line together, you could always count on them showing some tightly coordinated and exciting new dance steps. Eddie himself is an accomplished singer, songwriter, and actor as well as the nephew of Nat "King" Cole. Over the years, his accomplishments ranged from working with performers such as Aretha Franklin, Diana Ross, Tom Jones, and James Brown.

SM: Was dancing always your passion growing up as a child?

EC: Dancing was my life! I loved dancing. Me and my siblings would dance for our mother's company. We'd make up little routines. I remember some very suggestive dances back then, like the dog and the hammer. People make a big thing about twerking and other dance styles, but we had ours back in the day, too.

SM: How did you become a *Soul Train* dancer?

EC: I had friends who were already on the show that had gotten picked up at Mavericks Flat. They told Wanda and me about the auditions

BACK IN THE DAY

CURRENT PHOTO

at Denker Park. We were so happy that Pam Brown picked us for the next taping. It was exciting! I was prepared to beg and plead to be on the show.

SM: What do you recall about the first time you stepped on the *Soul Train* set?

EC: The first time seeing the set and all the lights and camera crew was at first overwhelming. But then our friends were all there, either from school or the discos. There were rules like don't look in the camera, no talking, no chewing gum. Other than that, it was like a big party. When that red light is on, you're on!

SM: You and Wanda Fuller really had some tight dance routines and were one of the show's best dance couples. Did the two of you practice a lot?

EC: Wanda and I met in high school. We complemented each other's styles and moves and instantly adapted to each other! We could always feel what the other's next move would be. Eventually, we'd pick things randomly that one or the other did and put it into our routine going down the Soul Train Line. We could put together a routine in an instant!

SM: Did you ever do the Scramble Board, and did you get the solution the first time around?

EC: Yes! I'll never forget the fear after we were picked to do it. We had to be interviewed and say our names first. I had to practice saying my name in my head to make sure I didn't say my name was Wanda Fuller! [laughs] Then it was on! Two people trying to move those letters to spell The Intruders was close to impossible in a short time. But at the last minute we got it right.

SM: Who were the artists that you enjoyed watching perform on the show?

EC: Every artist that was there was awesome. I remember in particular

Aretha Franklin, the Queen of Soul! I remember sitting behind her in the stands. When I overheard her saying, "I just wanna tape this and split!" I thought, *Rude! Oh my God. I don't believe she said that!* But since we, the dancers, were having fun, I didn't relate that to her doing *Soul Train* as a job. I do now!

SM: Did you ever have a chance to speak with any of the artists that came on the show?

EC: I remember speaking briefly to Lola Falana. I took a picture with her on the podium where Don Cornelius would do his announcements. I also shared a few giggles with Mary Wilson. I was really shy then.

SM: Do you have one favorite memory that stands out from your *Soul Train* days?

EC: One was when Wanda and I were featured on the creative dance spot in which we did a new dance. We tried not to do what everyone else was doing at that moment. We did some movement and called it the Tightrope, nothing like the things Marcel Marceau would do, but we did it.

SM: You must have been honored when you, Pat Davis, Damita Jo Freeman, and Little Joe Chism were chosen to be a part of several of Diana Ross's shows in Las Vegas. What was that experience like for you?

EC: The absolute highlight of my life was working with Diana Ross! We were kids, and we never called her Miss Ross! I'm sure she got sick of me saying, "Diana! Diana! Diana!" She was like someone in the family, a big sister. She took me and Little Joe shopping for our stage shoes in her Rolls Royce. We went into a shoe store in Beverly Hills, and she was asking which ones we liked. Our mouths dropped open, and our eyes bugged out. She called us her "wiggle tails." She nicknamed me "Easy Eddie!"

One night at Caesar's Palace, I started doing the Robot. I slid all the way to her side of the stage, and from the very first night, she joined in. That brought the house down! Berry Gordy said, "Great! Great! We have to keep that in!" I still love me some Diana Ross.

SM: You four were also a part of several of Aretha Franklin's shows in New York. What memories do you have of being a part of that show?

EC: That was something else! It was funny because when I got this call from some guy saying, "Hello. My sister Aretha wants you to come to perform at Radio City Music Hall," I said. "Hmmm... I don't know if I'm available at that time. Give me your number and I'll call you back!" Then I called Pat Davis and said some idiot is calling me, telling me he's Aretha's brother. She said, "No, no, no! Call back! It is him! He called me!"

It was a great experience with Aretha, like being with your own family. We spent a day at her house just hanging out. Everything was so relaxed. Being in Aretha's performances was like being in a dream.

SM: You, Pat, Wanda, Perry Brown and Jimmy "Scoo B Doo" Foster eventually left *Soul Train* in mid-1975 since you were a new dance group called Something Special. It must have been an incredible experience to travel the world and perform with big-name artists.

EC: We really groomed ourselves and faced a lot of challenges. We worked so hard! Everybody we worked with asked why we worked so hard. We danced like there was no tomorrow! What made us unique was that we also sang. We did all the commercial dances that originated on *Soul Train* and beyond while we were also developing and creating our own individual styles. Pat was "Madame Butterfly," Scoo B was still "Scoo B Doo," Wanda was "Electricity in Motion," Bert LA was "Pantera Negro," Perry Brown was "Sexy Brown," and me? When Diana Ross calls you "Easy Eddie," you don't change it!

SM: Other than performing, what other fun memories do you have of the days of Something Special?

EC: We really had a lot on our plate. Sometimes, we'd be invited to do TV shows in Japan or other countries, and we didn't want to use any of our routines in the show. So, we'd stay up late at night and train in the hallways of the five-star hotel! We were so silly. We got up in the mornings and did a dance class in the hallway. We bonded so closely. We all had hot plates for late-night snacks or tea. But on Sunday, we'd break bread together! We took turns cooking a meal for the group. So, that meant those five-star hotels were smelling like a restaurant on the eighteenth floor! We loved Japan. We went there first with Tom Jones, and we were invited back. So, we had fans and followers. A couple of ladies would turn up everywhere we were from the time with Tom throughout our career. SWEEEEEEEET! They'd find out when and where we would be or greet us in the hotel. Australia was another favorite place. It was easier there because of the language.

SM: Didn't the group record a single or an album?

EC: Yes, we recorded the singles "Got to Get Ready" and "Keep My Love."

SM: Eventually, you moved to Vienna, Austria. Patricia Davis moved there as well, and you became a duet called Essence. How did that come about?

EC: Pat and I joined forces after Something Special went our separate ways. Pat actually got me in touch with another singer who had been over here in Vienna. They needed a break dancer who could sing for a tour. I was never a break dancer, but I could dance and had my robot skills down. I was asked to sing something, so I sang "Everything Must Change," and before I could finish, she said, "OK, you leave for Vienna on..." I was in shock and not really believing this was happening. Long story short, we hit it! We toured all over Austria and Germany and went to Spain and Italy. We made a pretty good name for ourselves. As the duo Essence, we kept the same standards as we had in Something Special. It wasn't easy because there were only two of us. We'd dance a number, sing two numbers, then dance again and again, sing and jump and run, do sketches—everything! Whew!

SM: Did Essence ever record any songs?

EC: We did a song called "Black Out." I was so excited. When the intro of the song started, she said, "That's 'The Bird' by Morris Day!" I said, "No, it's not!" Then I learned it was the same playback with different lyrics. Sad-faced, I told Pat, and we were in shock. We had to record another song and decide which would be the A or B side. The song was "Kahlua Sun." I wasn't really happy about the song style, but I was proud that we did make it to the hit parade.

SM: In 1997, Little Joe Chism and Thelma Davis Martin put together the very first Soul Train Gang Reunion. What was it like for you to reunite with so many people you haven't seen in years?

EC: I was over the moon! It was emotional on many levels because not everybody was there. Some faces were missing; some faces you didn't recognize anymore. We were grown–not old, older! But when we hit that dance floor, all of a sudden, we had a Soul Train Line again! I hung out with Tyrone Proctor and Little Joe deeper in the nights of Hollywood. I never had that pleasure before.

SM: Speaking of Little Joe, he was a very close friend of yours, mine, and a lot of other people, and his death in 1998 touched many people. What do you want to say in his memory?

EC: I was devastated, to say the least. I learned he had passed after returning to Austria. He and I were featured in *Right On! Magazine*. When we performed with Diana Ross, Joe came to work with corn rows in his hair. We suggested he take them out and fork his hair out. He said, "I'm not taking my corn rows out!" Diana said, "Little Joe, come here for a minute." The next thing we saw was him taking those rows out! Funny! I miss him. There's so much we'd talk about today, so much to share and exchange.

SM: You overcame a battle with cancer some time ago. Do you wish to talk about that experience?

EC: Well, I had a regular abscess on my cheek. I had it drained many years ago, but it kept coming back. I went to the hospital, and they did a nasty long and deep biopsy. I was told it was cancer. I had twenty-four-hour a day chemo and daily radiation. I thought if this is it, I'm not going to be sad about it; this experience is a part of life and death. I'm not afraid to die. I lost loads of weight and had a colostomy. After finally getting over everything, my sister was diagnosed with cancer. Unfortunately, she passed after I came back to Vienna. We had a great time visiting my dad in Vegas, who also passed away.

SM: Tell me about some of the things you have done in recent years.

EC: I did a project called Cole & Keys, which includes just me and a keyboardist. We did all sorts of easy listening music by artists such as Cole Porter, Billie Joel, Nat King Cole, Michael Franks, Al Jarreau, and so on. I have also worked with the Vienna Ballroom Orchestra for the Bon Bon Ball in the Vienna Concert House. I also did a rock project called *Die Gruppe*, where I wrote the lyrics and did the vocal arrangements. One of my closest friends and I put together a soul/funk band called Prime Cut. We have a chance to do all the things we can't normally do. We've grounded a project called "A Tribute To Black Icons," which covers our history from Billie Holiday, Ella, Nat, and Fats Waller to Motown. We left it open so we can constantly change and add to it. It's a great show!

SM: What do you want to say in memory of Don Cornelius?

EC: When Don passed, I was shocked and deeply saddened. My first time on the show, I was intimidated by him and stayed out of his way. But once he got used to seeing the regulars, he became a gentle giant to me. We'd share a smile and a nod. He made us all feel special in that way, like a parent does their children.

SM: Do you have any words of wisdom you want to share?

EC: My advice to everybody is just don't let anyone stand in your way. There is only one road to life, and it's the one you choose. That's where your lessons are. People talk about the generation now just like they talked about ours. We also had crazy styles and looks. My sister always said if you can dream it, you can achieve it. I cherish a plaque we got from Soul Train from George E. Johnson, which read: *Make no small plans for your future but literally reach for the stars. Some might not reach the stars, and some might fall, but if you try and you fail to reach the stars, you might fall on a mountain top.*

And yes, I still have that plaque with me in Vienna, Austria. Love, peace, and *sooooul*!

*This interview was originally conducted in 2015. Eddie sadly passed away in August 2022. May he forever rest in peace. I am truly thankful for his friendship and kindness.*

BACK IN THE DAY

CURRENT PHOTO

# Wanda Fuller Robinson

(1972–1975)

Anyone who watched *Soul Train* in its early days could not take their eyes off one of the program's most dynamic dance couples, Wanda Fuller and Eddie Cole. Their routines were always in sync, always tight, and, in short, they knew just how to get down! Wanda was born with a special innate gift for dance, and she was blessed with many opportunities to showcase her talents and work with such entertainers as James Brown, Tom Jones, and Diana Ross. Wanda's effervescent dancing, along with her beauty, bright smile, and enthusiasm, were always a joy to watch every week on *Soul Train*. Here is her story.

SM: Who or what influenced you as a child to want to go into the entertainment business?

WR: When I was a child, I hung out a lot with my father. He was a saxophonist and performed with many entertainers, such as Louis Jordan, the Platters, and James Brown. When he went to the rehearsals for shows with those artists, I would attend with him. This was before I started school.

SM: Would you say dancing was a gift you were born with? After all, you are one of *Soul Train*'s all-time greatest dancers.

WR: Thank you! Well, I always wanted to dance. I loved to dance. I think it is a gift from God because when I would go to dance classes, I could just do the dance steps instantly. Of course, there were certain techniques I had to practice, but I could basically pick them up.

SM: How did you become a dancer on *Soul Train*?

WR: I went to high school with Connie Blackino, and she introduced me to another student, Eddie Cole. Eddie and I would dance together a lot and decided to go to an audition for *Soul Train* at Denker Park. The dance coordinator from the show, Pam Brown, was there, and she picked us to come to the show.

SM: What do you remember about your first day on the set of *Soul Train*?

WR: I remember all of the bright lights and was shocked at how small the set was! I also recall they had cheap tape laid out on the floor to resemble train tracks. Don Cornelius was bigger in person, and his voice was even deeper.

SM: Who were your buddies on *Soul Train*?

WR: Connie Blackino and Diana Price. We grew up together, and our families knew each other.

SM: You and Eddie were, hands down, one of the best dance couples in the history of *Soul Train*. You two were always in sync with one another. The two of you must have practiced a lot.

WR: Actually, we didn't. Eddie and I would just look at each other, and we knew what we were going to do. We just clicked and fed off each other and were having so much fun.

SM: Did you ever get caught by Pam Brown chewing gum?

WR: Yes! Everyone did! I remember taking my gum and giving it to her several times.

SM: Who were your favorite artists that you enjoyed watching perform on *Soul Train*?

WR: I have so many favorites, but the top one is The Jackson 5. I was shaking when they were in the studio. I remember Michael was eyeing dancer Connie Blackino and was trying to talk to her! As a performer, I could feel Michael's energy, and I cried and screamed as I watched him perform. I also enjoyed it when James Brown and Barry White came to the show. The music those artists created just moved you, and you could hear every instrument. That's what is missing in music now. I didn't like disco; I always loved live music.

SM: Because of the Soul Train Gang's popularity, several of the dancers had opportunities to work with certain recording artists and attend special events that they gave. What are your memories of those times?

WR: There are so many memories! Me and some of the dancers performed with James Brown. Also, several of us dancers attended a big party given at the mansion of Berry Gordy's sister after the wedding reception of Jermaine Jackson and Hazel Gordy. We also attended a party at Barry White's home and had a great time. We had so much fun during those times. The stars treated us so nicely.

SM: One special memory had to be when you, Eddie, Joe Chism, and Damita Jo Freeman performed at the NAACP Image Awards as a dance group called the Individuals.

WR: Yes! It was really a nice experience. I remember being so nervous when I met Sidney Poitier. Damita laughed at me so hard because I was literally trembling!

SM: Did you ever experience any jealousy from any of the other dancers?

WR: Not that I recall. If I did, it didn't faze me.

SM: Did you ever dance on Dick Clark's *American Bandstand* or the show he created to rival *Soul Train* called *Soul Unlimited*? If so, what do you recall about being on either show, and was Don Cornelius mad about his dancers dancing on those programs?

WR: Yes, I danced on those shows, and yes, Don was mad. Here he was doing his show, and another show came on to compete with his. Don gave us an ultimatum. He told us, "If you go there, you stay there!" So, we stayed with Don because *Soul Train* was our beginning.

SM: Did you ever experience any funny or embarrassing moments on *Soul Train*?

WR: I remember one time Eddie and I demonstrated a dance step on this platform in the middle of the dance floor. As we were dancing, the platform slowly began to come apart! The segment had to be taped over again, and that platform had to be put back together.

SM: In 1974, you and some of the other Soul Train Gang had the opportunity to work with Diana Ross during her Las Vegas shows at Caesar's Palace and at the Universal Amphitheatre in Los Angeles. What was that experience like for you?

WR: It was a really great experience. Damita Jo Freeman and I choreographed a lot of the routines, but Diana wanted a certain look for the background dancers, so she chose Joe Chism, Eddie, Pat, and Damita. I was disappointed about that, but I was fortunate to still be involved with the show doing choreography. Aside from performing, Pat and I held Diana's babies, we went shopping with Diana, and she made sure we had everything we needed. She treated us so good.

SM: Michael Jackson would attend some of those shows you and the other dancers performed in Vegas as well, right?

WR: Yes. He would be backstage watching and studying us dancers perform with Diana at Caesar's Palace.

SM: Later that year, you all performed with Aretha Franklin as well.

WR: Yes. I choreographed that show as well and performed in it this time. Aretha's children wanted to know the Soul Train Gang. Her son Clarence called each of us personally and asked us to audition and perform as part of her act. We also went to Aretha's home, and she even cooked for us. We had so much fun. Again, I just don't understand how people could say bad things about her or Diana. They spoiled us!

SM: You became a part of the Something Special dance troupe, comprised of several of the Soul Train Gang including you, Pat Davis, Scoo B, Eddie Cole, and Perry Brown, and became famous around the world. What are some of your greatest memories of being a part of Something Special?

WR: My fondest memories were traveling and going to all of the different countries and learning their customs. We toured with artists like Tom Jones and Natalie Cole. Me and the other dancers were like family. We even argued like sisters and brothers! To this day, the love among us is still there.

SM: Didn't Something Special release an album or a 45?

WR: Yes, we did quite a few songs, and they were quite popular in Japan and Europe.

SM: Did you do anything else professionally after Something Special disbanded?

WR: John Daniels, the owner of Maverick's Flat, and his wife had a group called Love Machine, and they were looking for background singers and dancers. Pat auditioned, but they were looking for a taller girl, so she told me about the audition. I auditioned and won. Eddie and Pat then went on tour in Austria as a singing duet called Essence. Love Machine toured the same places that Something Special went to. I was with Love Machine for four years. John Daniels was a good businessman. I remember that while we were on the road, auditions were being held for Michael Jackson's "Thriller" video. I was so upset that I missed it. After touring with Love Machine, I settled down and had a family.

SM: What are you doing currently?

WR: I'm a retired teacher's assistant with special education for over twenty years. It was the most rewarding and best job ever. I loved that job! It was wonderful helping the children and making a difference in their lives.

SM: What would you like to say in memory of Don Cornelius?

WR: Don gave the dancers a lot of opportunities, and for me, it was a life-changing opportunity. He was very serious about our image back then and made sure everything we did was clean and respectful, and he was concerned about how we portrayed ourselves. Don always made sure we had everything we needed and was a father image away from our homes. He also made sure everyone respected us.

SM: What word of wisdom do you want to share?

WR: Let your mistakes be lessons. Move on and realize that a lot of times, you don't get a second chance. So, just take that chance and go forth—and take God with you.

# Bobby Washington

(1972–1976)

From a very young age, Los Angeles native Bobby Washington was determined to use his talents somehow to be seen as well as heard. His eye-catching, enthusiastic energy as a *Soul Train* dancer and his career as part of a gospel choir and as a professional photographer gave Washington the opportunity to see the world. In fact, he was a part of a classic gospel album by the Queen of Soul herself. He is also responsible for bringing the legendary Jody Watley on board the *Soul Train*. Here is his story.

SM: What were your aspirations growing up?

BW: Dancing was one of them. My sister and her friends always danced around the house. I also wanted to act. I did an audition for a commercial, but I didn't get it. I always wanted to be on TV, and I loved to dance. Music and dance are my life. I expressed myself through dance.

SM: You were also a part of Reverend James Cleveland's Southern California Community Choir, right?

BW: Right. I was already a gospel music lover, so when Reverend Cleveland started a gospel choir, I became a part of his choir for about seven years, starting in 1969 or 1970. After being a member of the

BACK IN THE DAY

CURRENT PHOTO

choir for a few years, Reverend Cleveland established the Cornerstone Institutional Baptist Church.

SM: Months before you became a *Soul Train* dancer, you were a part of another historic event, the recording of Aretha Franklin's classic *Amazing Grace* gospel album. How did this come about?

BW: Reverend Cleveland made an announcement that Aretha chose our church to come and record a gospel album. He used to sing at Aretha's church in Detroit, the New Bethel Baptist Church. Reverend Cleveland told the choir that thirty voices were needed, and thankfully, I was one of them! He also told us that we wouldn't be allowed to take any photos while she was there.

SM: All of you must have been so excited that you were going to sing on Aretha's album.

BW: Yes! This was Aretha Franklin, the Queen of Soul! When she came into the church, we were all starstruck with our mouths wide open. She stood about eight feet from where I was when she was performing. When she sang, I wondered, "How did she sing like that and so effortlessly and relaxed?" The rehearsals went on for several hours, but she was pleased with what she heard, and then filming began. Months later, each of us choir members got a copy of the *Amazing Grace* album. Being a part of the album and film was an awesome experience, and I am truly blessed for it.

SM: How did your journey with *Soul Train* begin?

BW: I met Joe Chism in 1972 at a club in Los Angeles. He told me to go to Denker Park, where the auditions for *Soul Train* were held. I went out there and danced, and the dance coordinator, Pam Brown, noticed me.

SM: What do you remember about your first time going to *Soul Train*?

BW: I was like a kid at a candy store! I remember being impressed by the stage set and the sound system. I also remember my first time on the show being somewhat intimidating because I did not know what to expect. I didn't even have a partner, but Joe told me not to worry.

SM: Who eventually became your dance partner?

BW: A girl named Doris was one of my first partners, and then a girl nicknamed "New York" was another partner. Ella Walker, Queen Turner, Rhonda Brown, and Jody Watley were also my partners.

SM: Who were your favorite dance partners?

BW: I would say Jody, Queen, and Rhonda were my favorite partners.

SM: Speaking of Jody Watley, you were responsible for getting her on *Soul Train*. How did that come about?

BW: Jody's mom and some of her family and friends and I were part of the same church. I contacted Jody, and I brought her to *Soul Train*. She was real nervous when she first came on the show, but I loved her energy and attitude.

SM: Being that you were instrumental in Jody's first nationwide exposure, how do you feel about all of the success she had later with Shalamar and as a solo artist?

BW: It was like a sister or cousin made it big! I was so proud of my former dance partner. When I saw her at the memorial for Don Cornelius, my eyes lit up.

SM: What are your memories of Don Cornelius?

BW: Don was strange to me but in a good way. He stayed within his parameters. He was low-key and quiet. I remember he would be off to the side as the makeup lady would touch him up, and he would go over his script.

SM: Did you ever fall victim to Pam Brown's gum ritual?

BW: Yes. Twice! [laughs] She would come to me with that paper cup and say, "You know what I want!" Pam was adorable.

SM: What was it like for you going down the Soul Train Line?

BW: It was intimidating! You didn't know what you were going to look like on TV, but after a while, you do what you do and make the best of it.

SM: Is there any funny or special memory that stands out from *Soul Train*?

BW: We had been in the studio for five hours into the second show. We had a break, and all of a sudden, music came on. The dancers got up from the bleachers and started partying, but the cameras weren't on. [laughs] One song kept playing after another. No one ever told us to sit down, and no one ever explained what that was all about.

SM: Several Soul Train dancers also danced on Dick Clark's *American Bandstand*. Did you ever dance on his show?

BW: Yes, I did. When word got back to Don that his dancers were on *Bandstand*, he did not like it at all. Dick was very happy we were on his show, but it didn't last long.

SM: You and many of the other dancers were featured extras in the wedding scene of the movie *Five On The Blackhand Side*. What was that experience like?

BW: It was a fun experience. The shoot took all day. Virginia Capers, who was a star of the movie, gave us some advice and told us about her experiences in movies. The producers were very pleased with what we did.

SM: Did you ever do any other films or projects while you were a *Soul Train* dancer?

BW: Some of the other dancers and I did a commercial shown only in Japan for a brand of wine or champagne. We all did the bump dance move and pretended we were drinking.

SM: Wasn't there some sort of book or magazine that was published about the Soul Train Gang?

BW: Yes. It was sort of a gossip-type book about the dancers, what the dancers were wearing or how certain dancers wore their hair.

SM: What are your favorite memories of stars that came to *Soul Train*?

BW: Patti Labelle! I was really impressed by her and her group, Labelle. They killed it! They had on those space outfits and feathers. [laughs] Patti was very personable, and she took the time to talk to us dancers during a break. Also, I had a chance to talk personally with Eddie Kendricks, who is one of my favorite artists. He was on stage, and he took the time to talk with me and even wanted me to go on the road with him. I also have great memories of when Diana Ross, The Supremes, and The Jackson 5 came to *Soul Train*. I remember Michael was nervous and extremely shy.

SM: I'm going to throw at you some names of other artists that came to the show. The Staple Singers.

BW: I had been following them since their gospel days, so when they came to the show, I was so happy. Don pointed his microphone at me to ask them a question during the Q&A session.

SM: Marvin Gaye.

BW: He wore a green beanie when he came on, and he was so smooth.

SM: James Brown.

BW: Now, that was a great moment! The Godfather of Soul! We were like, "This brother can work!" He had a live band, and he sang live.

SM: Richard Pryor.

BW: [laughs] He was so funny! I liked his style.

SM: Being that you sang in the choir that backed Aretha Franklin on her *Amazing Grace* album, what do you recall when she first came to Soul Train a year later?

BW: We all cherished her when she was on Soul Train. That was quite a moment! I think she remembered my face from the *Amazing Grace* recording session.

SM: Have you done any other film work since leaving Soul Train?

BW: I was an extra in a Halle Berry movie in the early nineties. I was in a church scene, and I sat in the audience right behind Halle. Also, I was shown during an old *Soul Train* Line segment in a Halle Berry movie called *Frankie & Alice.*

SM: What else have you done professionally over the years?

BW: I sang with a local choir in Los Angeles called the Pentecostal Community Choir. We appeared at a *Grammy Awards* ceremony with Albertina Walker singing "Spread the Word," the same ceremony where Michael Jackson won many awards for his *Thriller* album. We also sang with Albertina Walker doing three shows at Adventure Land in Disneyworld during gospel night, which was a great moment for us. We backed up Mariah Carey, Patti Labelle, and Luther Vandross, as well as Dionne Warwick at the Minority AIDS Project, and we toured the Holy Land and Africa in 1993. In September 1995, thirteen people from the choir backed up a popular recording artist from Italy. I am still part of the choir, and we continue to do benefit concerts.

SM: You were also part of the Millennium Choir, right?

BW: Yes. The Pentecostal Community Choir became a part of this large interdenominational choir comprised of different races. We went back to Italy, and we were in this concert hall in front of a large audience, and it was televised. It was a wonderful moment for us.

SM: You are also an established photographer. How did this come about?

BW: I was always interested in all kinds of cameras, and I started doing more camera work in high school and college. I've done a few shots for albums for artists like Billy Preston, Reverend James Cleveland, Albertina Walker, the Kurt Carr singers, other local artists, and for local papers. I also did work for Bishop Blake's church, Magic Johnson, and

Denzel Washington. I submitted work for the Smithsonian Institution, and it is still on display.

SM: Generally, what kind of subjects are you most interested in photographing?

BW: I love photographing people at large events such as weddings and reunions. I also would love photographing animal wildlife. I would eventually love to expand my photography.

SM: What was your overall experience with *Soul Train*?

BW: *Soul Train* was and still is a wonderful family. I had such a positive experience. It was a party all day for eight to ten hours and was a way of life. I am proud to be a part of its history and legacy, and I have no regrets. Whenever I hear certain songs of the seventies, I think of Don, Pam, and the dancers. They say Disneyland is the happiest place on earth, but to me, *Soul Train* was the happiest place to be!

SM: Don's passing was shocking and very tragic. If you could say something personally to Don, what would it be?

BW: Don, thank you so much for giving us the opportunity to display our talents.

SM: Is there anyone else you want to give thanks to?

BW: A big thanks to Pam Brown. She gave all the dancers tremendous support. I also want to thank you, Stephen, for helping to keep *Soul Train* alive and remembering us.

SM: Thanks, and you're most welcome! The dancers deserve recognition for all they have done. What was it like to reunite with the dancers at the party celebrating the life of Don Cornelius and *Soul Train*?

BW: It was like seventh heaven! To have Pat Davis and Damita Jo Freeman in the same room and to see Jimmy "Scoo B Doo" Foster and Vicki Abercrombie made for some very touching moments. We laughed. We cried. It was quite a high. We hugged and kissed. I am honored to know these people. It was a happy moment for us all.

SM: Many of the dancers also gathered for the memorial for Don Cornelius at Forest Lawn Cemetery. What was it like for all of you coming together for a man who helped give many of you your big break?

BW: I remember Pat Davis, Tyrone Proctor, and myself walking toward the entrance, and we were happy to see the other dancers, but then the reality of Don's death came upon us. He was gone. It hurt just like Joe Chism's death. After the memorial, twenty-five or thirty of us went to a restaurant, just eating and remembering.

SM: Do you have a word of wisdom you want to share?

BW: Always be yourself. It pays off. If you just be yourself, you'll be surprised at what you can accomplish. Whatever you are into, do the right thing and be yourself, and it will pay off!

BACK IN THE DAY

CURRENT PHOTO

# Tyrone "The Bone" Proctor

(1972–1978)

Tyrone "The Bone" Proctor is one of *Soul Train*'s all-time popular regulars. His unique style of dancing and his fashions—from pink jumpsuits to fur coats—as well as his upbeat persona, were a treat for viewers every week. He helped to popularize a new style of dancing in the early days of *Soul Train* called "waacking," which he teaches in classes around the world. This Philadelphia-born kid was determined to jump aboard the *Soul Train* and become a star.

SM: You're one of *Soul Train*'s all-time, best-known, and most popular dancers. Would you say dancing is in your blood? What inspired you to dance?

TP: My family would always congregate at my aunt's and grandmother's houses over the weekend. I was one of the younger cousins. The elders would stay upstairs, and since I was the youngest, they didn't want me upstairs listening to the adult conversations, so they put me downstairs with my cousins. My cousins would be making up steps to the cha-cha and doing the bop and all of these other things. So, I'm just sitting there taking this all in, and that's how it started.

SM: In late 1971, you saw a television program called *Soul Train,* and it changed your life. You've said in past interviews that you were determined to get on that show.

TP: When *Soul Train* first came on the air, it defined our generation by who and what we are. It was a defining moment to see kids up there doing dances that normally weren't being done. The only Black people who would be acting up on stage were entertainers such as James Brown. So, I'm sitting there watching the show, and I said to myself, "I'm going on there." I was in twelfth grade, and I was telling people I was going on that show. They laughed and said, "You ain't going on that show." Lo and behold, September 22, 1972, at 10:22 p.m. Pacific Time, I arrived in Los Angeles!

SM: When you first came to Los Angeles, you didn't know anybody. One night, you went to a club called The Summit when "Papa Was A Rolling Stone" was playing, and you met Little Joe Chism, who danced on *Soul Train*, and he helped get you on the show's November 1972 taping, right?

TP: Yes. I befriended Little Joe there, and from Little Joe, I met everyone else from *Soul Train*.

SM: There's a funny story that you hid in the trunk of someone's car when you went through the gate at the studio where *Soul Train* was taped. Tell us about that.

TP: In the early days of *Soul Train*, Pam Brown, the teen coordinator of the show, would often go to Denker Park to audition and choose dancers to go on *Soul Train*. Since it was too late for me to audition, Little Joe took me to the television studio in the trunk of his car so we could get past the guard who was at the front with a list of names. So, Little Joe devised the plan to put me in the trunk of the car, and we drove right through the gate. That's how I got in!

SM: What do you recall about that first day at *Soul Train*?

TP: I recall thinking that on television, it looks a lot bigger than when you see it in person. The set was small. I could see everyone milling around. This was the first time I had ever been on a television studio set in my life, and I had to act like I fit in, hoping that Don Cornelius didn't see me since my name was not on the list. Unbeknownst to me, Little Joe had already started telling other dancers about me. I met Pat Davis and my heart is going, "Oh my God! Pat Davis!" At that very same time, she was talking about another dancer named Sharon Hill, who had just begun dancing on the show a few tapings earlier. I didn't have a dance partner, so she asked, "Why don't you dance with me?" I turned around to see the prettiest Black girl I had ever seen in my life! Sharon Hill was unbelievably beautiful. That's my memory of my first day at *Soul Train*.

SM: What are some of your favorite memories of recording artists that came to *Soul Train*? Who stands out?

TP: Marvin Gaye, Donna Summer, The Temptations, and Aretha Franklin are among them.

SM: You told me that there was one time James Brown came to the show very late.

TP: We had to stay on the set very late because he had either missed his flight, or his flight came in late. We waited and waited and waited. When he came, he set up his show, and we got out of the studio about 2:00 in the morning.

SM: When The Jackson 5 was on, you gave Tito Jackson a birthday card that was signed by all of the dancers because many of you were friendly with them.

TP: That's right. I remember one time when me and Gary Keyes went to the Jacksons' house and the only person that was there was Janet. But Pat Davis, Damita Jo Freeman, and some of the other dancers would go over to their house often and dance.

SM: You were one of several Soul Train dancers chosen to go on the Soul Train road tours, and you would all travel to different cities with groups like the Sylvers, The Moments, and other artists. I know that must have been an honor for you. What was that experience like?

TP: I couldn't get past the fact that I was going on the tour with Pat Davis, Damita Jo Freeman, Gary Keys, Don Campbell and Jimmy "Scoo B Doo" Foster! I couldn't get over that. I remember we would rehearse at Denker Recreation Center. The first concert we did was at the Cow Palace in San Francisco, and the Soul Train Gang opened the show. I clearly remember that right before Sharon and I went on, I went up to Don Cornelius and said, "But Don, the audience doesn't know who I am." Don said, "Bone, they know who you are. Just go on out there." So, we went out there, and the crowd just went up, and they started screaming. Then, Pat and Gary Keyes came out, and the crowd got even louder. When Damita and Don Campbell came out, the screaming was at a fever pitch. This place held thirty thousand seats, and it was sold out.

SM: You were very fashionable on *Soul Train*. You wore every hair-style—the Afro, cornrows, and the process. You wore fur coats coming down the Soul Train Line. Do you feel you were influential to future *Soul Train* dancers?

TP: I think I influenced Sharon, Jody Watley, and a couple of other people. I wouldn't exactly say influence, but more guidance.

SM: Did you ever have any problems with jealousy while you were on the show?

TP: I don't remember it. I'm sure there was. I didn't have time to get involved in that.

SM: I remember you told me you were one of the only dancers allowed to go downstairs in the studio and have your hair professionally done by *Soul Train*'s hairdresser, Ruby Ford.

TP: Right, because I had a perm and had to have rollers in my hair. I went downstairs, and the only dancers who were allowed to go downstairs were me and Jeffrey Daniels. One of the reasons for this was that Jeffrey and I took the lunches and put them in the recording artists' rooms.

SM: You guys served the recording artists fried chicken? [laughs]

TP: [laughs] No, they had something else besides chicken. The dancers had the two pieces of chicken from either Kentucky Fried Chicken or Golden Bird and one can of soda. We had to stick our hand in a basket filled with ice and take out our can of soda!

SM: Now, you brought a new style of dancing to *Soul Train* that people had never seen before called Waacking. Where did that style of dance come from?

TP: Waacking came from a certain community. To be honest and to be fair, a lot of the dances that were done on the show were brought to the show. They weren't invented on the show; they were invented in the clubs. The Soul Train Gang was basically the first generation of club kids, and we would go to different clubs every night of the week. There was a group of dancers who would be waacking on *Soul Train* that I have a fondness and respect for: Lamont Petersen, Mickey Lord, Gary Keyes, John Pickett, David Vinson, Dwayne Hargrave, Blinky, Arthur, and Andrew. They have all passed away, and it's important that the readers understand and recognize the importance of their influence on dance and on *Soul Train*.

SM: Waacking is still being done to this day all over the world.

TP: That's right! The dance groups that came from the show were The Lockers, Something Special, and the Outrageous Waack Dancers that included myself, Jeffrey, Jody, and Sharon. All of the dances that those dance groups performed are still popular to this day. Out of all those dance groups, those were some of the most popular people on the show.

SM: It was Don Cornelius that gave you the nickname "The Bone," right?

TP: Yes. He gave me that name because when I was a young little whipper snapper, he would always say, "Bone, up on the riser! Bone, come here!" He would always call me that because I was so thin. I had other nicknames, but I affectionately kept that one because I always had a huge fondness and respect for Don.

SM: You and other *Soul Train* dancers danced on *American Bandstand* from time to time. In fact, you and Sharon participated in and won a dance contest on *American Bandstand*. That must have indeed been a wonderful experience.

TP: Yes, it was! When I first met Little Joe, he and Damita had just won a dance contest on *American Bandstand*, and they were going to Hawaii as part of the prize. Dick Clark asked Damita and Little Joe if they knew a couple that could be in their next dance contest, and they gave him my name and Sharon Hill's name. We went to Dick Clark's office, and we did a couple of quick dance routines right in his office. To ensure that Sharon and I would win, we would often make up routines and try out the routines in different clubs like the Total Experience. We would tell the club owners we were in this dance contest, and we wanted to take five minutes to do a little show. Most of the club owners knew that we danced on *Soul Train* and said, "Sure, go ahead." Then we would hand out the index cards to the people at the clubs. They would sign the cards, and we would fill them out and mail them in. It was good that we did that, but we didn't need to, because a guy who worked for Dick Clark told us that out of all of the seven contestants, there were 100,000 votes and Sharon and I got 60,000 of the votes!

SM: What did it feel like when you and Sharon won the contest?

TP: We were shocked and surprised! We each won brand new cars, the 1974 Mazda RX4 Coupe. But in order to get the cars, we had to pay the taxes and licenses for them, which was $334.25. So, I told Jeffrey Daniel, whom I call my little baby brother, that I needed to get the money to pay the taxes for it. So, he told me, "Why don't we go to Don Cornelius?" I said, "Don? Are you crazy? Don's not going to give me any money for this. I danced on another dance show." So, we went to Don and talked to him about it. He pulled out his drawer, took out his checkbook, wrote out a check for $334.25, and gave it to me! I'm assuming the reason he did it was because me and Sharon winning the contest was more or less *Soul Train* vs. *Bandstand*. I was ever so grateful to him. That was one of the nicest things Don did for me, personally.

SM: You and the dancers were in many issues of *Right On!* Magazine, and you got letters from a lot of fans. The adulation must have been great.

TP: Even though we had all of this fame and had press and media attention, a lot of us tried to do other things in the entertainment industry through SAG and AFTRA, but it didn't work. We danced on *Soul Train* for years, and SAG and AFTRA told us that all we were doing was not good enough. That didn't sit very well with me because with just *Soul Train* on your resume, that should have been enough to allow you to join.

SM: You were also one of the instructors in the *Soul Train* dance studio, correct?

TP: Yes. Don Cornelius opened up a dance studio in Los Angeles in 1978, and Jeffrey, Jody, Sherri Green, and I would teach the Hustle to classes.

SM: You moved to the East Coast after you left *Soul Train*, right?

TP: Yes. After I left *Soul Train*, I moved to New York. Before that, the Outrageous Waack Dancers got a chance to do a gig in Japan. Dick Griffey and Don worked with Jeffrey and Jody Watley so other dancers from *Soul Train* joined Sharon and me. When I came back to Los Angeles, a girl named Sherri wanted to go to New York to pursue a modeling career. So, I left Los Angeles and moved to New York.

SM: Somewhere along the line, you began to choreograph acts in the music industry.

TP: One day in 1987, I was working in a store, and I got a call. It was Jody Watley. I was surprised! She told me she was coming out with her next single from her first solo album, and she wanted me to work with her on her "Still A Thrill" music video. She flew me out to Paris, and I choreographed and danced in the video with her. At that point, it went uphill for me. I started to do choreography for people like Sweet Sensation, The Isley Brothers, Levert, Keith Sweat, Johnny Kemp, Perfect Gentleman, and Taylor Dane. I was also nominated for an MTV Award for choreographing New Kids On the Block. I had met Maurice Starr at that time, who formed New Kids On the Block and we clicked and we're friends to this day. I did choreography for all of his acts. Jody opened up all of these other possibilities to me back on that day in 1987.

SM: At the *MTV Awards* ceremony, you reunited with Don Cornelius after a number of years.

TP: When I got there, I saw him, and he said, "Bone! What are you doing here?" I said, "I am here because New Kids On the Block were nominated and I am working with them." As he was turning around to walk away, he said, "Make sure to tell them where you come from."

SM: In 1997, the first Soul Train Gang reunion was put together by Little Joe and Thelma Davis Martin. You hadn't seen a lot of the dancers in years. I remember when you got there and you saw Sharon, you had such an outpouring of emotion. I was happy to see that.

TP: It had been years since I had seen a lot of those dancers. The emotional part was seeing Sharon because she was like my sister. Even now, her kids call me Uncle Ty. And to see Pat Davis, Don Campbell, Eddie Cole, Bernard Thompson, and Nieci Payne was a great experience. *Soul Train* is my family. I'm a blessed man. I've lived a wonderful and gifted life.

SM: A year later, Little Joe passed away, and he was one of your dearest and closest friends as well as one of mine. I remember when you called and told me the news. What do you want to say in his memory?

TP: I miss him. That's all I can say. If it wasn't for him and his kindness, I wouldn't be where I am today. Little Joe was the glue, and he kept all of the dancers together.

SM: The loss of Don Cornelius was shocking to us all. What do you want to say in Don's memory?

TP: Don helped a lot of people explore their dreams. He helped people ignite their talents and possibilities. I don't think he had an opportunity to realize what he had. It's a wonderful experience to watch people's talents blossom like Rosie Perez and Darnell Williams. I'm honored to be a part of *Soul Train*. When Don died, many were more focused on the artists who performed in the show than the dancers. The *Soul Train* dancers were hurting, so we decided to put together a memorial for him at Maverick's Flat. That's why I am honored that the Smithsonian Institution is putting together an exhibit honoring Don, the show, and the dancers in its African American Museum that is being built right now. Don Cornelius was a revolutionary.

SM: What word of wisdom do you want to share?

TP: What I have learned about dance is this: If you don't reach back and teach the young people, there will be no history. Dance basically comes from Black people; all of these dances come from Black people, but it's for everybody. I want to say thank you to all of the people reading this, and I love you so much. And as I always say in parting, if you don't understand the music, you will never understand the dance.

NOTE: This interview was originally conducted in 2013. Proctor passed away in 2020. He was a dear friend of mine, and I enjoyed meeting up with him in Harlem where he lived, our many conversations, and how he helped me get in various projects. When his family had his funeral in Brooklyn in 2020, it was at the height of the coronavirus pandemic, and many dancers from the West Coast could not fly out, but because I live in New Jersey, I spoke at his funeral on behalf of the Soul Train dancers. The rest of the *Soul Train* family and I extend our deepest condolences to Tyrone's family. May he forever rest in peace.

BACK IN THE DAY

CURRENT PHOTO

# Sheila Childress Kuniyuki

(1972–1976)

> There was a popular GIF online for quite some time showing an old Soul Train Line clip of Fred “Rerun” Berry doing a slow matrix-style dance with a young lady in a red shirt. Many wondered, “Who is that girl in the red shirt dancing with Rerun?” The mystery has been solved. She is Sheila Childress Kuniyaki.

**S**M: How did you get on *Soul Train*?

SK: I went to one of the auditions at Denker Park and was selected from there. I was just out of high school at that time. One of my really good friends, Doris, told me about the audition and said that I should go.

SM: What was the audition process like?

SK: They had two Soul Train Lines that different groups had to go down. I was in one line, and Fred “Rerun” Berry was on another line, and after the audition, Don Cornelius put us together.

SM: Tell me about your friendship with Fred Berry.

SK: Fred and I were like brother and sister at the time. I first met Penguin (Berry’s nickname) at a club. I went over to him and said, “Hi,” and we eventually became friends. I helped him enter dance contests and get exposure because he didn’t have a job at the time. I also remember that he had a curfew and always had to make sure the window to his house was open. [laughs]

SM: What do you recall about your first time on *Soul Train*?

SK: It was really exciting to see all the other young people like Damita Jo Freeman that were dancing on *Soul Train*. She was the first dancer from the show that I truly admired, and that's one of the reasons I wanted to go on the show.

SM: There is a Soul Train Line in which you and Fred are coming down the line doing what appears to be a dynamic matrix-style routine!

SK: This was Fred and I's first time going down the Soul Train Line, so we made up something called the Slow Motion prior to going down the line.

SM: That clip of you and Fred is very popular now and is even a GIF image on social media.

SK: Yes! Many wondered who the girl was dancing with Fred. I am the mysterious woman with the red shirt on. [laughs].SM: Do you recall the long tapings and that some of these tapings went into the wee hours of the morning?

SK: Yes! I surely do. We would tape Saturday and Sunday, and we would tape two shows each day. So, there were some very, very long days. But it was so much fun! We didn't care. All we wanted to do was just dance, so it didn't really matter.

SM: I call taping *Soul Train* like going to a club with long breaks between songs and artist performances.

SK: Exactly! Everybody had fun, we were all around the same age and it was like we were out partying all day and half of the night!

SM: Did you ever do the Scramble Board?

SK: No, unfortunately, I never did the Scramble Board. I would have loved to have done it.

SM: Did you get your share of fried chicken? [laughs]

SK: [laughs] Yes, I did! Golden Bird! It's so funny because one of my friends said she got high cholesterol from all the chicken she ate on *Soul Train*! But it was so good and so welcoming because all that dancing made you hungry!

SM: [laughs] And I heard the early dancers could only have one soda each out of that garbage can.

SK: Yes, one soda for one entire day! But it didn't really matter much. I was young, and I don't think I ever finished drinking my soda in one taping. I would just drink some, go out and dance, then come back, drink some more, then go back out and dance.

SM: I'm going to throw some names of recording artists who were on the show while you were a dancer and ask you to tell me what you can recall. First, Marvin Gaye.

SK: Oh my God! He sat between me and Rhonda Brown right before the Q&A session. Then he was holding my hand and singing "Let's Get it On." That was really, really exciting! I enjoyed that more than anything until a camera hog came and jumped in front of us and did her thing. She did not want to let him go! [laughs]

SM: What was Marvin like during breaks? Did he interact or speak with any of you?

SK: Well, I got his attention because he was chewing gum a lot. Don had asked him many times, "You've got to get rid of the gum, man." So, he would take it out but then put another piece in his mouth. So, I made a comment like, "That gum is going to get you in big trouble." That's what made him come over and talk to Rhonda and me because of that comment.

SM: What about Al Green? He's been on the show a number of times, but there was one time in particular when he had performed with his arm in a sling, but he gave one of the best live performances on the show I've ever seen. Do you remember that?

SK: Yes, I do! We used to tease him too! [laughs]

SM: For someone who had broken his arm, he was hopping around on the stage and passing out roses to the ladies like he was in no pain at all. He had all of you under a spell and took *Soul Train* to church!

SK: He truly did! But we were silly and young, so our nickname for him was Al "Hot Grits" Green. We didn't call him that, but that was an inside joke among us dancers.

SM: How about Smokey Robinson?

SK: Oh my God! He was such a crooner and was so smooth. He was very gracious, and he had the most beautiful eyes.

SM: One particular time, he sang "Baby Come Close" live. He had his band that included Jeffrey Osborne as his drummer, and all the dancers were seated and standing around as he sang on stage.

SK: We were totally mesmerized by him!

SM: Any other memories of artists that you recall?

SK: I remember The Pointer Sisters when they first came on.

SM: Yes, they did "Yes We Can Can" live and then another tune from their album called "Cloudbursts," and they had you all excited with their scatting and vocalizations on that tune.

SK: Oh yes, we loved The Pointer Sisters! Me and my friend Doris bought some handkerchiefs because they always had their hankies when they performed. So, we had our hankies too, so we could wave them in the air like they did.

SM: I noticed some of the times you and Doris went down the Soul Train Line, you both would be cutting up while holding your handkerchiefs. [laughs]

SK: [laughs] Yes, we got that from The Pointer Sisters. Then there was Barry White. As a big guy, he was just so smooth. He was like a Teddy Bear. He had a beautiful complexion with a dark mustache and goatee.

SM: And the perm!

SK: [laughs] Yes! And his wife, Glodean, sang with him as a background singer in the Love Unlimited group. I also remember when Ashford & Simpson came on. I just loved them!

SM: How about The Jackson 5?

SK: Oh yes, when they did "Dancing Machine." Sometimes, when you're starstruck, you can't really say anything. All you can do is just look at them and see how awesome they are! I didn't even dance on the floor when they were performing. I was just looking at them from the stands. I was so mesmerized!

SM: Who can forget when the Godfather of Soul, James Brown, came on the show!

SK: Oh yes, Mr. Brown!

SM: He had his J.B.'s, Lyn Collins, and little daughter Deanna with him. He had *Soul Train* rocking with that live setup. What do you remember about having him in your midst?

SK: Seeing him dance and perform was just truly awesome because he was an all-around performer! Kool & the Gang was another act I enjoyed. They were so much fun. All of the artists from that time were really good.

SM: Absolutely, like Rufus featuring Chaka Khan.

SK: Chaka Khan! Yes! She would get in trouble with Don too.

SM: I was told at one taping she kept asking for water, and Don was getting irritated.

SK: Yes, he did! And Billy Preston was great! He was a godfather to the daughter of Rhonda Brown.

SM: As I tell other dancers from your era of *Soul Train*, you were all blessed to have had all those legends in your midst on the show, many of whom are no longer with us.

SK: It was so exciting. That was the highlight of our young lives.

SM: Back at that time, many dancers were profiled in *Right On!* magazine. Were you ever profiled?

SK: Yes! They were showing how some of the dancers relaxed during tapings, and I was one of the dancers they featured, so that was exciting.

SM: When you started getting seen on *Soul Train*, what was the recognition like from your family and friends and the general public?

SK: It made you feel special. That's for sure. One time, one of my little brothers had taken some of my hair from my brush and was trying to sell it! [laughs] He would tell people, "My sister dances on *Soul Train*! Do you want to buy some of her hair?" [laughs]

SM: Who were your favorite dance partners?

SK: A guy named Steven who had a beard and curly hair. Another guy was Phillip.

SM: You and Steven did your thing down the Soul Train Line.

SK: Well, thank you!

SM: Now I know some of the dancers experienced jealousy from other dancers. Did you ever experience any jealousy?

SK: No. We were all pretty mellow. If there was any jealousy, I didn't experience it.

SM: I remember seeing some situations on the set with some dancers while I was on the show, and they were told to stop, or else Don would throw them off the show.

SK: Yes, he would! He wasn't going to stand for it. I remember when a certain dancer was going around trying to get donations to give Don a gift. We were looking at her like she was crazy. We were like, "Don should be paying us!" One of my friends told her, "Get out of here, Mary Poppins!" She got so upset that this girl came down the aisle with a big trash can, headed straight for her, but she was stopped before she could get to her.

SM: Wow! Did Don find out about this?

SK: Yes. He was like, "You two coming on the set acting like Muhammad Ali and Joe Frazier." [laughs]

SM: Another dancer from the early days told me she actually had a fight on the set with another girl. I was like, I thought there was nothing but love, peace, and soul on set.

SK: No, it was not. You never know who's jealous of whom. I just enjoyed dancing on the show and having fun. I didn't care about all of that other stuff.

SM: Did you ever dance on *American Bandstand* or the show that was created to rival *Soul Train* called *Soul Unlimited*?

SK: No, I never danced on those shows.

ME: Any other standout or special moments on *Soul Train*?

SK: When I met Stevie Wonder! He is just a genius. When I was growing up, we used to have 45 RPM records, and I would sleep with the picture sleeve of the Stevie Wonder 45s under my pillow! [laughs] He is the most fantastic and talented young man that I have ever seen. Meeting Stevie Wonder was just awesome. I went to the studio where he was making his *Songs In the Key of Life* album, and I was so mesmerized. He came out and introduced himself to Rhonda and me. He kissed our hands and said something to us in another language. He had just had his first daughter, Aisha, and I told him I had just had my daughter, Crystal, so we had something in common. That was so very special.

SM: A lot of the dancers told me about all the clubs the dancers frequented back in those days.

SK: Maverick's Flat! That was the place! We would leave *Soul Train* and go to Mavericks and dance even more! They had bands and artists like Bootsy Collins playing live there.

SM: Do you still dance?

SK: I still dance, and I love line dancing. My oldest daughter and I would go line dancing all the time. My daughters and granddaughter have rhythm. When I was growing up, I loved to skate. I did it every weekend. It's funny because my daughters would always volunteer me to be a chaperone with their class to take them skating. I was skating until I got sick. I had lung cancer twice, but I am doing much better now and am cancer-free. I was on *Ellen* in 2006 after I beat cancer, and another time I was on her show, I danced down the aisle. I'm proud that I overcame cancer, and I love sharing that.

SM: Thank you so much for sharing this story, and I am so happy you are cancer-free.

SK: Thank you! I have also been married for forty-four years to my husband Yukinori Kuniyuki

SM: Congratulations! What are you doing currently?

SK: My husband and I own our own business, Pacific Associates, an employment and training company that has been around for about forty years. We also have job developers that contact other companies to get our people as they complete their training. We have been very successful and weren't affected by COVID-19 or anything. I retired in 2019, and my husband is going to be retiring soon, so our youngest daughter is going to be taking over the business.

SM: What do you want to say in memory of Don Cornelius?

SK: All I can say is that he put on a hell of a good show for young people with a desire to dance. He made a way for us to come on and show our talent, our hair, our clothes, and our dancing.

SM: What word of wisdom do you want to share?

SK: I think you should always follow what you desire because by me watching *Soul Train*, I never thought I would be able to go on the show, and I did. Whatever you want to accomplish, remember that you can do it with hard work and by following your dreams.

CURRENT PHOTO

BACK IN THE DAY

# James "Skeeter Rabbit" Higgins

(1972–1974)

> James "Skeeter Rabbit" Higgins is one of the funkiest dancers that came out of South-Central Los Angeles. His locking, roboting, and trademark Skeeter Rabbit dance moves are legendary. What is really important to him is that the true history behind locking is told and never forgotten. The roots and foundation of locking were born out of the struggle of the civil rights movement, and friendship and brotherhood are at its core. This is what Skeeter has been teaching in locking workshops around the world for several years, the importance of "educating before recreating." Although his nickname was bestowed on someone else, James Higgins is the original "Skeeter Rabbit."

SM: Who or what inspired you to dance?

JH: I saw dancing all my life. It was part of the culture I grew up in. My mom would be in the kitchen cooking with rhythm as she listened to the Motown music jamming on radio station KGFJ and its DJ, the Magnificent Montague. My first dance partner was my mom. She taught me how to do the Stroll and the Madison. My mom didn't have any sisters, so her friends were like my aunts. When they got together, they would do dances like the Dog and the Shotgun.

SM: You are originally from South Central California, right?

JH: I grew up in South Central California at 46th and Central, which was two blocks from Dolphin's of Hollywood where KGFJ would broadcast from their windows. I caught the bus every day on Central and 46th into Watts, where I went to a private high school.

SM: What was it like growing up in South Central California with all of the gangs?

JH: We had so much respect from the gangs for our dancing. Me, the GoGo Brothers, Buddy and Tony Gogo, the Yo-Yo Brothers, and the CoCo Brothers could go anywhere in any territory, and the gangs would say, "That's the GoGo Brothers! That's one of the Yo-Yo Brothers!" So, we didn't have a problem with the gang situation. As a matter of fact, I tell this all the time: the ace deuce hats, the hats that you see The Lockers wear, were hats worn by gangs like the Crips. The only reason that Greg "Campbell Lock Jr." Pope, Shabba Doo and the rest of The Lockers could wear those hats is because the price was paid in the streets by the GoGo Brothers who earned wearing the ace deuce hats. So, when Greg and Jimmy "Scoo B Doo" Foster started coming to Watts Writers Workshop, they earned the right to wear the ace deuce hats.

SM: How did you get the nickname Skeeter Rabbit?

JH: The nickname and the step are synonymous. I've been called Skeeter all of my life. The story my grandmother tells is that when I was born on January 21st, 1955, my dad looked at me through the glass window of the hospital saying "Skeeter, Skeeter, Skeeter," and that became my nickname. I started to create the step the Skeeter Rabbit from watching the kids in the neighborhood I lived in playing hopscotch, but they would hop in a rhythm. I also watched the legendary Nicholas Brothers doing their shuffle steps, and they would end their shuffling steps in the old traditional tap dance shuffle and throw their hands out. As I was doing locking, I started putting my footwork in it like Jimmy "Scoo B Doo" incorporated his Scoo B Doo steps into locking. I started combining moves and shuffling. One time, I didn't shuffle and end the move, but I kept kicking and spinning, kicking and spinning, and shuffling, and everyone started laughing, including the GoGo Brothers, Buddy and Tony Gogo. So, one night we went to the Citadel, and they said, "Come on, do that thing you do Skeet." So, I started doing the step. Behind me, I heard some laughter, and it came from Fred Berry, a.k.a. Penguin. He looked at me and said, "Skeeter, you look like a rabbit doing that stuff, man. You're like a Skeeter Rabbit." And the name Skeeter Rabbit stuck. That became the name of the step, and it became my full nickname.

SM: Wasn't there another dancer from the Electric Boogaloos that went by the nickname of Skeeter Rabbit?

JH: Skeeter Rabbit is a unique name. It's my name from the time I was born in 1955, and the rabbit part was added to it because of my dance. I met Steven Nichols, who also had the nickname Skeeter Rabbit, in 2004 in Japan, and believe me, he was a wonderful dancer with the Electric Boogaloos. We sat down and talked, and he told me, "Hey Skeet, I meant no disrespect. I used to watch you when you had your yellow Chevy, and you went to 110 and Broadway and would dance in the front yards." That's true. I had a girlfriend on 110 and Broadway, and I used to dance in the front yard. Some kids from the neighborhood would come down and watch.

SM: Before you became a *Soul Train* dancer, you were part of the Watts Writers Workshop which included a lot of other future dance legends such as Greg "Campbell Lock Jr." Pope, Jimmy "Scoo B Doo" Foster and the GoGo Brothers.

JH: Right. The Watts Writers Workshop had existed since 1966, after the Watts Riots in 1965. It had writers, bands, and even a recording studio. I became a part of its dancing classes around 1971 or 1972.

SM: How did you become a part of the Watts Writers Workshop?

JH: The GoGo Brothers, Tony and Buddy, were traveling from school to school with an acapella singing group called the Free Expressions.

My school would allow me to go and tour with the Go-Bo Brothers and Free Expressions, and we would be doing dance skits and steps that included locking and roboting at all of the neighboring high schools. Watts Writers Workshop heard about this from Arnetta Johnson, one of the best lock dancers I have ever seen. She was called "Netta Bug" and had an uncle who worked there. He asked us to bring this dancing we were doing to the workshop. When we got there, we put a dance crew together there that included myself, the GoGo Brothers, the Toota Woota Sisters, and sometimes Freddie Maxie, Greg "Campbell Lock Jr." and Jimmy "Scoo B Doo." We called our group Creative Generation. We would teach the local kids who were in the Watts Writers Workshop how to do this style of dancing, and we would travel and work with them.

SM: So, would all of you teach locking and roboting at the workshop and perform at different places?

JH: Yes. We traveled up and down the West Coast and would do a lot of colleges, such as Cal State and Berkeley, doing full locking routines. This was before The Lockers dance group was formed.

SM: There was a time that you changed from a party-style dancer to a locker-style dancer, right?

JH: Yes. Down the street was a guy named Charles Washington. He was the first one I would see go to a social party and dance with females doing the Robot as a dance style. I would see him dance in his front yard, and he would start talking about these clubs that existed where this dance was going on. So, Buddy, Tony Gogo, Kevin Yo-Yo, and I traveled to the Citadel. That's where I met Greg "Campbell Lock Jr.," Fluky Luke, and Fred Berry. That's where I got "Rabbit" added to my nickname, Skeeter.

SM: How did you become a *Soul Train* dancer?

JH: Shortly after that night at the Citadel, we heard about this show coming out from Chicago called *Soul Train*. I didn't go to the first season's auditions, but when *Soul Train* first came on and I saw how hot and popular the people from the club became, I couldn't wait to get to the second season's auditions. They were held at Denker Park. Pam Brown, the show's dance coordinator, was there, and Dick Griffey. It was the longest Soul Train Line I had ever seen, from one end of the gym to the other. Pam and Dick would stand at the end of the line and would play Lyn Collins's "Think" over and over and over again. I must have gone down that line twenty times to that song! Pam Brown called me and my dance partners, Candi Boon and Gerri Turner, and said that our names were on the list for the next show. I was going to get in anyway because I knew Don Campbell and Greg were already on the show, and they said if we didn't get in, they were going to help us get in by hopping us over the fence or opening the gate or whatever. But I actually got on legitimately because Pam Brown put me on the list.

SM: What artists did you enjoy watching perform on *Soul Train*?

JH: The most prominent act I remember definitely was James Brown. I will never ever forget being on that episode. Most of the time on *Soul Train,* a lot of the acts lip-synched. When James Brown came on, there was some conversation over whether he was supposed to lip-synch, and it was delaying the production. But when he came out on the stage, everything was plugged up live. That entire day, the music flowed live, from the time the show started all the way through breaks. James Brown had his band, The J.B.'s, play for us even during the breaks.

SM: Did you have a chance to meet or speak to James Brown?

JH: I got a chance to stand right next to him in front of the stage, and he said in that rough voice, "Hey, you dancers, you guys really cutting up and doing your thing."

SM: Years later, when I was a *Soul Train* dancer, the powers that be on the show tried to diffuse locking and roboting. You told me before you experienced that on the show too, right?

JH: Yes. Absolutely. When Don Campbell became very popular, he allegedly asked for payment and got thrown off the show. The show tried to diffuse the dancers who were locking from getting popular, so they would place them on the outskirts of the stage. Sometimes, the dancers were told to stop locking, and it wasn't to be done down the Soul Train Line. But the dance had become so popular and there were so many great dancers doing it that they couldn't hide it all from the camera. Eventually, Don Campbell wound up back on the show when The Lockers came back to perform as professionals. Don Cornelius laughed and made light of the time he had Don Campbell kicked off the show. As you know, *American Bandstand* started almost recruiting the dancers who were doing roboting and locking over onto their show, so it became a competitive thing.

SM: I recall some episodes of *American Bandstand* from the 1970s, and they had some White guys and a White girl dressed in locker-style clothing imitating what they considered locking, but it seemed fake.

JH: It wasn't real at all.

SM: Did you ever dance on the Black dance show that Dick Clark produced to rival *Soul Train* called *Soul Unlimited*?

JH: I never danced on that show. I went on *American Bandstand* one time. A lot of people at that point were trying to imitate what they saw on *Soul Train* because locking and roboting had become so popular. *American Bandstand* didn't have the funk and soul feel. When I grew up in the sixties, *American Bandstand* was known for only having one or two Black couples on just to accentuate the Black artists that came on the show. I was told that two Black couples could not dance next to each other on *American Bandstand*, and they were separated.

SM: Other dancers told me Don Cornelius gave the dancers a warning if they danced on *Soul Unlimited* or *American Bandstand*.

JH: Yes. If you went on one of those shows, it was said you weren't going to be welcomed back on *Soul Train*, so you had to make a choice.

SM: What was your overall experience on *Soul Train* like?

JH: I had a great time on *Soul Train*. I was on from 1972 to 1973 and for a short time in 1974. Sometimes, I wouldn't even try to go on camera. I would party near the bleachers or on the outskirts of the stage and just have a good time. I didn't push to be a camera hog or to get down the Soul Train Line. My main focus was on enjoying dancing and seeing the artists. That was more important than being seen per se. My mom would sit and watch *Soul Train* and say, "There goes Skeet!" After leaving a *Soul Train* taping, me and other dancers would go to Maverick's Flat, The Summit, the Citadel, and just dance all night long.

SM: I guess you danced off all that fried chicken that was given to the dancers! [laughs]

JH: Yes! [laughs] The show brought in lots of boxes of Golden Bird chicken. Golden Bird was a Black-owned business that closed out of Watts some years ago.

SM: You were, at some point, part of The Lockers dance group, right?

JH: Right. I was with them on the Frank Sinatra tour in the spring of 1974. I received a phone call from Greg and Toni Basil then, and they said, "Skeet, we're ready for you to come out to New York. We're going to put you in the group. We need you to do the Robot numbers and other things."

SM: At this time, you were going to Long Beach State College on a baseball scholarship. How did your mom feel about you going to New York to do this show?

JH: My mom was furious. "Skeet, you're going to leave Long Beach State and leave a baseball scholarship and run out on your education just to go do this?" But those opportunities were not that frequent. It was very rare to have a professional dance group. That didn't exist before, so I wanted to go. So, I got on an airplane and flew out to New York. I had to put the light suit together and the whole bit. I had worn light-up suits before at Maverick's.

SM: What was that experience like?

JH: It was the first professional show I ever did, which was at Carnegie Hall in New York. I wound up being the robot for that entire Frank Sinatra tour. During the Robot number, I lay on the floor in a West Side Story-like skit. I'm lying on the floor after being "beat up" by the West Side Story gang, and I come up off the floor like a robot to Deodato's "2000." I'm looking down at the opera seats, and I see Lucille Ball in the audience. I met her, Frank Sinatra, and Sammy Davis Jr. that night.

SM: How long was the tour?

JH: It was for a few months. I toured with them, and I came back to Los Angeles. I was working and training with them because I was supposedly on alternate status, and I was supposed to get a contract on that tour, but I never did. So, when the tax paperwork came out, there was huge confusion, and it upset my family that I never got a contract. Never getting a permanent contract with ICM (talent agency) or The Lockers changed the course of things for me and caused me to do other things.

SM: What did you do professionally after that experience?

JH: I became a dancer on the *Cher* show for part of a season. Damita Jo Freeman connected me with her. I was so despondent about not actually being given a contract with The Lockers that I contemplated going into the service. I had given up my baseball scholarship and had to deal with all this pressure from my family of why I left school to go do this. So, I'm contemplating going into the service, and I actually signed up for the late entry. But then I got a call from Damita Jo Freeman. She told me to go down to CBS TV for an audition. I got there late after accidentally going to CBS Radio first, but I was still allowed to audition. For some reason, they knew my name and who I was. So, I was picked to be one of the dancers on the *Cher* show along with Lionel Douglass a.k.a. Big B, Deney Terrio, and some White dancers that knew how to do some dance styles, but not the inner-city stuff. We were there to teach and show Cher how to do some of the numbers in the funky street dance style.

SM: How were you able to get out of the service since you had signed up?

JH: I was able to go back and talk my way out of the service. I was actually let out because the commanding officer was a fan of the *Cher* show, and I told him I had a double contract, one with Cher and another with them, and they let me out.

SM: What was it like working with Cher?

JH: She was remarkable, just like Frank Sinatra. They had this certain aura, and they gave me a greater appreciation for other kinds of music and other talents. Growing up in the hood, you hear funk and soul, and you don't really appreciate other talents and other forms of music. Frank Sinatra had an energy about him that he could walk into a stadium and everyone just stood up. I was like, "He's done nothing yet." It was just his energy. Cher had that same ability. I could demonstrate a step, and the choreographer would call the step according to jazz moves, and Cher would somehow translate that into our style of dance. It was remarkable.

SM: Did you do any more touring after that?

JH: On the *Cher* show, I met one of the dancers named Cam Walker from Utah, one of the funkiest dancing White guys that I ever saw. He wanted to learn our style of dance as well as its history. He said to me, "Hey Skeet, let's put a real group together from out of the hood. Do you know any of the dancers inside the hood that did not get into The Lockers or did not get real famous outside of the hood?" I said, "Yes, I know several of them that danced with me up through the years." So, he asked me to put a group together, and we called the group 33 RPM. We went and got Michael Peek-a-Boo Frankie from out of South-Central Los Angeles, we got a Robot dancer and a Locker by the name of John Oke-e-Doke and others. All of these guys were on various episodes of *Soul Train*. So, we formed that group, and Cam introduced us to Sid and Marty Krofft. They were puppeteers, and they had the H.R. Pufnstuff show on the air, but the main thing is that they put on great puppet shows. So, they sent 33 RPM on a southern tour with our home base in Atlanta, Georgia, from 1975 to 1976. That was a heck of an experience.

SM: Did you do any other TV appearances?

JH: 33 RPM did the fiftieth anniversary of the Harlem Globetrotters TV special out of that theatre. The Globetrotters did their basketball performance there, and we performed during halftime. We also toured Utah and had some of the craziest experiences where it was hard for a Black person to get accepted, but they loved our style of dancing. So, many great things happened during that time.

SM: Going into the eighties, did you do anything entertainment-related?

JH: I stayed away from the new commercial scene when videos came out. I became a detective, and I opened a beauty supply store called Skeet's Hair Needs. I actually owned four stores at one time. I also became a community activist, becoming president of the Vernon Central Merchants Association and president of Teens Against Gangs (TAG). So, I stayed in the inner city of South Central and Watts, working from that standpoint.

SM: That's quite impressive! I can imagine it must have been quite an experience being a detective.

JH: It was challenging because the movement of street dance that came along in the 1960s was about the oppression of Black people. The Watts Riots started because of police brutality. I've been a victim of police brutality myself. I came up in the era of the Black power movement, which was not a negative movement from the inner-city but was a positive movement. I came up seeing the gestures that were used on the streets in locking before there *was* locking, such as pointing at each other, raising fists, giving yourself five, and the handshakes. So, I came up in that movement. I became an investigator working with the transit police, trying to get them to work with children, and I got my degree in criminal justice. But to work in community service and law enforcement, you had to be a bonafide cop with all of the training and all of the experience to get there. So, I was willing to do that to get inside and help, but I almost quit being in law enforcement at one point in time when I witnessed police brutality. So, I went home, meditated, and talked to my wife, Arlene, to whom I've been married for forty-five years. She said there are going to be other young Black people who are going to need you as a resource to fall back on when they encounter these problems. Arlene has always been supportive, inspiring me to continue to contribute to the needs of our community. She blessed me with two wonderful children, and we have six grandchildren.

SM: That's beautiful! Congratulations! For quite some time, you have been teaching locking around the world.

JH: Over the last ten years, I've been traveling and teaching dance workshops all over the world and talking about *Soul Train*. It was much more than entertainment and dancing. It bridged a gap to unity and an open dialogue with dance. It was the dance movement for change. It's the way the rest of the world saw people inside the inner communities dance for unity. So many people never saw where the dance came from. They saw it on TV on *Soul Train*, *The Carol Burnett Show*, *Doris Day*, and other shows. They saw the act, but they never saw the roots and the foundation of the street dancing that was taking place. They never saw the nightclubs after we left a *Soul Train* taping or the picnics we were at when people would just dance for the heck of dancing. All they saw was the show. I teach that you have to submit to the music. If you don't submit to the music and the culture, you're only imitating funk and soul.

SM: Indeed. For those who don't know the history of locking, it's just entertainment. While it may be entertaining, there are roots behind it. You, The Lockers, the Go-Gos, the Yo-Yos, the CoCos, Jimmy "Scoo B Doo" and Creative Generation are the roots. It predated breakdancing in the late 1970s and 1980s. There's a reason for the handshakes and the pointing. It's not playing around, and it comes from a real experience.

JH: Right! It's not a minstrel, and that's when the embarrassing part comes in. Some of the people saw the style of dance and not the art form and don't understand the history of where it comes from and where our people come from. So, they try to imitate the style, and they think it's just the wearing of hats. One time, I was at a preliminary dance contest in France where a dancer came out and he had the Elvis Presley wig on, a cape and a guitar on his back, and he started to point and shake and flip the guitar around and fake like he was playing music and would then freeze. When he wasn't selected to travel in the locking competition, he asked me why he wasn't selected. In his words, "locking was all about creativity," and as long as he posed in a locking move, he was locking. I had to explain to him that locking was a culture from the streets inspired by the Civil Rights era, and there were certain things done that are not to be compromised.

SM: I'm really into roboting and not playing around. When I do the Robot, it just takes over me, and I go into another zone.

JH: When you Robot to party music, not pre-arranged Robot music, such as when you walk into a party and hear the Chi-Lites' "For God's Sake, Give More Power to the People" for instance and you go inside that music and become the robotic instrument of that music, that's part of you illustrating what the lyrics and the expression of what the songwriter put in that music as a robot, total concentration.

SM: That's why it irked me in the late nineties and early 2000s on *Soul Train* when the dance coordinator would tell me to stop locking and roboting. I would say that these dances are still being done and taught overseas, and that Michael Jackson and Usher were still incorporating those dances in their steps. So, quite often, he would have me placed at the end of the Soul Train Line, or I wouldn't go down the line at all.

JH: That's why I believe that locking and popping are synonymous.

These dances should be deemed African American cultural art forms. Evidently, in the later years of *Soul Train*, there was self-hatred where we didn't want to showcase what our culture and history really is. What you did should have been celebrated.

SM: Thank you, Skeeter, bro! When I was on *Soul Train* it was a different time. If you watch any *Soul Train* show from the nineties to when it ended, the main focus was on the girls being cute and shaking around, not the dancing. I was happy that I was a part of the show and its legacy, but it was really different. They tried to water me down. I was told to watch what the other guys do, and I would say I'm not the other guys, I'm me.

JH: There's something throughout our history that's remarkable. Whenever anything becomes powerful, and you take the purpose out of it and turn it into straight entertainment, you can stop people from following the purpose. At the end of the sixties and the first part of the seventies, the Afrocentric movement was so powerful that there was a force it seems that tried to water it down so what they did was we as African Americans received a lot of benefits from the Civil Rights struggle such as educational opportunity programs (EOP), grants, and affirmative action. To do that, they took the purpose out of the music, and they took it to disco.

SM: Hence, *Saturday Night Fever*.

JH: John Travolta actually rehearsed at a dance academy directly after 33 RPM. So, Cam Walker knew Deney Terrio, who would come out to the dance contests and sit and watch Don Campbell, myself, Greg, Scoo B, and Alpha Omega Anderson. He would watch all of us dance, and then he began to train John Travolta. They didn't know how to do locking, so they called the rolling of the wrists "supper supper" and the pace part of locking they called "punch punch." They began to teach John Travolta "supper supper," and that's why he imitated locking in the movie *Saturday Night Fever*. They took the purpose and movement out of the dance and made it a disco dance. They changed the location of where it took place and ended the purpose of it. But you cannot stop a boiling pot from boiling over.

SM: Indeed. That's when breakdancing and the hip-hop movement came in out of the South Bronx.

JH: The same issues manifested themselves on the East Coast with hip-hop. Hip-hop began to tell stories of the street experiences and it boiled that pot right back over. But this time the East Coast was smart enough to put a tag on it called hip-hop. They again tried to take the purpose out of it, but there was such a strong movement of real brothers and sisters that they wouldn't allow that to happen. A lot of the second and third generations saw the dance on TV and tried to imitate it themselves. A lot of those places want to classify themselves as foundational and original, but they came along after the original era.

SM: It all goes back to the civil rights movement, the anger, and the pride that came out of that movement. Our people have a rich heritage, and it's sad that during the time I was on *Soul Train,* they tried to diffuse that. There are schools all over the world that teach popping, roboting, and locking. Those dance styles are looked upon by some people as mere dance crazes, but they're not. They are movements born out of a period of time and are timeless.

JH: I'm amazed as I travel, so many people want to know the history and the purpose of locking. Dance has always been spiritual in our history, all the way from the slave fields. There are a lot of kids around the world who are searching for their spiritual roots and want to know where it came from and about the struggle. Sweden has one of the biggest and strongest connections to our total movement because they study and understand the struggle. There are so many underprivileged kids that don't have the money to pay for some of these workshops, but they are flying all around the world to learn the dance. I wish there was an inner-city academy that would allow these talented kids to be able to learn their roots and heritage without having to pay that kind of money or being subsidized by the government. In Japan and China, the government sponsors the cultural exchanges. The United States hasn't recognized what we have done as a cultural heritage.

SM: What about people who try to take what you teach and try to take credit for it?

JH: Some people meet me and Scoo B, and then they go back to their countries and say they are full-fledged teachers of locking and exploit the dance. When I teach, I tell people that funk and soul are not things that can be bought or sold. They have to come from within. If the creative forces are in our souls, the funk is the sweat that pours off that soul. The only way you allow sweat to come off that soul is to hear with the ears of your soul and not the ears of your ego. I teach kids that it's just like going to church. You teach them that if they really want to feel the funk and soul of the eras we came out of, then you submit to the music, its culture, and the real funk and soul. If not, I feel sorry because you will only imitate but never feel it.

SM: It reminds me of some people who don't know the experience and culture of Black people, and they try to use our language to fit in and supposedly be hip. You had to have lived the experience and history.

JH: When you look at the James Brown episode on *Soul Train* when he is being interviewed, he is talking about going back to Black colleges to see why the educational standards are not up to par. He was an advocate for the movement of improving Black education. When you look at the early *Soul Train* scramble boards, they weren't just about Black entertainers but about the Black history experience. The Frederick Douglass Afro Sheen commercial was showing Black pride in our hair. So, the people who don't want to teach us what the cultural impact of *Soul Train*, locking, and street dancing means, those are people who are trying to erase things out of history.

SM: What do you want to say in Don Cornelius's memory?

JH: He needs to receive the credit not just as a producer or the host of a television dance show, but for allowing the generation to express themselves and their allegiance and alliance to the movement through dance by stepping out and risking himself and risking what he wanted to do and holding fast to his commitment. By throwing up his fist at the end of each *Soul Train* episode and declaring "love, peace, and soul," he affirms his connection to our roots. His program was one of the most remarkable things that ever happened to open the doors for what you see in hip-hop today.

SM: What word of wisdom do you want to share?

JH: Continue to put out what we as a people were about, what *Soul Train* was about, and take great pride in what we did that had such an effect on the world.

*To learn more about Skeeter Rabbit, as well as the history and roots of locking and the pioneers that helped to invent it, please visit www.lockerlegends.net.*

# Anthony "Tony GoGo" Foster

(1972–1974)

Anthony Foster, a.k.a. Tony GoGo, is one of the pioneers of locking. As a co-founding member of the original GoGo Brothers dance group, he has preserved the art of locking and has been teaching this dance movement in Japan and other territories for over two decades. As a history/dance teacher, Tony instructs his students on the importance of knowing the history behind the locking phenomenon before executing the steps. Before this, he was a dancer on *Soul Train*, which served as a catalyst for what he is doing currently.

SM: Who or what inspired you to dance when you were growing up?

AF: I was inspired by many, including Fred Astaire, Gene Kelly, Bill "Bojangles" Robinson, James Brown, The Temptations, and most of the vocal groups of the sixties and seventies, such as The Four Tops, Stylistics, etc.

SM: How did you get the nickname "GoGo?"

AF: I was given this name by Fred "Rerun" Berry at the Citadel. Rerun called me off the wall and shouted to everyone, "This is GoGo, Tony GoGo!" The Citadel is where I got my first lesson from a Campbell Locker. After this, Edward Lombard and I decided to create a group

BACK IN THE DAY

CURRENT PHOTO

called the GoGo Brothers because we both loved dancing, and it was more about brotherhood. Togetherness is our motto. Our best friend at that time was James "Skeeter Rabbit" Higgins. We later added him to our GoGo Brothers family, and we are still together now. We have chapters of our name now in Japan, the US, Sweden, China, Taipei, and other places.

SM: Skeeter told me during my interview with him that you, he, and the GoGo Brothers all had respect from the neighborhood gangs due to your great dancing skills.

AF: Yes, this is true. I was not as well off as my brothers at that time in my life, so I was able to connect with the less fortunate in the hood. Like Skeeter stated, our dancing helped us to survive and make friends with the street gangs. They respected us because we respected them.

SM: What was the experience like being part of the Watts Writers Workshop?

AF: Watts Writers was a grand experience for me. Working as a group with my brothers and sisters helped me to overcome my shyness. Also, to be challenged with reading actual scripts written for stage and television was a beautiful experience for all of us. Our teacher, Sue Baker, was a grand blessing also. She was also a performer on most of the Black sitcoms at that time.

SM: How did you become a *Soul Train* dancer?

AF: During that time, Greg Pope was a dancer on the show and a member of The Campbell Lock Dancers. He came to my mother's home and asked me to come with him to the *Soul Train* auditions at Denker Park. He said I had the talent to become a dancer on the show. Ms. Pam Brown was the talent coordinator at the time. Out of two hundred people, only ten guys, including myself, and ten girls were chosen for the show that day. I thank Ms. Pam Brown for the chance of a lifetime. Always much love and respect.

SM: Do you recall your first weekend on *Soul Train*?

AF: Yes! I can never forget this. I was so excited, and all my brothers were as well. Like I told you, I was a little less fortunate than my brothers. On that first weekend, we met at Jovannie Mabrie's house and had breakfast there. It was a beautiful morning. When it was time to go, Jovannie said I could use his car to go to the studio. What a blessing. He had just bought a new blue Volkswagen. I backed out of the driveway and bam! The car from across the street was also backing out at the same time. I felt as small as a pea. While I was backing out, I felt like King Kong. After the "bam," I was a pea.

SM: I hope that didn't ruin your excitement about going to *Soul Train* that day.

AF: I felt bad that first day I did the show. What a bummer. But this is why the GoGo Brothers stress brotherhood. Jovannie made me go to the show even though I wrecked his new car, and he has never said anything about it to this day.

After making it to the studio and getting to the gate, Greg ran up to me and introduced me to Jherri Turner. We decided we would first do the Mashed Potato and then dance freestyle. It worked. So, we got to say our names to Don Cornelius and go down the line. This was a great experience of heartache and happiness at the same time that day! It was hard to handle without the support of family and real brothers.

SM: Who are some of the artists you enjoyed watching perform on *Soul Train*?

AF: James Brown, Sly and the Family Stone, Marvin Gaye, War, The O'Jays, Aretha Franklin, and The Lockers.

SM: How did it feel to be a part of the finals of the *Soul Train* Dance Contest that Jimmy Scoo B Doo Foster and Damita Jo Freeman ultimately won?

AF: This was very rewarding in many ways. Damita was like the Queen of Soul Dance at this time. Seeing her and Scoo B was a great accomplishment for all of us. It felt so good to be dancing with Damita, Scoo B, Pat Davis, Lamont Peterson, and all the other contestants. From shining shoes in front of the Houston, Texas, Greyhound bus station in junior high school to dancing in the finals of the *Soul Train* dance contest, I was feeling pretty good as a person. And to top it off, the person I admired most at the time, Mr. James Brown, was judging the contest. I was blessed tenfold and felt it.

SM: Were you ever told to stop locking while you were on *Soul Train,* or did you get limited camera time because of locking? I ask this because I was told that after Don Campbell was kicked off *Soul Train*, Don Cornelius didn't want locking to be featured on the show any longer.

AF: It wasn't that Don Cornelius did not want to feature locking. This was something between Don and Don Campbell. Scoo B and I kept on locking, and I started bringing all my brothers on the show after this. Scoo B was picked for the finals, and so was I. All I did was lock. Don Cornelius wanted us to do soul dance steps of other genres. This made sense to me and Scoo B to do other types of dancing and not just locking.

SM: Did you ever do any professional work outside of *Soul Train* like theatre, TV shows, movies, etc.?

AF: Yes, I did spots on the soap opera *General Hospital* as an extra, *The Big Show* featuring Shabba Doo and the *Dick Van Dyke* variety show as a Locker. I also did the opening show for Ella Fitzgerald at the Detroit Plaza, an opening show for Bob Hope, the Orange County Fair's first laser show, *The Dating Game*, and a show with the Ink Spots in San Bernardino. The GoGo Brothers and I did the 4A Championship Basketball halftime show.

SM: Did you ever have the chance to teach choreography to celebrities?

AF: I was able to teach Michael Jackson a few steps of soul and locking at NBC Studios once and at a personal place of his choice another time.

SM: You are now one of the master teachers of locking all over the world. How long have you been teaching locking?

AF: I have been teaching for over thirty years.

SM: What message do you have for those who try to duplicate locking without knowing its history?

AF: I would say please respect all of the originals. We all have something others can learn from and use as a base. Also, *Soul Train* is the base for all of us, not just seven people who got a break on television or in low-budget movies. We are all brothers and sisters in the craft of dancing to make a better world, not to put our people down for material things or fame. Love the craft and take care of it, and it will take care of you.

SM: What would you like to say in memory of Don Cornelius?

AF: I would first like to give my condolences to his family and friends. This was a person who gave many generations of kids a chance to have popularity, fame, and so on. Now, we can say he gave us something that we can be proud of in achievement and cultural identity. I always give respect and honor to this individual. Rest in peace, Mr. Cornelius, and may our cultural entity live on.

SM: What word of wisdom do you want to share?

AF: Always give nutrition to the generations under you. They will be the ones to keep you focused, alive, and on time.

# Edith Lynn Pickens

(1972–1975)

Many who have the official *Soul Train* DVD boxed set have seen the picture of a shapely female *Soul Train* dancer wearing a striped midriff and an Afro that adorns its cover. That is Edith Lynn Pickens. Although her energetic dance moves won fans, garnered coverage in *Right On!* Magazine, and found her a spot on the Soul Train Revue tour from August 1973 to January 1974. Lynn, as her friends call her, was never an attention-getter, nor did she want fame. All she wanted to do was just dance and let the joy of her dancing take over. Indeed, one felt those vibes by watching her dance on *Soul Train* from late 1972 to early 1975. Lynn was someone who danced simply for the joy of it.

SM: What were your aspirations as a child?

EP: I wanted to be a physical education teacher. I was athletic and was also a cheerleader. In college, I took physical education classes to be a teacher or a trainer. While I was in college, I began to dance on *Soul Train*.

SM: How did you become a *Soul Train* dancer?

EP: I used to hang out with The Lockers and dance with them. Greg "Campbell Lock Jr." was a good friend of mine, and we went to St.

BACK IN THE DAY

CURRENT PHOTO

Albert's High School together. But it was Leo "Fluky Luke" Williamson from The Lockers who first brought me to *Soul Train*. I clearly remember The Four Tops performed "Ain't No Woman (Like the One I've Got)" the first time I was on *Soul Train*.

SM: What else do you remember about your first time being on the show?

EP: I was so shy. I only danced to a couple of numbers on the floor.

SM: What were your impressions of Don Cornelius?

EP: I've seen all sides of him, the good side and the bad side. He never disrespected me and was always pretty cordial with me. But I saw the way he treated some of the other dancers, which I didn't like. But he was just Don.

SM: You were one of the dancers chosen to be on the *Soul Train* Revue tour from 1973 to 1974. Do you recall the selection process?

EP: I got a phone call from someone from *Soul Train* asking me to meet him at a hotel in Hollywood to be a dancer on this tour. My dad took me down to the hotel, and he met with Don, and they discussed the tour. Later, my parents told me that the tour would be a chance for me to travel and see the world. They said I could always go back to school.

SM: What do you remember about the tour?

EP: It was beautiful! We got a chance to meet, travel, hang out, and interact with the Sylvers, the Whispers, the Moments, Sylvia, and other artists. Don Campbell and I were dance partners during the tour. We did a whole week at the Apollo on one tour stop.

SM: Other dancers on that tour told me that the reaction was great everywhere but especially at the Apollo.

EP: I remember many people from the Apollo audience coming up the fire escape trying to get to us! They wanted a part of us. I remember they gave us things to wear on *Soul Train*. The fans were really good to us.

SM: I read somewhere that one time the tour bus broke down in some remote part of North Carolina. Do you remember that?

EP: Yes! The bus broke down in some tiny little town in North Carolina. I was like, "Where are we?" We were stuck for hours.

SM: After a long day's taping of *Soul Train*, were you craving that fried chicken?

EP: [laughs] Oh yes. We ate a lot of that Golden Bird chicken.

SM: What artists did you enjoy watching perform on *Soul Train*?

EP: Wow, there were so many. Al Green, Marvin Gaye, Tina Turner, The Ohio Players, and Barry White to name a few. When The Jackson 5 came on the show, they were just phenomenal! They gave us J-5 T-shirts to wear while they performed. But for the most part I didn't get into the stars and wasn't starstruck. I remember some of the artists asked me to go out with them to dinner, but I was only eighteen and nineteen, and at that age, you're still developing and going through your own trips.

SM: To this day, you and Freddie Maxie are the best friends after meeting on *Soul Train*, right?

EP: Absolutely. At one taping, she needed a ride home. At that time, she was living in Fullerton, California, and at the time, I also lived in Fullerton, and I told her that I would drive her back home, and we have remained friends ever since.

SM: Do you remember the one and only time Don Cornelius came down the Soul Train Line?

EP: Oh, yes! I loved that Soul Train Line. Everyone was cracking up at Don when he came down the line. He tried to do some kind of dance move in those big platform shoes, and he fell! We all just lost it! [laughs]

SM: Little Joe Chism told me that when "T.S.O.P." was first played on *Soul Train* as the new theme song, all of the dancers just partied, and the dancers eagerly looked forward to it being played at each subsequent taping.

EP: Everybody just cut loose when "T.S.O.P." was played on the set!

SM: Did you ever dance on *American Bandstand*?

EP: I did, and it was different. But Don didn't want the Soul Train Gang to go on *American Bandstand*. I remember meeting Toni Basil at The Summit on the Hill, and she wanted me to do the TV special *Rock & Roll Years*, which was produced by Dick Clark. Fred Berry, Denny Terio, and I were among the dancers on that special. I wore a wig so just in case Don Cornelius saw the special he wouldn't recognize me.

SM: What was it like to be featured in *Right On!* Magazine?

EP: It was great. I also appeared in *Newsweek* Magazine, which featured an article on *Soul Train*, and it had a photo of me, Slim the Robot, and Don Campbell. I still have most of the *Right On!* magazines I appeared in.

SM: What was the overall recognition like of being a *Soul Train* dancer?

EP: I mainly received recognition from my family. On *Soul Train,* I was basically in the background and didn't stand out. I was never a social butterfly. I just danced on the show for fun, not to be an aspiring dancer.

SM: Did you ever experience jealousy on the set of *Soul Train*?

EP: I did. A couple of things might have been said to me, but I rose above it. I didn't want to get into all of that.

SM: There were a lot of clubs that the Soul Train Gang used to frequent. Do you remember those clubs?

EP: There was Maverick's Flat, Whiskey-A-Gogo, the Citadel, The Summit on the Hill, and Disco 9000, to name a few.

SM: What was it like when you decided to stop dancing on *Soul Train*?

EP: I danced on *Soul Train* just for fun. When it became a job, it changed for me. I lost interest, and I made a quiet exit from the show.

Then, I started working for many years at some prestigious companies.

SM: What has it been like to go to the reunions and see other former Soul Train dancers?

EP: It is so nice to see everyone. I'm always surprised when people remember me from *Soul Train.*

SM: What are you doing currently?

EP: I retired from working in the medical field and married Bernard Toller, another former Soul Train dancer, on May 8, 2021. We actually dated over fifty years ago, but none of the other dancers knew about it except Freddie Maxie.

SM: What do you want to say in memory of Don Cornelius?

EP: I want to thank him for his vision. He had a very big vision that worked. I will always be appreciative of him.

SM: What word of wisdom do you want to share?

EP: Whatever your dream is, follow it!

# Jesse Johnson

(1973–1975)

An army veteran, he showed his fellow soldiers that he could hold his own on the dance floor, and he eventually got on *Soul Train* as well as *American Bandstand*. In the years since his *Soul Train* days, being of service to others has been really important to this brother, and he is still doing so to this very day.

SM: During the time you were in the army, *Soul Train* was a "must watch" for you and other soldiers, right?

JJ: Right. I was in the army, and all of the soldiers ran home, especially the Black ones, when they were off duty, to righteously watch *Soul Train* to see the latest dances and fashions. I won dance competitions in different places I was stationed, before and after I was in the service.

SM: How did you get on *Soul Train*?

JJ: Actually, it was through a friend of mine, Joseph Chism, better known as Lil Joe Chism. He was my boy. I met him after I came home from being in the army. He said, "You can sure dance. You need to be on *Soul Train*!" Unless you knew someone on the show, you had to go to certain parks to audition to get on *Soul Train*.

SM: What were your reactions when you first came on the set?
JJ: I recall it really being an exciting moment to be around all those stars.

BACK IN THE DAY

CURRENT PHOTO

I was just overwhelmed and taken aback by having the opportunity to be on *Soul Train.* Little Joe also connected me to *American Bandstand.*

SM: Who are some of the artists you remember seeing during your time *on Soul Train*, which I call the show's golden era?

JJ: Labelle, the Sylvers and Gladys Knight & the Pips. I also remember when Barry White came, and he had his whole orchestra there.

SM: Who was your dance partner on the show? JJ: My partner was LaQuinta Gross. I haven't seen her since she got married in the late seventies or early eighties.

SM: Did you ever go down the Soul Train Line?

JJ: Not often, but every now and then. I remember going down the line to Gladys Knight & the Pips' "Daddy Could Swear I Declare."

SM: That chicken was mighty good after those long tapings, wasn't it? [laughs]

JJ: [laughs] I was craving anything! I remember that Golden Bird chicken.

SM: Any other memories from *Soul Train* that stand out or other fellow dancers you connected with?

JJ: One memory is of Don Campbell. He was such a nice guy. I grew up in St. Louis, Missouri, and that's where Don Campbell is from. I remember that on set, we reminisced about the times we had growing up in St. Louis. I'm glad I had that opportunity. They renamed Crenshaw and Stocker Street in Los Angeles to Don Campbell Square. I was there, as well as several other Soul Train dancers, when they did that dedication. I was happy to reminisce with him again before he passed. Tyrone Proctor was also my boy. He is really missed. There was an *American Bandstand* reunion at Oil Can Harry in the Valley, and he was there. We chitchitchatted a long time, and he told me about his experiences all around the world teaching waacking. He had also told me he was having some challenging times because his knees were so bad.

SM: Did you get caught by Pam Brown during her "spit out the gum in the cup" ritual?

JJ: No, I don't even chew gum. It makes me hungry! [laughs] Pam Brown still looks good for her age. She used to work at LA Parks & Recreation in addition to being the coordinator for *Soul Train.* She is a sweet lady.

SM: Did you frequent the clubs in Los Angeles?

JJ: We would always go to Maverick's Flat. That's where we all met up. That club goes all the way back to my high school days when we used to party there. Sometimes, some of us would sneak in before I was twenty-one. [laughs]

SM: You mentioned you danced on *American Bandstand.* What was that experience like?

JJ: It was great. But that's when things were getting tight for me, having two jobs and going to school full-time. I told LaQuinta that it was a great two years, but it has been challenging, and I've got to stop. She said, "No, you can't stop. Dick Clark wants us to do the dance of the month." Dick Clark also used to do shows from the beach in Malibu. I think the Sylvers had performed at the time, and Dick Clark really liked LaQuinta and me, so I danced on Dick Clark's beach show and *American Bandstand.*

SM: What have you accomplished in the years since leaving *Soul Train*?

JJ: I got a Bachelor of Science in Business Administration with Marketing and Transportation at California State University. At the time, I was working for the City of Los Angeles and attending college. Then, I went on to work for the city of Long Beach. I was the Purchasing Director for many years in the Department of Diversity and Economic Opportunity. The last position I held there was as its coordinator. I have also done a lot of volunteer work, and I have been involved with the NAACP for many years.

SM: Tell me about other charitable work you have done in recent years and other organizations you are involved with?

JJ: I founded 100 Black Men of Long Beach thirteen years ago. The umbrella organization, 100 Black Men of America, was formed in 1963. Jackie Robinson was one of its founders. We have one hundred chapters all over the world. Another one of the original founders, Dr. Bill Hayden, really respected what I did and what I do for 100 Black Men. He passed away some time ago. Since I am originally from New Orleans, I am part of an organization called Louisiana to Los Angeles. The acronym is LALA, and we give scholarships to graduating seniors. We also keep the Mardi Gras tradition alive.

SM: What do you want to say in memory of Don Cornelius?

JJ: I just want to thank him for the opportunity he gave me to be one of the Soul Train dancers. I idolized all of the dancers prior to ever thinking I would be considered to be a part of the show. I also thank him for what he did for the world with *Soul Train*. It has been an inspiration, not just nationally but internationally. The spirit of *Soul Train* and the Soul Train dancers will live forever thanks to Don Cornelius.

SM: What word of wisdom do you want to share?

JJ: You want to enjoy your life because tomorrow is not promised to anyone, young or old.

BACK IN THE DAY

CURRENT PHOTO

# Debra Heard

**(1973–1975, 1984–2003)**

> Hailing from show business royalty, this young lady had entertainment in her roots. She showcased her dance skills on *Soul Train* and years later came back to the show, not only to dance but to help present the show with a new and fresh look in its later decades.

SM: Long before you came to *Soul Train*, you were already in some way affiliated with show business, right?

DH: Right. My uncle, Jimmy Lewis, was an original member of the Drifters; then, he became a solo artist and started to produce for Ray Charles. I have an album where my uncle produced an entire album for Ray Charles. He also worked with Jimi Hendrix and Otis Redding, with whom he was best friends. I met a lot of artists through my uncle, including Little Richard, who spoke at my uncle's funeral. He gave me a book about coping with the loss of a loved one. He signed it, and I still have it.

SM: Growing up around all these legends must have truly further inspired you to get into show business.

DH: It did. I was naturally gifted as a dancer. From elementary school all the way up to high school, I trained in school with jazz dancing and ballet. I didn't really care for it, but it made me flexible. I was also very active in athletics. I was a cheerleader, a gymnast, and in a group called Dance Performance. I attended Dorsey High School, where future Soul Train dancers Cheryl Song, Jody Watley, and several others attended.

SM: What are your memories of when *Soul Train* first came on the air?

DH: I was from a large family. My mom had twelve kids; she lost one but had seven boys and four girls. On Saturdays, we looked forward to watching *Soul Train*. We would sit in front of the TV waiting for it to come on. If someone was not in the room, we'd yell, "Hurry up! *Soul Train* is coming on!" Everyone would run out, and we'd all sit there planted in front of that TV. I'm telling you it was the highlight of my life on Saturdays. Sitting there looking at it I told my mom I was going to be on that show. She was like, "Sure, right." [laughs] I was only sixteen years old, but I don't know why I believed I was going to dance on that show. I didn't know anyone connected to the show at all, but I believed somehow, I was going to dance on that show.

SM: How did your journey to get on *Soul Train* begin?

DH: Shelly Zapata, a fellow classmate who attended Dorsey, was on *Soul Train* one Saturday. We could pass for sisters. When I saw her in school that Monday, I said, "Oh my God! I saw you on *Soul Train* this Saturday!" I told her how much I enjoyed her and all the dancers on the show. I asked her how to get on the show. She said I had to audition and that they would be at Denker Park. She said I had to have a dance partner, and I was like, "Oh oh! I have to find someone to dance with." So, I went on a mission! Finally, I found my dance partner, who also attended Dorsey High. He was a really heavyset guy like Rerun and was Korean and Black. I asked him if he would be willing to audition with me for *Soul Train,* and he said, "Sure! I have a car so I can drive us there."

SM: What do you recall about that day you auditioned?

DH: On that day, they had about four Soul Train Lines going at the same time with music playing. We danced up and down that line for hours. At the time, Pam Brown was the *Soul Train* dance coordinator, and she walked over and placed this number on me and my partner, saying, "Congratulations! You made the show." We lost our minds. I was screaming! I went home and told my mom.

SM: What was it like for you when you were inside that studio on the *Soooul Train*?

DH: I was like, "Oh my God, I'm living my dream." There's nothing like your dream coming true. I remember that certain dancers would get recognition over other dancers. They had their regulars, which were guaranteed placement at that time. We just went in and followed directions wherever we were told to dance. Wherever we were placed, we did our thing.

SM: Who were some of the artists you enjoyed watching perform on *Soul Train* during the period you first came on the show?

DH: Barry White! My family actually knew Barry White because he used to play in the front yard with my older sister. When I told my mom that Barry White was going to be on the show, she said, "This is what you tell him..." and I told him what she had to say. I also remember James Brown; Labelle was another one, as well as Chaka Khan. I must say that it was a blessing to see the celebrities I always admired

SM: Who were your other dance partners?

DH: I danced with Gary Keyes and a lot of different people. I was always dancing with someone different.

SM: Did you ever have to deal with Pam Brown's gum ritual?

DH: Of course! Luckily for me, I never had gum. I was a mint kind of girl. I always had mints.

SM: How did you enjoy the cold chicken? [laughs]

DH: [laughs] I did not complain about that chicken. It was something to eat after all that dancing, and we needed to refuel. I was used to eating cold chicken. I'm from a large family, so that cold chicken didn't bother me at all.

SM: During the seventies, you were part of a dance group, right?

DH: Oh, yes. Sheri Byers and I were best friends. She was also best friends with Jody Watley. My dance troupe was The Lady Lockers because I was very influenced by The Lockers. I could lock as good as they could, and I can still lock like that! I was the choreographer for the group. I also came up with the attire we were going to wear. You could not tell we were girls because we had big apple caps on our heads. We got a standing ovation and won shows. When we took our bows and took off our caps, our long hair fell down, and the crowd went wild! They thought we were guys!

SM: Did you ever do the Soul Train Scramble Board?

DH: Absolutely. I did it in the nineties after I came back to the show after returning from Europe. I left the show in 1975 and moved away from California and got married to a guy in the military, and we moved to Germany. We would leave and travel every three to four years. Once one of our tours was over, I'd always come back home because I'm a native of California, and I would go back to *Soul Train*.

SM: When you returned to *Soul Train* in the mid-eighties, you had no problem getting back on the show?

DH: No, not at all. At that time, it was about who you knew because they were not holding auditions anymore. It was about knowing the right people so you could walk through those doors. You really did not even know how to dance well. The show became more about image and your attire.

SM: What memories do you have of being on the show in the eighties? I know there are many.

DH: Absolutely! Coming back to the show during the eighties, I found the music and everything had changed. I danced for a while, but I also wanted to really bring something more to the show because of something my uncle shared with me: "Sometimes, you do better behind the scenes than out in the front. You don't always have to be in the forefront." He always stressed that. During the eighties, I started to pretty much dance for a while, but things were different. The attire started to change to girls wearing big, padded shoulders, leggings, and the hair was bigger. It took a while, but the eighties dancers came into their own. They are getting the recognition they deserve because they also brought a lot to the show. They were unique and had a different kind of energy. Their whole vibe was electric.

SM: I know you went down the Soul Train Line several times in the seventies, but did you go down the line in the eighties?

DH: I would get in the line but never made it down the line. I would just stand there doing the little two-step they would have us do, and you would have five or six people who went down the line, and then that's it. Then they would place you where they wanted you to stand in that line. That's how you knew whether or not you were going to make it down the line. They would only have certain girls start the line and certain guys start the line. They just had their favorites. That was the politics we had to deal with.

SM: What artists stand out during your time as a dancer when you came back to the show?

DH: Janet Jackson! I stood very close to the stage when she performed. One time we had Big Daddy Kane on the show, and me and several girls were in front of the stage. While he was performing, he pulled some of us on stage with him. We made it through the whole number. Then Don walked over to him and said, "Hey, we have to shoot that again." So, Don put the girls up on stage that he wanted to dance with him. When they reshot his performance, none of the girls Big Daddy Kane selected were included. Don picked his favorites to dance with him. There were things like that that happened all the time with the dancers.

SM: I understand the dancers had trailers back in the eighties and early nineties.

DH: Yes. At one time, the Soul Train dancers had their own trailers where we changed clothes four times for each of the four shows we shot each weekend. So, that was four different outfits we had to have. Sometimes, the girls wanted to change their hair for each show. We had the whole nine yards with makeup and curling irons. But all of a sudden, the trailers went away, and we were stuck with repeating the same outfit all day for Saturday and all day for Sunday. There have been so many changes over the years. I think that when rap came in is when *Soul Train* really started to die.

SM: Did you ever appear in any music videos?

DH: I did a Heavy D video and a lot of extra work in videos. I would also do talk shows and sit in the audience.

SM: At some point in the nineties, you were looking to do something different with the show, right?

DH: Right. In the early nineties, I started my own management company in San Diego. San Diego people knew me. I was either a part of or associated with anything that pertained to entertainment. One evening, I was at this club, and I saw a couple of females and told them they were attractive and asked if they ever watched *Soul Train*. They said yes. Then I asked them if they would be willing to dance on the show, and they said, "Are you serious?" And I said, "Of course I'm serious." So, this is when I started to bring females to the show. I did this on my own and Eric Casem and Don Cornelius took sight of what I was doing and paid attention to it. The different hosts and later hosts, Mystro Clark and Shemar Moore, would compliment me. Mystro was like, "Keep doing what you're doing. Keep it one hundred!" [laughs] "We love what you're doing." Shemar would say, "You keep doing what you are doing. You are winning!" They were always so very positive. Reggie Rutherford (the show's operations manager) adored my team of girls. I would come in with all these gorgeous females, and the guys would bow down. Seriously. They would bow down in front of me like, "Oh my God!"

SM: I remember when I first came to the show and met you and saw how you were bringing all those lovely girls to the show.

DH: When I first brought a group of girls to the show, Eric Casem said, "They look clean, they look fresh, they look wholesome." I never forgot that. Eric and Don's favorite girl I brought to the show was Flower. She was Filipino and Black. Even the show's photographers and other crew adored her. She danced with Shemar on the center riser during the opening and closing numbers. She had the Flower power! She was just herself and very down to earth. She was beautiful inside and out. Autumn is another one of my girls who danced with Shemar. It got to the point that the show wanted a certain type, Eric would come to me and say he needed a beautiful dark-skinned girl for the show for instance. Or if he needed some salsa dancers, I would bring them to the show. I kept it very diverse. I had a diverse team of girls, Black, White, Asian, Latina, and biracial. One time some of the girls wore red, white, and blue to the show after 9/11 and another time they wore military but sexy Kandis to support the troops. The girls also did the Soul Train Christmas Starfest too, where everyone dressed in white.

SM: I remember how many of your girls were placed on different spots on the stage and risers.

DH: That became a problem. As soon as I walked through that door, some of the girls that were already on stage were taken down and replaced with my girls. So, that created a great deal of jealousy and animosity. There were some girls on the show who were being catty, and they got jealous of one another, so there was that kind of drama.

SM: In general, I remember Don and Eric were always very particular about all of the females that were placed on the stage and risers.

DH: One time, I recall very clearly there were some girls on the risers that Don didn't want. He came over to Eric and me and told us to take those girls down, because there was not enough beauty up there. I could not believe he said that, but we did exactly what he told us to do.

SM: Did your girls ever do any work outside of *Soul Train*?

DH: When one of the Super Bowls was in San Diego there was this Super Bowl Jam, and I was able to have some of the *Soul Train* girls perform with Destiny's Child on the stage. We also did publications and magazines, and some of the girls were featured as Beauty of the Week in *Jet* magazine. Some of them were also in the *Source* magazine and on the cover of *Low Rider*. We did a lot of work, because we were associated with *Soul Train*. It opened up a lot of doors for me. Do you remember Black Entertainment Television (BET) Sprite night? Our girls did that. That event was amazing. Don really didn't mind if you received work outside of *Soul Train* because you were still representing *Soul Train*. We were representing *Soul Train* to the nines in San Diego. We were getting in clubs for free. Me and my girls came in and they could dance on stage and perform. Sisqo came one time to San Diego to do *Sisqo's Summer Shakedown*, and it was a big hit. Every single one of my girls was on his show.

SM: Although the production staff loved the girls you brought to the show, were there ever any issues concerning the way they danced, dressed, or things of that nature?

DH: Sometimes Don or Eric would tell me that some of the girls I brought were not bringing the kind of energy that they needed on the show. I also talked with Don and Eric about the cameramen going up the girls' dresses, which I did not like.

SM: As you know, when Don didn't approve of something, he would let it be known.

DH: He sure would! I was on set that day when Don cursed out one of the cameramen, fired him on the spot, and threw him out. He was a

White guy. I never thought I would see a Black man be able to talk to a White man like that in my life!

SM: When you were working with the girls, you also had mentoring sessions with them, right?

DH: Right. We'd be in a conference room, and I would call a meeting. I would express to the girls that I did not like groupies; *Soul Train* was a place of business. I represented them, and they represented me. I wanted them to be professional. They listened, and we discussed attire. We'd go shopping together, and we were family. So, my *Soul Train* family of girls in San Diego brought a lot to the show.

SM: I remember for a time you worked with another woman, Veronica, who we all called Ms. V, who assisted you and your girls with makeup. How did this connection come about?

DH: Eric wanted me to bring a beautiful dark-skinned girl to the show. Veronica's daughter was a girl I met when I was recruiting some girls for the show. I approached her and asked her if she would like to dance on *Soul Train*. She discussed it with her family, and her mom gave me a call. She said, "I'm so excited for my daughter. I'd love to meet you." We all got together and met. Veronica told me she was a makeup artist, and I told her I could really utilize her talent. The girls could pay her for doing their makeup per set on the show. That's how Veronica got involved with the show: coming in with me as the makeup artist for my girls.

SM: You two were a great combination and did a great job with the girls!

DH: Thank you! When we attended the *Soul Train* awards shows, we were given free passes, and I would receive my credentials to go backstage. Some of the girls would be allowed to come backstage with me and mingle. From there, Veronica met some of Don's people who had been with him for about twenty years, and they gave her an opportunity to do makeup at one of the *Soul Train* Music Awards backstage. That was the beginning of her makeup career in Hollywood.

SM: I also remember meeting Ms. V's son, IV, who attended some of the show's tapings a few times. He was really cool.

DH: Yes, IV was a rapper. I would hang out in the studio with him and his crew while he was laying down his tracks. It was exciting. IV sounded just like 2Pac. He is doing gospel rap now.

SM: When did you leave the show?

DH: My last show with *Soul Train* was in 2003. When I gave it up, I gave up working with the girls. None of them continued on *Soul Train* when I decided to leave the show. I started focusing more on a career in fashion design because that's what I went to school for. I also went to school for makeup artistry and worked as a manager in retail management as a stylist. I would also dress corporate women for corporate America.

SM: What are you doing currently?

DH: I decided to start my own business as a fashion doll designer. My work is in fashion doll magazines, and I attend a great deal of fashion doll conventions. I'm just passionate about it. I also designed fashion dolls based on some of the *Soul Train* dancers. This is something I always wanted to do because of my love of the dancers.

SM: What would you like to say in memory of Don?

DH: I respected Don for what he did and what he brought to the entertainment industry. He gave an opportunity to artists who may have never been seen, and for that, I know they should be grateful, and I am grateful. A lot of people out there would not have been seen if it weren't for *Soul Train*. It opened a great deal of opportunities for us. It gave so many artists an opportunity to shine and be seen, even those who were just starting their careers in the entertainment industry. Don gave so many people a shot. I appreciate everything he did for Black entertainment.

SM: What word of wisdom do you want to share?

DH: I come from a family of eleven children and my mom always said I was her wisest one. I always like telling people to stay true to themselves, find their purpose, and continue to dream because dreams do come true. That dream of being a *Soul Train* dancer came true for me. Whatever a person is trying to achieve, it is totally achievable. Surround yourself with like-minded people who are filled with love and are supportive and who believe in you as much as you believe in yourself.

BACK IN THE DAY

CURRENT PHOTO

# Alvin Wallace

(1972–1974)

Little did this Detroit native and aspiring actor know that while he was attending UCLA he would be climbing aboard the hippest trip in America with memories lasting him a lifetime.

**S**M: How did you become a Soul Train dancer?

AW: I'm originally from Detroit, but I spent my last years of high school in Los Angeles and then went to UCLA. I was part of a group of ten to fifteen people from UCLA who auditioned to go on Soul Train. We went to Denker Park and met Pam Brown, the coordinator of the show. We did some Soul Train Lines, and all of us were selected to come to *Soul Train*.

SM: What do you recall about that first day on the set?

AW: I was in awe of the studio! I remember meeting Diana Ross, who was there to introduce Billy Preston. She talked to us as she was waiting to go on stage. I also remember the Ojays and Aretha Franklin being on the show. She was from Detroit, too, so I had a connection with her, and I definitely wanted to ask her a question during the Q&A session.

SM: Did you ever do the Scramble Board?

AW: Yes, I did. Me and my partner had to try and figure out the solution since the answer wasn't given to us.

SM: Do you recall any funny or interesting incidents on the set?

AW: I remember Little Joe Chism and Don Campbell almost got into a fight right before Willie Hutch was going to perform. Willie was already on stage about five feet away from them, and the taping couldn't start until Joe and Don's altercation was settled.

SM: You were involved in theatre while at UCLA, right?

AW: Right. I also auditioned for an early pilot for the TV show *White Shadow* and was an extra as a Detroit police officer in an ABC series *Detroit 187,* in which Robert Hooks was the director.

SM: What have you done since your *Soul Train* days?

AW: I graduated from UCLA, worked at General Motors, and then retired. . I also did freelance journalism and was a Midwest reporter for Jack the Rapper's magazine *Mello Yello*, which was given to Black radio stations. I also gave music conventions in Los Angeles, where I met 2Pac and many other celebrities. I still dabble in theatre, wrote a movie script and a book which isn't published yet, and a commercial entitled "The New International Pledge of Allegiance" and I do private home inspections.

SM: Did you ever think in those early years of dancing on *Soul Train* that it would be the phenomenon it became?

AW: I was just enjoying myself and having fun. We were all just in the moment.

SM: What do you want to say in memory of Don Cornelius?

AW: He was a trailblazer.

SM: What word of wisdom do you want to share?

AW: For people to search their souls deeply and be not afraid to go as far as they can.

# Diana Price

(1973–1981)

For nine years, Diana Price was one of *Soul Train*'s most fashionable and effervescent dancers. Whether she was dancing in sync with her then-husband and fellow *Soul Train* dancer Erwin Bernard Thompson or other dance partners, she always stayed in the groove and the flow of the music. Today, she is a successful businesswoman running her own business. Here, she reflects upon her days dancing on *Soul Train* and how she is currently her own boss.

SM: What or who inspired you to want to dance?

DP: When I was growing up, I was always outside skipping rope, jumping around, and playing. I was like a tomboy. I was climbing trees all the time. In school, I was a cheerleader, and I was always dancing along with the cheers. I was always the cheerleader that the guys would throw up in the air, and I would be screaming, "AHHH!"

SM: I hope they never dropped you! [laughs]

DP: [laughs] No, thankfully, they never dropped me.

SM: How did all of that parlay into you becoming a Soul Train dancer?

DP: There were a couple of friends I hung out with, and they said to me, "Hey, there's this Soul Train dance show, and a couple of people

BACK IN THE DAY

CURRENT PHOTO

told us we should try to get on there." I was like, "I don't know about that." I was always into my studies. At that age, I was thinking, 'What do I want to do with my life?' So, I had mixed feelings when I was asked to go on *Soul Train*. But then I thought that it might be fun. I could always take my books and study at the studio when there was a late break. So, I was talked into going to *Soul Train*.

SM: What do you remember about your first weekend at *Soul Train*?

DP: I remember being really excited. I was like, "Wow, this is how they really put together a television program." One of the things I had always wanted to do was be behind the scenes in radio and television, so I thought being on *Soul Train* was kind of cool! I would scope the set out and see who was in charge of doing this and doing that.

SM: So, you were excited more so from seeing *Soul Train*'s behind-the-scenes operations.

DP: Yeah! I wanted to see how the taping and broadcast of *Soul Train* was put together. It was really intriguing to me since it was something I always aspired to do.

SM: Who were some of your favorite artists you enjoyed watching perform on *Soul Train*, and do you have any memorable stories associated with them?

DP: Yes! I have two favorites: Marvin Gaye and Diana Ross. Those were my two absolute favorite guests. I met both of them. Marvin Gaye was on the show a couple of times, and I really enjoyed his music. I enjoyed the way he moved and his energy. To me, he was a spicy entertainer. I remember at one of the tapings, I was right smack in the middle of Marvin Gaye. That was where I wanted to be!

SM: When Marvin Gaye sang "Let's Get it On" on *Soul Train*, all of the girls were surrounding him on the dance floor. He gave you a nice big hug! You looked like you were on cloud nine!

DP: Yes! It was a great big hug. It was for a few minutes, but I thought it was forever! I thought he would not stop hugging me. I was like, "Oh, this is fabulous!" I was so calm and collected, but on the inside, I was coming apart!

SM: Did you ever have any opportunities in the entertainment business as a result of dancing on *Soul Train*?

DP: Diana Ross was performing in Las Vegas a lot, and there was an opportunity to audition to be a dancer in her show. I thought about it hard and long, thinking how exciting it would be. But then I thought, *Is that the kind of career that I want, a showtime dancer?* I was really analytical when I was younger. I didn't have a lot of people to talk to me, give me guidance, and be a mentor to me, so I just thought long and hard about it. I really wanted to dance in Diana Ross' show, but I ended up not going for it.

SM: You and Erwin Thompson were the only married couple on *Soul Train* in the program's history, I think. Did you two meet on *Soul Train*?

DP: I met Erwin through Wanda Fuller and Eddie Cole, but not on the *Soul Train* set.

SM: You and Erwin danced together so well and always in sync. You were one of *Soul Train*'s best dancing couples ever. Did you two practice a lot of your routines together?

DP: We practiced a lot! Dancing was just fabulous to me. I just love to be free and express myself. I also loved for us to be matching in our outfits and to be fashionable. I was always like, "What should we wear? Should we wear this?" Even after I stopped dancing with Erwin, there was another guy I danced with named Billy who had a big Afro. I tell you; Billy and I would spend time going through routines and going shopping for outfits because Billy loved to dress. He would tell me, "You look good in this," or "No, you can't wear that!" We hit it off really well. Sadly, he passed away. We were really tight. He was like my brother.

SM: Were you ever caught by Pam Brown during her famous gum ritual?

DP: I think Pam caught everybody chewing gum at some point! So, yes, she caught me. She would either have her Dixie cup or put her hand out and say, "Give it to me! Give it to me! Spit it out! Spit it out!" [laughs]

SM: Do you recall any funny or embarrassing moments that happened on the show involving you or another dancer?

DP: It had to do with the Scramble Board. There was this couple that wanted to do it so bad, and they weren't called upon to do it, and they were like, "We can do it! We can do it!" They were conspiring in the background. They were like, "Everyone else did it, and we never did it!" They were really upset! So, when they actually got called to do it, they were so excitable and really making fools of themselves.

SM: Did you ever dance on Dick Clark's *Soul Unlimited* show that tried to rival *Soul Train*?

DP: I never went on that show. I know a lot of my friends from *Soul Train* went on the show, but I never did.

SM: You wore some dynamite fashions on *Soul Train*. Did you make a lot of your own clothes, or were there certain shops you would go to?

DP: My mother is my hero. She taught me how to sew. She actually helped me make a lot of my outfits, but I would make some of my outfits, too. Billy and I would also go to this boutique, and we would mix different things together. I lived in a small town called Monrovia. I would drive from there to Los Angeles to shop for different things. Billy lived in Los Angeles. I had a good friend named Evelyn who was like the fashion queen. She didn't dance on *Soul Train*, but she was a good friend of mine, and I would go shopping with her and find a lot of things. I really enjoyed dressing up.

SM: Did you ever frequent the clubs Maverick's Flat or the Total Experience?

DP: Oh, yes! I went to Maverick's Flat, the Citadel, and the Total Experience. There was another club on Sunset Boulevard which was really highfalutin and upscale, and then there was another one on La Cienega. We were really hanging out at those clubs. We hung out hard! We danced until the wee hours of the morning.

SM: One of the things many of the dancers told me was that back then in the seventies, there was no violence or fighting in those clubs. You didn't have to worry about things like that. It was all just fun, and everyone had a good time.

DP: We would meet at each other at the clubs and club hop all night long. There were so many fun clubs, and people would not get in trouble. It was a lot of fun—no worries about gangs or getting beat up. I really miss those days.

SM: What dances did you enjoy doing back in the day?

DP: Wow! I don't even remember the names of a lot of those dances. We would just make up a lot of our steps. Of course, we would copy some people, too. There was a jerk-like dance we'd like to do. Billy would be shaking, and I would be shaking!

SM: What are you doing in your career currently?

DP: I am having a great time doing the things I want to do. I started off working in corporate America. When I was doing all of that studying and bringing my books to the *Soul Train* set, I was taking all kinds of classes. I later managed fourteen international travel offices that I worked for and several offices for big corporate companies. But I stopped doing that because I always wanted my own business. So, I did something about it. Now, I am an entrepreneur, and I can't tell you how happy I am. My business is called Diana Price & Associates, and it was one of the most rewarding things I have ever done for myself. I'm the president and CEO of my own company, and I do a lot of speaking engagements about customer service management, leadership, personal and professional sales growth, confronting change, and social media. So, I teach companies and leaders how to communicate and really be successful in living out their dreams. In addition, I have been a Forensic Travel Expert witness since 2012, and I help law firms assess risks and opine on the travel industry and tourism standards for travelers.

SM: That is wonderful! Congratulations!

DP: Thank you!

SM: What was your overall experience with *Soul Train*?

DP: *Soul Train* was a really valuable and exciting part of my life, a part of the thread that makes up the person I am. It played a role in my wanting to pursue a career in corporate America. After graduating from the University of Southern California with my master's degree, I decided that corporate America was the career for me. *Soul Train* influenced the broadcast show I am doing today. It really had a positive impact on my life. Years later, when I began advancing in the corporate ranks, people would come up to me asking, "Didn't you used to dance on *Soul Train*?"

SM: What would you like to say in memory of Don Cornelius?

DP: When he died, we lost an American icon. To Don's credit, he started a culture that no one ever thought about or did. Don knew what he wanted. He had the mentality that said, "I can do anything I want to do." I so respect him for that. We all need to have that kind of mindset in our lives and help others to have that frame of mind and teach them how to really live out their dreams.

SM: What word of wisdom do you want to share?

DP: You've got to be a leader and choose what you want to do in your lives. At *Soul Train*, we all chose to have that wonderful part of our being to be genuine, to dance, to have our culture, and value really show up in that show for all those years. As we continue, it doesn't matter how old you are, you have to confront your status quo and comfort zone and be fearless. When you choose the lifestyle you want, you might make mistakes like I did, but mistakes will catapult you to success if you learn the valuable lessons. We have to refuse to quit and be committed to other things as well as help and support each other in getting that done.

# Michael Khalfani

(1973–1974)

> This New York native and aspiring actor as well as journalist didn't initially come to Los Angeles to dance, but as fate would have it, he made his way onto Soul Train but at the same time began a great career in journalism, which he is still doing to this very day.

**SM**: You come from a show business background, right?

MK: Right. My family was in show business, so we knew a lot of actors like Roscoe Lee Browne, Godfrey Cambridge, Lincoln Kilpatrick, Calvin Lockhart, Billy Dee Williams, James Earl Jones, and others. My family knew them first as stage actors in New York before they moved on to doing films. When those Black films came out in the early seventies, producers in Los Angeles were looking for New York-trained actors, so I moved to Los Angeles to pursue acting. There were a lot of Black movies coming out around this time, like *The Mack* and *Sheba Baby*.

SM: How did this journey begin?

MK: After I got out of the Air Force, I was wondering what I wanted to do with my life. Did I want to stay with a career in acting? I was twenty-one, trying to figure out what to do. One night, I met this girl at a party in New York who was a friend of a lady who I was dating. She

CURRENT PHOTO

told me she was having a New Year's Eve Party in San Francisco, and she would send me a plane ticket to come. So, I decided to move out to California, and I lived out in San Francisco for a while. But I couldn't get a job as a theatre actor, not even a job at Jack in the Box. So, I ended up staying with a lady who was a friend of the girl who got me the ticket to San Francisco.

SM: How did you get on *Soul Train*?

MK: In 1973, I was staying with my cousin in Los Angeles. Luckily, being a veteran, I was able to go to Los Angeles Community College (LACC) with the Servicemen's Readjustment Act of 1944 (GI Bill) and majored in broadcasting. My cousin's best friend was Thelma Davis, who was one of the Soul Train Gang. I was sleeping on the living room couch one Saturday morning, and when I woke up, Thelma came by and asked me if I wanted to come with her to *Soul Train*. I was like, "Hell yeah!" I called my mom and told her I was going to *Sooooul Train*!

SM: What do you remember about that first time Thelma took you to *Soul Train*?

MK: The fried chicken, because I was hungry! [laughs] When you dance, you get hungry, especially when you're doing multiple takes. They didn't do a lot of takes in the early days because it was expensive.

SM: Do you remember any of the artists who performed your first time on the show?

MK: The Ojays! What I remember about that is that they rehearsed their numbers in five takes. They didn't miss a step! When a group like them or The Whispers came on the show, both of whom have been performing for years, their steps and choreography were tight. When I was growing up, I saw the Ojays at the Apollo, but I was in the balcony. At *Soul Train*, I was right there by the stage!

SM: So, you never had to audition for *Soul Train*?

MK: In the early days they held auditions, but around the time I came to the show the dance coordinator Pam Brown as well as Dick Griffey would go to teenage clubs, parties, and dances to look for dancers. Back in 1973, there was a restaurant called the Proud Bird that Thelma Davis had taken me to. I was dancing and doing my New York moves, and I guess I stood out because Pam Brown came up to me with Dick Griffey and said, "Wow, we like the way you dance. Would you like to be on *Soul Train*?" This was about two weeks after Thelma had taken me. The first time she took me to the show, I was just a guest to *Soul Train*, but this time, I was on the list of dancers. I said to myself, "It was meant for me to be in Los Angeles."

SM: What other acts do you recall performing on *Soul Train* during your time as a dancer?

MK: Rufus featuring Chaka Khan, Curtis Mayfield, and Gladys Knight & the Pips were among the standouts. The people who worked closely with Don knew which artists would be on the show. Sometimes bookings were made at the last minute. I remember during the Q&A session with Kool & the Gang, I asked them if they felt that Black artists had a responsibility to the Black community, and Kool answered my question. Then Don said, "That's the end of this heavy interview!" [laughs]

SM: Did you go to most of the tapings?

MK: I didn't come to all the tapings because I started getting involved with the Inner-City Cultural Center and the Quincy Jones workshop, which was started by Quincy and another giant in the industry, Ed Eckstine. It was a workshop for singers and musicians and only lasted two or three years, but during its run, you learned show business one-on-one from the ground up. Quincy and Ed had all the people they worked with to do seminars, and they talked to us about the business. We had to produce our own shows and put them together as if we were putting together multimillion-dollar productions. We learned the responsibilities of videographers, choreographers, stage managers, and everything in the business that goes on around the talent. We put together singing groups and named them. So, I was doing this as well as a program called *Black Awareness in Television.* I would get press passes to attend the NAACP Image Awards as well as attend Saviors Day, which is given every year by the Nation of Islam. So, I was doing a lot of things besides *Soul Train* when I moved out to Los Angeles. LACC was the school to go to for broadcasting.

SM: What were your impressions of Don Cornelius?

MK: A Black man with a Black show, a moment to remember. I was in my early twenties when I was on the show, but I can remember when I was ten there were no Black shows on TV: no *Jeffersons,* no *Sanford & Son*, nothing, just shows like the *Real McCoys, Ozzie & Harriett* and *Beverly Hillbillies* [laughs]. When there was a Black person on TV, someone would say, "Mom, Dad, there's a Black person on TV!" When *Soul Train* came along in the seventies, that was the game changer. Not only was a Black man on the show as the host, but he also owned the show.

SM: Did you ever do the Scramble Board?

MK: I never did the Scramble Board, and I only went down the Soul Train Line once the whole time I was on the show. I didn't stand out because the other guys were doing backflips and stuff, so my line was edited. They would shoot the lines over and over, and then in editing, the producers would choose who and what they wanted to show. If you did something incredible down the line, it would be kept in. If you came up with a great routine, you would be highlighted. Competition drove creativity. At the end of the tapings, everyone would go home and start to work on what they were going to do for the next taping. Also, your Afro had to be tight! Since I was a television major, I watched what was done with the camera work. They would also do pickups if the lighting or sound wasn't right. Sometimes, songs would be chosen for the line that weren't that well known or popular like War's "Ballero." Don was probably trying to help promote certain songs that may not have been hits on the radio, but he played them on his show on the Soul Train Line.

SM: There were always a lot of lovely girls on *Soul Train*. Did you crush on any of them while you were on the show?

MK: The one lady I fell in love with on the show was Pat Davis! I never could tell her because I was too shy. I was her greatest fan. I wasn't her dance partner, but she was the most spontaneous woman I ever danced around. When she came to the tapings, all eyes were on her, with people wondering what she was going to wear or do. She was so creative and spontaneous. She never made the same move twice. I remember the movie she was in, *Disco 9000*. The movie bombed, but the scene of her coming out of a cake made the movie!

SM: You didn't come to the show often, but did you ever experience any issues or pettiness with other dancers?

MK: There were cliques on the show from the very beginning. That's what prevented me from getting to know Pat Davis. I was a new dancer. I remember she had a birthday party in either 1973 or 1974. She gave a party, and only certain members of the Soul Train Gang were there. Thelma took me to the party, but I just could never say to Pat Davis what I wanted to say. Plus, she was such a head-over-heels dancer that I didn't think I could keep up with her creativity.

SM: So, you did go to Pat's birthday party but didn't get a chance to talk to her.

MK: Right, because she had a little circle of friends. But I was just glad to be there and stood from afar. A lot of people don't know she was the first choice for Shalamar, not Jody Watley. But she was busy at the time, and no one really knew if Shalamar was going to get anywhere since Don had some other groups that didn't go anywhere. Shalamar, in the beginning, was just a concept. Can you imagine if Pat was in Shalamar? They would have had a hell of a stage show. Pat Davis was *baaaad*!

SM: Indeed! Outside of *Soul Train*, you were also doing broadcasting.

Tell me about that experience.

MK: While I was attending LACC, someone told me that I had a nice voice, so I switched my major to broadcasting and became a newscaster. I did some interviews with people like Muhammad Ali, Isabel Sanford, Marvin Gaye, James Brown, and Brock Peters for the radio show *Black Awareness in Television*. These were all radio interviews, some of which I did at the fifth annual NAACP Image Awards. I interviewed James Brown, Rev Ike, the Delfonics—a whole lot of people. The guy who owned *Black Awareness in Television* was a Muslim brother, and we co-produced *Muhammed Speaks*, which was a television program on channel 68 in Los Angeles and sponsored by the Nation of Islam before Elijah Mohammed died in 1975. I was also able to get backstage at the Roxy or Total Experience to do interviews with artists such as Betty Wright, Eddie Kendricks, David Ruffin, and the Dramatics.

SM: You have an interesting story regarding the late Mary Wilson. Do you mind sharing?

MK: In 1979, I took my girlfriend to Cedars Sinai Hospital to have our baby. The person whose bed was next to hers was Mary Wilson. They were both in labor at the same time. Her son and my daughter were born at the exact same time. Fourteen years later, her son was killed in an accident in a jeep he was driving in the Hollywood Hills. I always wanted to introduce my daughter to Mary's son since they were both born on the same day.

SM: Currently, you have an online broadcast interview show. What is the name of it?

MK: Disco Daddy's Wide World of Hip-Hop & R&B. I interview a lot of R&B and hip-hop artists, usually the original gangsters (OGs) because I am always interested in the history and how things went down, the real stories behind certain things as opposed to rumors. I present a chance for the artist to lay it out and really tell it like it is instead of gossip.

SM: What was your overall experience on *Soul Train*?

MK: It gave me a base to start testing where I wanted to go in this business. I was part of a Black show in which, even then, I realized its historical significance.

SM: What do you want to say in memory of Don Cornelius?

MK: There are a few men who I can name on one hand: Berry Gordy, Muhummad Ali, Malcolm X, Martin Luther King, Quincy Jones, and Don Cornelius. When I was around Don, I felt I was in the presence of greatness. These are all men who achieved great things during a time when Black men were not given the avenue for that. They had to put themselves out there. One thing about show business: it's show, and it's business. *Soul Train* gave me that base to be able to dream.

SM: What words of wisdom do you want to share?

MK: Dream big! Why not? Dreams sometimes come true, and if you don't dream big, you have nothing! When you're at the bottom, don't take one step; take ten giant steps!

# Freddie Maxie

(1973–1976)

> Freddie Maxie was one of the first female dancers to do The Lock dance move professionally. Her locking movements were a visual treat for *Soul Train* and the Soul Train road tours. Her journey before and after *Soul Train* is truly incredible.

**S**M: My first question is: where are you originally from?

FM: I am from Shreveport, Louisiana.

SM: When you were a child, did you have any desires or ambitions to dance or be in show business?

FM: I come from a musical family. I loved singing more than dancing. Several of my relatives sang in church, but I was shy and quiet, and I never sang in front of anybody. My older sister was more talented, and she was a big inspiration in my life.

SM: When was the first time you sang in public?

FM: I was twelve years old when I first sang in public in church in front of my family. My uncle, my grandfather's twin brother, and my mother cried when they heard me singing "Oh Rugged Cross," and they could not believe my delivery of that song.

SM: When did your love of dancing occur?

CURRENT PHOTO

BACK IN THE DAY

FM: I was about eight or nine when I began dancing. Me and my older sister, other relatives, and I always danced around the house, and being a Pentecost, we danced during church service, too.

SM: When did you and your family move to Los Angeles?

FM: In 1970. My mom wanted to move to Los Angeles, where her sisters were living, to get a better job. So, we rode from Shreveport to Compton in a big yellow Cadillac. We arrived on July 4, 1970. That car was packed! We rode "ten deep" in that canary yellow Cadillac!

SM: How did you become a Soul Train dancer?

FM: The story began at the Watts Writers Workshop, a program for young people who aspired to be in the arts; they put on productions and plays. It was at this workshop where I met Jimmy "Scoo B Doo" Foster, and we became good friends. He trained me on locking movements. He was already a dancer on *Soul Train*, so one Sunday, he took me to the show for a taping.

SM: What do you remember most about your first time being on *Soul Train*?

FM: Becoming friends with Pat Davis. You see, that previous Monday I had beaten Pat in a dance contest at a club, and she and her partner, Gary Keyes, were so nice to me afterward. So, that Sunday when I went to the show, Pat remembered me. She told Pam Brown that I beat her in a dance contest, that I was a great dancer, and that I could lock. Pam was looking for dancers to be a part of *Soul Train*'s upcoming road tours. So, after Pam watched me dance, she invited me to come back to the next tapings so that the TV audience could become familiar with who I was by the time the tour began.

SM: So, your friendship with Pat Davis helped you get opportunities with *Soul Train*?

FM: Yes! Pat was always kind to me and looked out for me. She always acknowledged me, never laughed at or made fun of me, and she always had a kind word for me. It was because of Pat that I became a part of the *Soul Train* tour. If it weren't for Pat, I wouldn't have had those great experiences with *Soul Train*.

SM: What was your experience with the Soul Train road tours?

FM: Wonderful! The tour consisted of eight to ten dancers, myself, Pat Davis, Sharon Hill, Tyrone Proctor, Jimmy "Scoo B Doo," Edith Lynn Pickens, Gary Keyes, Connie Blackino, who left after the Apollo show, and Don Campbell. We were paid a hundred dollars per performance and fifty dollars a day for food. Before our first show at the Los Angeles Forum, I had to take the SAT at Long Beach State. Then I had to rush back to the Forum. We opened up for The Whispers, the Sylvers, Eddie Kendricks, and the Moments. While touring, I was going to California State University of Fullerton, and Don Cornelius would fly me in on Fridays to perform with the dancers. But I was so nervous! There were thousands of people there, and I had butterflies in my stomach. I had never experienced that before.

SM: How did you deal with being nervous in front of the large crowds?

FM: I said to myself, "Don't look at the crowd; don't look at the people's faces; just look at my partner." The other dancers also helped me get over my nervousness. So, when Don Cornelius called out me and my partner's names, and we did our routines, I was fine. After that, we played the Cow Palace in San Francisco and then an arena in San Diego. By the time we played the Apollo in New York, I was okay.

SM: Performing at the legendary Apollo must have been a truly memorable experience!

FM: It really was, but it almost didn't happen. Not too long before the Apollo gig, *Soul Train* had a national dance contest, and the winners were a couple from New Orleans. Don Cornelius wanted them, as well as Damita Jo Freeman, who was also part of that contest, on the tour. So, during a rehearsal at the park that Tuesday night for the tour, Don told Connie Blackino and me that we were eliminated from the tour, so he paid us for coming to the rehearsals, and they went to New York without us.

SM: That must have been very disappointing for you,

FM: Yes. Even the other dancers on the tour were unhappy that we were not performing with them at the Apollo. Pam Brown felt really bad about it and told Don to put us back on the show. It turned out that Damita didn't join the tour, and the dance contest winners could not go because they were going to school. So, one day, a black limo pulled up to Connie's house in Los Angeles and to my house in Compton. We got our suitcases packed and flew first class to New York City!

SM: What kind of dance routines did you do during the tour?

FM: Since I am a Locker, I would do locking routines with Scoo B Doo and Don Campbell. They would do these handshakes and hand claps, but they were so fast... and rough! [laughs] They would also go between my legs, then jump out into the audience and kiss the girls, then hop back on stage! We performed in arena venues and huge stadiums.

SM: Traveling on the road with acts like The Whispers and Sylvers and performing on the same stage with them must have been exciting.

FM: It was! Sometimes, the owners of the clubs didn't want to pay The Whispers. The Whispers are from Watts, and they didn't play! They could fight, and they made some phone calls, so they got paid. While we were in New York performing at the Apollo, we would grab a bite to eat and then head back to our hotel. So, me, Sharon, Pat, Connie, and Edith, as well as Charmaine and Olympia Sylvers of the Sylvers and their keyboardist Patrice Rushen would sit around with nothing to do, so we would sing songs. This is where Don Cornelius found out that I could sing! This would come up a few years later when he formed his Soul Train Gang recording group.

SM: The *American Soul* miniseries depicted that the dancers faced racism during the road tour. Did you or the other dancers on the tour deal with any racial problems?

FM: I never experienced any racial problems during the tour, nor did any of the other dancers ever mention being harassed or facing racism. We were heavily chaperoned most of the time. We didn't experience any racism during the tour. We were well-mannered and respectful to Don Cornelius, Pam Brown, and everyone we met. Also, we never picketed *Soul Train* for pay.

SM: Did you ever experience any jealousy while you were on *Soul Train*?

FM: No, not really. One time, though, I was in the park in Compton. The music was on, and we were all dancing. Several guys saw me locking and wanted me to teach them the moves. The other girls there got jealous. One of them was a member of the Crips. She wanted to fight with me, but then she said, "Don't I know you?" She remembered me from a talent show we performed in together. That saved me from getting beat up! [laughs]

SM: Do you have any OMG moments from *Soul Train*?

FM: Yes. Two actually. First was when The Jackson 5 came on the show. I sat with Katherine Jackson and Janet Jackson while a Soul Train Line was being taped. Afterward, Pat and I went to The Jackson 5's dressing room. She knocked on the door and said, "Hey, I want you to meet my friend, Freddie." The door opened, and Michael and Marlon stood there. The dressing room was full of feathers in the air and on the floor because the group had just finished having a pillow fight. They weren't even in their stage outfits yet! [laughs]

SM: [laughs] That's a funny way of being introduced to The Jackson 5. What happened next?

FM: Pat told Michael that I could do the Robot real good, and that I could make my arms go behind my back. Michael got excited and asked if I could come to his house later for a party his family was giving and show him how to do the Robot. I said, "Michael, you just have to practice." But Michael pressed further and asked, "Are you gonna come?" Suddenly, Pat and I heard Pam Brown's voice saying, "Pat and Freddie!

I know you are back here! We need you downstairs!" Pat and I ran into the ladies' room, went into the stalls, and stood on the toilets. Pam came in and said, "I know you two are in here. Come on downstairs!"

SM: [laughs] That's hilarious!

FM: It sure was! A little later on, Michael and his brothers came out to the stage in their outfits looking neat with their Afros picked out, not like how they were in the dressing room. When they performed "Dancing Machine" and Michael did the Robot, I said to myself, "Michael, you don't need me to teach you to do the Robot!" That was a fun day! Many of us wore J-5 T-shirts passed out to us by the production staff.

SM: Did you ever accept Michael's invitation to come to his house to the party his family was giving after the taping?

FM: I did, but after the taping, Edith and I were supposed to go to a party hosted by the grandson of William "Buckwheat" Thomas (The Little Rascals character). I told her that Michael had invited the dancers to his home for a party, but she said we would go later. Plus, we also had to tape other segments of the show. So, we went to the other party, and it was great. Afterward, Edith and I went to the Jacksons' home in Encino. But it was midnight! I rang the bell. Mrs. Jackson answered the intercom and said, "I'm sorry, baby. Everyone went home."

SM: You wanted to strangle Edith, didn't you? [laughs]

FM: Yes! [laughs]

SM: What was your other OMG moment from *Soul Train*?

FM: Marvin Gaye! We had no idea he was going to be a guest on the show; So, when he walked in the studio and stood near Don and the production staff, we just all stared at him. Don Cornelius literally let Marvin run the whole show that day, and everyone just wanted to talk to him. We were so happy he came to *Soul Train*. There was magic in the air when he came on.

SM: What was Marvin's personality like?

FM: He was very relaxed but seemed a bit down at first. But once we started screaming when he performed, he felt all right. The dancers grew up in an era where people wanted to be able to meet and see people like Marvin, Michael, and Aretha, and there they were on *Soul Train* for us to meet and see.

SM: The Soul Train Gang was featured heavily in *Right On! magazine*, and a series of photos were taken of all of you for numerous issues of the magazine. Looks like all of you had fun during those photo shoots.

FM: Did we! The photos were shot at Griffith Park in Los Angeles. Flo Jenkins wanted to spotlight the members of the Soul Train Gang who were part of the Soul Train road tours. The photos were used to promote the Soul Train tours, not the *Soul Train* show. Some of the other dancers who were not part of the tour showed up at the shoots and pushed their way into the photos.

SM: There was a certain 1940s style that several of the girls were into during the time you were on the show.

FM: Yes. The Billie Holiday look influenced the style of dress of some of the girls on the show, like Pat Davis. When The Pointer Sisters first came to the show dressed in 1940s fashions, Pat and Fawn Quinones began to dress in those styles.

SM: Was it hard for you to leave *Soul Train*?

FM: It was difficult. Pat Davis and I left about the same time. I wanted to go to college but didn't feel mentally ready for it. Don and Dick Griffey knew I could sing and wanted me to be a part of their new musical group, which would be recording, traveling and touring. But both my grandmother and Pam Brown advised me to go to school. It was rough leaving the life of entertainment and just going to school. It was heartbreaking, but it was something I had to do. So, I enrolled in California State Fullerton and earned my Bachelor of Arts degree in Performing Arts in 1978.

SM: What was your journey like in college?

FM: During my time there, I enrolled in a Black Ensemble class. My professor, Stan Breckeridge, wanted me to sing the Rufus song "Sweet Thing." When he and the rest of the class heard me singing, they were blown away. After that, I began to work with my professor, and I performed at shows in beach areas and at weddings. When I formed my band, Maxie, we performed all over Orange County's beach cities, Disneyland, and Knotts Berry Farm.

SM: What was it like performing in Disneyland?

FM: Disneyland had held an audition, but I wasn't hired because I was too light; they only wanted brown-skinned singers. But some years later, the All-American College Band couldn't play at Disneyland, so my band, Maxie, performed. I was the first Black female to sing in Orange County Beach cities.

SM: That is quite an honor! Did you ever do any recordings?

FM: My uncle worked with artists like Willie Hutch and Paul Anka, so I did some backup singing in the studios.

SM: What are you doing currently?

FM: I worked for General Mills for twenty-eight years while still doing singing gigs here and there and show tunes with my family at restaurants. I also met my husband through his aunt in church. We have been married twenty-seven years, and we have a twenty-six year-old son named Cana Maxie Gordon.

SM: Has Cana  seen footage of you dancing on *Soul Train*?

FM: [laughs] My son gets tickled when he sees me in those old *Soul Train* episodes. I was gratified when I went to my husband's job and saw how they reacted to me because I was a former *Soul Train* dancer.

SM: Since you were one of the first girls to do locking professionally, what do you think of how this dance step has evolved into a movement?

FM: To see a dance move that was introduced over fifty years ago that is still being done today is incredible.

SM: You must be honored to have the outfit you wore when Marvin Gaye appeared on the show on display in the Smithsonian Institution's African American Museum as part of its *Soul Train* exhibit.

FM: That is something that I never expected to happen! That was my best day on *Soul Train* when Marvin Gaye appeared, and the second was when The Jackson 5 appeared, and I got a chance to meet Michael, Marlon, Janet, and Mrs. Jackson.

SM: It is wonderful that the Soul Train Gang gets together often for reunions and parties.

FM: When we get together, we are all one. The Soul Train Gang is so important, and in many ways, we are an inspiration to others.

SM: What would you like to say in memory of Don Cornelius?

FM: Thank you, Don Cornelius. I am truly proud, blessed, and honored to be a part of the history of *Soul Train*.

SM: What word of wisdom would you like to share?

FM: Dancing is just a part of my life. It's like breathing. It makes me happy. We need to keep dancing. Dancing is good for you and very healthy. Don't stop dancing.

# Bill "Slim the Robot" Williams

(1973–1974)

Bill Williams, a.k.a. Slim the Robot, was an original member of The Lockers dance group. He was always a standout for his eye-popping and intriguing mannequin robotic routines. His mechanical movements inspired and influenced many, including the "King of Pop," Michael Jackson. He shares his memories of being a part of The Lockers, dancing on *Soul Train*, and the staying power and durability of the Robot dance step.

**S**M: Who or what inspired you to want to get into the entertainment industry?

BW: My mother was a fashion designer and entertainer, and my father was an artist. I got all my talents and skills from them.

SM: What about your dancing talent? Where did you learn that from?

BW: I learned dancing from a blend of my parents and their friends at reunions and parties. They would do all of the latest dances. They would also throw parties and big events.

SM: You are one of the greatest mannequin dancers in the world. You were one of my inspirations. Your light-up suits and mannequin Robot skills were always on point.

BW: Thank you! I actually got involved with mannequins because my mother did window designs at the store she worked in, and I would help her dress up the mannequins. I would just start posing like the mannequins.

SM: So, it's apparent that your talent of mannequin moves, roboting, and miming were just a God-given gift.

BW: Absolutely. I remember I posed as a mannequin at Clifton's department store. There was a mannequin in front of the store. I would just go up there and pose right next to the mannequin. People thought I was actually part of the display! I just started posing like a mannequin in front of department stores everywhere next to the real mannequins. At the clubs, when the music started playing, I would just start moving and posing like a robotic mannequin.

SM: How did you become a part of The Lockers?

BW: Don Campbell and I went to Trade Tech together, and we were friends. We would compete in all of the dance contests. All of the ladies would like you, and all of the guys would hate you. We'd go to all of the clubs in Hollywood, Santa Monica, and Long Beach like The Summit, The Showcase, The Imperial West, The Whiskey, Blueberry Hill, and the Citadel. Don always wanted to be the best at everything. He was great at art and playing football. Fred Berry, a.k.a. Penguin, was my biggest competitor and buddy. He just had a lot of speed and personality. He was great at doing the Slow Motion. Fluky Luke was very fluid, and Greg Pope danced a lot like Don, and that's why he got the nickname Campbell Lock Jr.

SM: You first danced on *Soul Train* in 1973. What do you remember about your first day on the set?

BW: It was a house party atmosphere! I just had the same attitude I had in the clubs, to compete and dance, just showing out!

SM: When The Lockers began performing professionally, you wore some amazing outfits. I was always intrigued by your light-up suits.

BW: My father built electronic displays for department stores, and I would help him. That inspired me. I made my first electronic bow tie with light-up bulbs. I was C-3PO before *Star Wars*. I *was* close encounters, not just of the third kind, but every kind!

SM: What are some of your greatest memories with The Lockers?

BW: All of them are great memories! We traveled around the world, and performed on the *Roberta Flack Special,* the *Midnight Special* and *Carol Burnett*. We had a Saturday morning children's special and did a commercial for Schlitz Malt Liquor. We also performed in Las Vegas with Frank Sinatra, Dean Martin, and Roger Miller. Michael Jackson was intrigued by all of us. Other dance troupes tried to mimic us, but we were the originals.

SM: What do you recall when The Lockers broke up? I know that must have been a difficult time.

BW: Some of us were business-oriented, and some of us weren't. Egos work well on stage, but off stage, they don't.

SM: What did you do professionally after leaving The Lockers?

BW: I built robot man suits, did laser shows, and was a lighting director on tours such as *The Night I Fell in Love* tour with Luther Vandross and Cheryl Lynn. Marcel Marceau and I were going to do a remake of *Westworld,* but it fell through.

SM: What do you want to say in memory of Don Cornelius?

BW: I remember he was fascinated by my light-up suits. He told me that I should patent the lighting designs on my outfits, but I never did.

SM: What word of wisdom do you want to share?

BW: The future is coming, and the robots are coming back!

# Francesska Berry

(1973–1975)

Franchesska Berry is all about the dance. As she states, she lives it, eats it, and breathes it. She knew from the time she was a little girl that she wanted to devote her life to dance. She was a standout dancer on *Soul Train* and, for a time, married dancer and actor Fred Berry. She discusses her childhood, her history with *Soul Train*, her fond memories with Berry, her dedication to maintaining the history and legacy of African dance, and the accolades being bestowed upon her in Senegal.

SM: You are an excellent, vibrant dancer. Was dancing your passion as a child?

FB: Yes! I believe I was born to dance. My first paid dance performance was when I was three years old.

SM: Who were your dance influences?

FB: I believe that dance chose me. I remember in school, I would be asked what I was going to be when I grew up. My answer was that I was going to grow up and be me. But my first influences were Shirley Temple and Bill "Bojangles" Robinson. My mother knew I loved to dance, and she would put me in front of the TV when I was two and three years old, and I would watch Shirley Temple movies. I remember

BACK IN THE DAY

CURRENT PHOTO

watching one movie and thinking, "Why couldn't a little girl the same color I was be able to dance with that tall, suited man?" In another movie, she was having a birthday party, and some little Black girls wanted to attend, but Shirley Temple told them they had to wait outside. From that day on, I said to myself I was going to start rehearsing and preparing myself to dance with Mr. Robinson. From the age of three, I rehearsed every day. I always had a new dance performance to show our postman, Mr. Jaguar, every day. When I was four, he asked my mother if I could dance at a party he was giving. So, at the party he asked me what I wanted to dance to. I told him, "Put on James Brown." At first, I was nervous, but the music came on, and I just started doing the Philly Dog. All the people cheered and started clapping. I never had that response before. This was my first gig, and I will never forget the joy I brought to them. After I performed, Mr. Jaguar put a five-dollar bill in my four-year-old hand. At that moment, I realized dance was something I was supposed to do. The rest is "herstory."

SM: Beautiful! What or who were other influences?

FB: My mother knew how much I loved to dance and would let me stay up late to see the African-based movies, which had scenes where the tribes would go into the forest. They would always have the indigenous tribes dance in the area they were in. I would always wait for those African dance scenes, and I was doing exactly what they were doing.

SM: When you were fourteen, you first went to *Soul Train* by way of Chuck Berry, right?

FB: Yes. It was my dance destiny. My mother met Mr. Chuck Berry, and he told her he was in town to tape *Soul Train*. She told him about me and asked if he wouldn't mind if I came with him to *Soul Train*. My mother came home and told me I would be going to *Soul Train* with Chuck Berry, and that would be my big opportunity. I was like, "Mom, this means so much to me! You know how much I want to be on the show!" So, when he came to get me and pick me up, he was so kind. I just spoke to him like he was my grandfather. Keep in mind, at that time, I didn't really know his legacy as the King of Rock and Roll since I was too young. I just spoke to him about my passion on the way to the studio and thanked him. He said, "I'm only here (to tape *Soul Train* on Saturday), but it's up to you to do your thing. I promise you if you do what you do, they will request you to come back." I think you had to be eighteen to be a dancer on the show, but I was only fourteen, so I knew I had to be quiet and not let my age show. I danced my heart out and enjoyed it so much. It was Pam Brown, the show's dance coordinator, who came to me at the end of the taping of the two shows and invited me back that Sunday.

SM: As time went on, what artists did you enjoy watching perform on *Soul Train*?

FB: I would say James Brown, Graham Central Station, The O'Jays, and Al Green. I was a huge Al Green fan! He sang "Sweet 16" to me on my sixteenth birthday. He was so kind to me. Others I enjoyed were Labelle, Tower of Power, Ohio Players, and The Jackson 5. In fact, Michael and I actually had a few conversations. I remember when Barry White and his entire orchestra came, as well as Elton John and Gino Vanelli. I had a personal conversation with Teddy Pendergrass when he came to the show with the Blue Notes. The list goes on and on.

SM: You told me that when James Brown came to the show, the taping was held up for quite some time because he wanted certain notes to be just right.

FB: Right. The dancers would find out who the artists were that were going to appear, and when they learned James Brown was going to appear, some of the veteran dancers grumbled. I wondered to myself, *Why were they upset?* I just knew that since James Brown was coming, it was going to be something like I had never experienced. I was blessed to be on the show a couple of times when he appeared; he was such a consummate artist. But this particular time, we were on the set for hours! We didn't get out of the two tapings until twelve or one in the morning.

SM: Being that you were younger than most of the other dancers, did you make friends with them easily?

FB: Dancers like Pat Davis, Damita Jo Freeman, and others eventually came to adopt me as one of the Soul Train Gang. My mother would take me to the show once a month, and she would leave me in the care of two dancers, Rhonda Brown and Reuben Williams. I love them so much. They would watch over me. I appreciated them so much.

SM: Did you have any favorite dance partners?

FB: I would dance with Mark Moore. Before him, I danced with a guy on *Soul Train* named Derrick. He had a big gold Afro and was very slender. He just stood out from the rest whenever he would dance. I would see him on TV, and I would say, "Mommy, I want to dance with him so much." I happened to be blessed to dance with him when I went on the show. He was my first dance partner, and he was so sweet. I remember Tyrone Proctor and I would do a swing dance. I danced with Jeffrey Daniels for a while when he first got on the show. I've had some wonderful dance partners.

SM: Do you recall any funny moments on the show?

FB: I remember Don Cornelius being very clumsy and always falling off the risers. He would also fall going up the stairs to the stage. Every time he would walk on set, I was on needles and pins thinking to myself, "Please don't fall, Mr. Cornelius." I remember one time he fell on his face right on the bottom of my shoe, and he looked up at me. I almost passed out!

SM: Did you meet Fred Berry on *Soul Train* or outside of *Soul Train*?

FB: Actually, we did meet on *Soul Train*. My father used to love it when Peng, my nickname for Fred, would go down the Soul Train Line. This was before I came to the show. So, when I did come to the show, The Lockers had this avant-garde, "we're The Lockers clique" kind of thing. But at one taping, I was eating my chicken, and Peng sauntered over to me and said something like, "One day I'm going to eat you like that chicken." He scared the crap out of me! I was surprised he even noticed me with all the other beautiful women there. I would eventually travel with the Soul Train Gang and The Lockers. We'd often get requests to perform on TV shows like *In Concert* or clubs like Maverick's Flat, The Citadel, The Speakeasy, and the Total Experience. I would see Peng at these venues, and I think I kind of grew on him. When I was fifteen, we started dancing together, just hanging out. This was when I became aware of his kindness and big heart. He was very sweet.

SM: What are some of the warm, happy, and fond memories you have when you later married Fred?

FB: He taught me things about dance. He knew my passion and discipline for dance. We both wore tams and dressed alike since we had similar styles. He also taught me how to "go hungry" and eat potatoes all day. I was like, "Look, I can go to my mother's house and get a steak from the freezer. She won't even notice it's gone." But he said, "No. You're a dancer. You have to learn how to go without." I asked, "Why? I never heard of that." He said we were going to eat potatoes all day. In the morning, we'd have smothered potatoes for breakfast, we'd have french fries for lunch, and for dinner, we'd have a baked potato. I have never had that experience before! Peng made this a lot of fun. He was trying to say that this is the life of a dancer. Sometimes, you have to sacrifice to have your dancing at a certain level. That made a very strong impression on me.

SM: Do you recall when Fred got the role of Rerun on *What's Happening?*

F B: Yes. I remember he called me saying there was an audition for this new TV show. All of The Lockers were in Los Angeles for some event, and they all auditioned. Fred wasn't going to go since the part was for a tall, skinny White guy, but I just further encouraged him to go. When he came home, he was a little nervous, but excited! He told me he got this gig for a sitcom. He had to have a headshot and was nervous about it. I literally gave him the shirt off my back. He didn't have his tam on that day, but I had on my tam. I gave it to him, and he wore that on his first headshot.

SM: What do you remember about Fred's days of being on *What's Happening*?

FB: When my husband came home from working, he would always bring home the script, and we would read it. Actually, it was me who created the choreography Peng would do with actresses on the show. With The Lockers, you held your own. My husband didn't actually know how to dance with actresses on the show because they were actresses, not dancers. He was like, "Baby, I need you to think of a count of thirty-two and four counts of eight that we could do together; then I'll branch off independently and do my own thing; then come over and pick her up on the last step." He didn't know how to do that. But I knew how to do that, and I told him, "Baby, it's just like when you dance with me." So, all of those episodes that you see my husband dancing with someone else, that was all me. I choreographed that. We literally danced twelve hours a day. That was our life. We danced all day and all night.

SM: You were actually in an episode with Fred about a dance contest at a disco, playing his girlfriend and dance partner, Charlene.

FB: Yes! Saul Turteltaub would always speak about my artistic prowess and my dancing. I would show Haywood Nelson (who played Dwayne) some things I had taught Fred. So, finally, Saul and the producers told Peng that he had to have his wife dance with him as opposed to another actress. That was when we did that episode, which was the fourth season premiere, and that was the highest rated *What's Happening!* episode ever. The producers likened Peng and me as the "Black Fred Astaire and Ginger Rogers." I actually choreographed our dance routine on that episode.

SM: Did Fred really take to heart the overweight jokes that would be made to him as Rerun?

FB: Peng grew up being ridiculed for his size. But he was able to turn something toxic into medicine and became empowered by it, so when he was a Locker as Mr. Penguin, he was being applauded for his weight. What people teased him about he was able to make it his strength. He traveled the world with The Lockers, and he was applauded. Now, here on this show, on every episode, there were fat jokes, and it hurt my husband. It caused him to put on a great deal of weight within a few shows. A lot of it was stressful, and he didn't know how to handle it. It was very difficult. He would cry to me. We would read the scripts at home, so whatever jokes there were, he would know about them ahead of time. It even hurt Haywood to tell those jokes to him. Those of us who knew and loved Fred knew how he suffered from it. During one hiatus, he lost weight, but when he came back to the show, the producers told him he looked really well, but it was not working, and he had to gain the weight back.

SM: After you and Fred went separate ways, what did you do professionally in your career?

FB: Peng and I still cared for each other and loved each other, but he had some lessons to learn, and I had my path. I was well into my career in African dance. After being a Soul Train Gang member at such an early age and dancing to funk, it was African dance that held my passion. I taught dance, and I even took classes. At that time, I was still dancing modern jazz and ballet. I am a technical dancer. Technique and polish are very important to me. I would watch African dance on television, and I didn't see the beauty, finesse, and depth of African dance, and that's when I decided that I would perfect African dance. I infused my modern Brazilian dance and all the techniques I brought to the table in African dance. That's what I specialize in. I'm a classical West African dancer.

SM: What do you think of dance today? For instance, when I was on *Soul Train* in its final years, the emphasis was more on how you looked as opposed to how you danced. Dance is from the soul. I think the roots and history of dance, particularly African dance, are not appreciated like they once were.

FB: You are speaking the truth! I eat, live, breathe, and bathe dance. Dance has taken me to so many places in the world to share this particular ideology and the value of dance. I continue to be a creator of dance. Dance is an implication of your spirit and soul. I consider dance to be something very sacred, so the expression you exude should be one that can be treasured. On any day I dance, I dance as though that day could be the last day I dance. I consider myself a keeper of traditional West African dance and the beautiful aspects of dance, and that's what I exude. Nothing less. But much like dance has deteriorated, I also think the quality and style that we have as a people has also lessened. Overtly, on the outside, it appears as though we have advanced, but covertly, on the inside, as a culture and a race, we are so far behind. That's why it is imperative that I continue to set an example of what we can be.

SM: You have received many honors and accolades. What are among them?

FB: I have taught at Antioch University in Seattle, which is where I graduated with honors. This was a 98.9 percent predominantly White university I went to, and I graduated at the top of my class. I actually performed at my graduation. I was the first to ever dance during a graduation ceremony at the university. I wore traditional African clothing. I have also taught in Australia and lived there for some time, and I am a Fulbright scholar to Egypt. While there, I was actually commissioned to share choreography and do a cultural exchange immersion with the Egyptian Royal Ballet. I consider dance to be the universal language. I danced in Guam, Senegal, and Canada. I performed and studied with the National Ballet of Senegal, and I am also an honorary member there. I am the Women's Director General of the Friends of the African Union. Being a voice for the sixth region of the diaspora, my goal and one of my passions is to somehow translate from a Eurocentric paradigm into an indigenous thought and language so that we can become one with those at home in Africa. I am a cultural ambassador to Senegal.

SM: You spoke in the *Unsung* documentary on *What's Happening*! with regard to Fred. What was that like for you?

FB: I was speaking about his true character, but the producers were looking for something else. It was like an interrogation. I was in that room for two and a half hours in this chair with a bottle of warm water and this light shining in my eyes. I gave them a lot of positive reflection, but what they chose to focus on was how Fred devolved and lost himself in this Rerun character with all of the pressure on him. The first hour I was smiling, but then they started insinuating and reading questions. I could see the angst and the sadness in my face with the clips that they used, and I was very sad. They used certain pieces and put them together the way they wanted; it was not the full story of Peng. It seemed that they strived to show negative aspects of him and had other cast members affirm them. So, I am hoping to have another opportunity to speak the truth about my husband and our life and dispel some of the rumors and myths. They left so much out and clearly strived to blur his legacy.

SM: In memory of Fred Berry, what would you like to say?

FB: When you have a gift the way he was gifted, you have to be protective of that gift. There is a lot of sacrifice and vulnerability that you have to exude to receive those blessings and anointing. I saw him as a human who was flawed, but who had great sensitivity and was very kind, sweet, and generous; and this was well before *What's Happening!* Once the show came it brought a lot of conflict within him. I am very protective of his legacy. He loved me, and I loved him. We had a storybook kind of love. We were called Mr. and Mrs. Penguin at Maverick's Flat! In our wedding vows, we vowed to never stop dancing until death do us part.

SM: What are you doing currently?

FB: I teach dance to kindergarten, elementary, junior high, and high school students. I also specialize in teaching women how to appreciate their flaws. I've been traveling back and forth to Senegal since 1999. I was invited by the artistic director of the National Ballet of Senegal at that time, Bouly Sonko. I was introduced to the ballet in such a royal fashion. I always wanted to pursue a diplomatic status in Senegal. I also taught two scholarly residencies at the University of Dakar. I always perform with the leading groups of Senegal, with them here in the States. I was honored in Senegal for all the work I've done there and in the States. To be honored there was a dream I had always had as a little girl when I was hopscotching. While I was in Senegal during the residencies, I created an institutional relationship between Antioch University and the University of Dakar. My plan is to do a documentary that will share their reflections on when I first came. I am also writing a book titled *My Life Has Been Dancing*.

SM: What do you want to say in memory of Don Cornelius?

FB: I loved him with all of my heart. He knew I was too young to be on the show, but he "overstood" my dance and the importance of that. I would tell him thank you for letting me be on his show. I didn't know all he had done as a civil rights activist and how his show came to be, but I know he was dapper and suited on every show. I remember his voice being so strong and articulate. He was always kind and very supportive. I loved him so much, and I am just so grateful.

SM: What word of wisdom do you want to share?

FB: I would like to personally thank all of the dancers that were much older than me at the time and who were so kind and so influential on me knowing that I could evolve. I continue to dance, and I am forever grateful for their love. We are the keepers of *Soul Train* and the greatness and the authenticity that came through.

CURRENT PHOTO

BACK IN THE DAY

# Carole Creekmore

(1973–1975)

> In the mid-seventies, there was a stylishly dressed and effervescent young lady on *Soul Train* by the name of Carole Creekmore. She and her dance partner, Ricardo, or "Rick" as he was known by his friends, were one of the program's most energetic dance couples. Creekmore had an enthusiasm that was contagious and won her several fans. She followed her dreams and, despite some setbacks, is still in the process of vigorously pursuing them.

**S**M: What were you most passionate about when you were growing up?

CC: My passion was to be an actress and a model, but my mother didn't think those professions were practical and thought I should be a nurse instead.

SM: How did you become a dancer on *Soul Train*?

CC: I was going to Compton College at the time. I was on their cheerleading squad. A guy named Darryl Mitchell knew a guy who danced on *Soul Train* who was looking for a dance partner. So, I chose the cheerleading captain, Sandra, to come to *Soul Train* with me. Darryl's friend, James, and a guy named Rick Bass picked Sandra and me up and drove us to the studio. I didn't have to audition at Denker Park, which was the way dancers were selected to go on the show initially.

SM: What do you remember about that first day at *Soul Train*?

CC: I remember a long line of people outside the studio. There was a shorter line for the regulars. James, Rick, Sandra, and I went on the shorter line. James and Rick's names were on the list, and we got into the studio with them. Inside the studio, I noticed the set had changed. I also noticed that the first two sets of bleachers were for the regulars, and the last set of bleachers was where the newer dancers sat. Pat Davis and Vicki Abercrombie were dressed so nice. Chicken was given to us for lunch, and we danced until ten at night.

SM: You've seen a lot of big-name acts come on *Soul Train* so I'm going to ask you what you remember when certain ones came to the show. First, Sly and the Family Stone.

CC: They played live! Most bands that came on *Soul Train* didn't play live. We waited two hours for him while he was in the back getting ready. He was even late getting to the studio. But he made up for his lateness. We partied! We had a live party on camera and off camera. Sly was, and still is, an icon.

SM: What about when Michael Jackson made a solo appearance on the show?

CC: Some of the kids didn't like a ballad he performed and made unpleasant comments. During breaks between performances, Michael remained on stage. Some dancers were so excited they jumped up to take pictures with him, but others were rude and clawed at him—not the regulars, but several unprofessional kids that the studio let in.

SM: What about James Brown?

CC: He and his J.B.'s played live! It was another on-camera and off-camera party. It was the biggest party. It was off the hook!

SM: Barry White?

CC: It was like heaven! He and his orchestra played live. I didn't care about anyone else when he sang. He was so down to earth. He even stood in line to have chicken with us. He was two people behind me. Don Cornelius was even in line. Someone yelled, "Don, we didn't know you ate fried chicken!" [laughs]

SM: What are some of your other favorite memories of other artists that came to *Soul Train*?

CC: Harold Melvin & the Blue Notes and The Commodores, Labelle, Chaka Khan, and Al Green. I made the dress that I wore the day Al Green came on.

SM: During the Q&A session when Al Green was on the show, you didn't ask a question but just said, "We love you, Al!"

CC: Yes! The session was coming to a close, so I just made that statement.

SM: Did you ever have any embarrassing moments on the show?

CC: Rick and I did this dance routine, and the heel of my platform shoe got caught in my dress, and I fell, and my embarrassing moment was caught on camera. Sometime after that happened, I was at a party, and a guy saw me and told someone, "Did you see that girl fall on *Soul Train*?"

SM: Did you ever experience any jealousy while you were dancing on *Soul Train*?

CC: After dancing on the show for a while, I became popular. There was jealousy, but I didn't care.

SM: In the early years of *Soul Train*, all the dancers changed clothes for all four shows, but an incident on the set changed all of that, right?

CC: Yes. A popular regular's outfit for the second show was stolen. So, it was announced from that time on that we would wear the same outfits all day for Saturday tapings and the same outfits all day for Sunday tapings; no more changing clothes for four different shows. We didn't have dressing rooms, so we changed our clothes in the bathrooms and put our belongings and outfits on the bleachers, so it was easy for someone to steal someone's belongings if they were unattended.

SM: Did you ever get caught by Pam Brown with her famous "gum ritual?"

CC: Yes, I did! One time, Pam wouldn't let me on the show because she felt I was dressed very provocatively. I had on a crisscross halter top and wide length pants with four buttons so it wouldn't show off my stomach. But Pam wouldn't let me in the studio. It's funny, but later in the eighties and nineties, the girls were dressed even more provocatively, and it was permitted!

SM: What were your impressions of Don Cornelius?

CC: I had a crush on Don Cornelius. I had his attention. I would see him say something to Chuck Johnson, and he would tell me to go on the riser.

SM: Did you ever do the Scramble Board?

CC: Yes. Rick and I did it. I was so nervous, but Don whispered the solution to me.

SM: What was it like going down the Soul Train Line?

CC: Everyone wanted to do it, but everyone didn't get a chance to. The regulars were positioned to go down the line, but Rick and I also made our way down the line several times.

SM: Did you ever dance on *American Bandstand*?

CC: Yes. I remember one time when I had my hair in braids, Dick Clark sat next to me on the bleachers and asked me about my braids. Don was not happy about his dancers going on Dick's show, and he made an announcement to everybody. He was like, "Y'all better not go back on *Bandstand*. If I catch any of you dancing on *Bandstand* again, you won't be allowed back on *Soul Train*."

SM: In my other interviews, the dancers told me about the clubs all of you used to frequent.

CC: Oh yes! Maverick's Flat, Whiskey A-Gogo, Citadel, and so many others. It was a freedom I enjoyed. I remember Little Joe Chism taking a group of us to all the clubs. He danced a lot!

SM: During your time on *Soul Train*, you were a flight attendant, right?

CC: Right. While I was going to Compton College, a lady who was a Pan Am stewardess was looking for people for an aviation class. She set up interviews with us, and eventually, I became a stewardess with Western Airlines. It was a fun and enlightening experience.

SM: Would your flight attendant job often conflict with *Soul Train* tapings?

CC: Yes. I had to work on some of those weekends when there were *Soul Train* tapings. That's how I missed when Marvin Gaye came to the show.

SM: Did you ever experience any unpleasant times as a flight attendant?

CC: Once I had to do a single flight to Salt Lake City. I met three other Black flight attendants. The actor Robert Redford was going to be a passenger on the flight. He was the Brad Pitt of our day, and I was a big fan of his. A cake was brought on board for him, and the other Black flight attendants and I were supposed to bring it to him. But there were White people aboard who said that Black flight attendants shouldn't be waiting on him. So, the cake was taken back, and Robert Redford was boarded on another flight. The whole experience was very racist. Other than that experience, everything was fine. Once Western Airlines merged with United Airlines, however, I got furloughed.

SM: What did you do in your career after that?

CC: After being furloughed, I went to school and got a regular job at the DMV. I did some modeling at Ames Department Store, and I ultimately put my dreams on the back burner. I eventually worked with Time Warner. While there, I was a producer/director and a seat filler for many awards shows. I also worked behind the scenes in production for networks. Currently, I'm on the crew for seat fillers for awards shows such as the *BET Awards, SAG Awards, People's Choice Awards*, and the *American Music Awards*. I saw R. Kelly and Lady Gaga and spoke to both of them, and they were very receptive. I was also able to meet Betty White at the SAG *Awards*, and I met and spoke to Jackie Jackson at the Billboard Awards, where there was a hologram performance of his brother Michael.

SM: Do you recall the day you heard Don Cornelius died?

CC: I woke up in the morning and saw it on the news. I had seen Don about six months earlier at the BET Awards. I'm devastated that Don is gone.

SM: What do you want to say in memory of Don?

CC: I really appreciated him so much for what he did for us. He was all about Black people. He saw how we were discriminated against. Don made a sacrifice for us and fought to make a difference because we were not being recognized. What he did will always be a part of history.

SM: How would you describe your overall experience being a Soul Train dancer?

CC: It was the time of my life! I am so grateful to Rick. If it weren't for him, I wouldn't have gotten on *Soul Train*.

SM: What word of wisdom do you want to share?

CC: Pursue your dreams. Don't listen to the dream killers.

# Adolfo "Shabba Doo" Quinones

(1973–1976)

Adolfo Quiones a.k.a. Shabba Doo is not only one of the original members of the Soul Train Gang but was also one of the members of the legendary, world-renowned dance group The Lockers, all of whom got their first national television exposure on *Soul Train*. After leaving The Lockers, Shabba Doo went on to do plays, television shows with major networks, movies, most notably his acclaimed, memorable role as Ozone in the classic movies *Breakin'* and *Breakin' 2: Electric Boogaloo*. He also choreographed music videos and even choreographed and appeared in a segment for the 2006 *Academy Awards* and began to pursue his new goal of being a filmmaker. In short, Shabba Doo is truly a legend.

SM: You are originally from Chicago. What were your dreams growing up as a child?

AQ: As an inner-city kid growing up in the projects, my aspirations were limited to the hope of making it to the next day. Dreams were reserved for people who were able to afford to make their dreams happen. I was supposed to be a little Black kid from Chicago strung out on dope, in jail, or a career criminal. I never dreamed I would have a career in show business.

SM: What inspired you to dance?

BACK IN THE DAY

CURRENT PHOTO

AQ: I grew up dancing around our living room apartment. We watched *American Bandstand* and the MGM musicals that would come on Saturday mornings. We also watched a lot of UHF channel programs like the *Big Bill Hill Show* and other programs that featured Rhythm & Blues recording artists.

SM: Speaking of UHF programs, *Soul Train* began as a local program on UHF station channel 26 in Chicago and, of course, that was one of the shows you watched.

AQ: *Soul Train* was amazing for all of us. It was a bit more organized than some of the other UHF programs. It had something a little different, like the introduction of the Soul Train Line.

SM: You and your sister Fawn danced on the local Chicago version of *Soul Train*. How did that come about? Did you audition?

AQ: No, we didn't audition. Kids just had to go to the Chicago Board of Trade building at certain times, and they were chosen on a first come, first served basis. There was no audition at all. The audition process didn't come until later when the show moved to Los Angeles.

SM: Did you and Fawn dance on the local *Soul Train* often?

AQ: No, we only danced on there a couple of times. I remember that the soundstage was very small, like a large living room! [laughs]

SM: When did you and your family move to Los Angeles?

AQ: Somewhere around the winter or spring of 1972.

SM: What were your impressions of Los Angeles?

AQ: I remember there was a party given at the Black Student Union on the campus of California State University Fullerton. Fawn and I attended the party, and we encountered the California flair. Where we came from, people dressed more seasonally, and our style of clothing was more muted. But here, people were decked out in colorful clothing like guys wearing yellow shirts and orange pants. [laughs]

SM: What was the style of the dancing in Los Angeles?

AQ: The style of dancing in Los Angeles was a release from the water hoses, the assassination of Martin Luther King Jr., the Vietnam War, being able to express yourself wearing big Afros and colorful clothing.

SM: When did you become a part of The Lockers?

AQ: At the Black Student Union party, Fawn and I met Greg Pope a.k.a. Campbell Lock Jr. We were in a dance contest. Fawn and I came in second, and Greg and his partner came in first. That was the beginning of the friendship between Greg and me and what eventually led to me becoming a part of The Lockers and dancing on *Soul Train*. We trained with Greg, and he taught us the locking steps while we taught him the stepping dance steps. In a couple of weeks, I learned how to lock.

SM: So, you and Greg were like brothers?

AQ: Yes. He, Scoo B Doo (James Foster) and I were roommates. Scoo B and Greg were like twenty, twenty-one years old. They were like big brothers to me. We would eat Rice a Roni and Tuna together. That was like Chinese Food to us! [laughs]

SM: What was it like when you went to *Soul Train* in Los Angeles, by this time airing nationally in major markets in the US?

AQ: For me, going to the national version of *Soul Train* was like the scene in *The Wizard of Oz* when Dorothy's house lands in Oz. When she opened the door, she stepped out of the dreary black and white into bright Technicolor. That's what it was like for me. It didn't even feel like a TV show. It was more like a social club. We'd be chatting it up about going to dances, clubs, and parties. We'd be on the bleachers telling jokes and, on long taping days, sneak out, and go to Fat Burger, then come back later.

SM: *Soul Train* was always noted for its beautiful girls. Was there any girl on the show you liked in particular?

AQ: [laughs] Pat Davis! I used to love me some Pat Davis! She, Fawn, and Freddie Maxie were known as the Butterfly Girls on *Soul Train* because of the Butterfly ornaments they wore in their hair.

SM: You, as well as all of The Lockers and members of the Soul Train Gang, danced at all of the popular clubs in Los Angeles, right?

AQ: Yes. We danced at The Summit on the Hill, the Apartment Club, Maverick's Flat, Blueberry Hill, the Citadel, the Total Experience, Under the Pier, and the Joker Room. A lot of times, when *Soul Train* had late tapings, sometimes to 1:00 a.m. in the morning, we were concerned about getting to the clubs before they closed because back then, clubs didn't stay open until 4:00 a.m. They closed at 1:00 or 1:30 a.m. [laughs] We couldn't get to the clubs often because of the late *Soul Train* tapings.

SM: Where did your nickname Shabba Doo come from?

AQ: My first nickname was Sir Lance-a-Lock, and that's what I went by. But one particular night at Summit on the Hill, the R&B group Bloodstone was performing and at one point, one of its members sang a line like, "Shabba doo bop, shabba doo bop bop, shabba doo bop." Greg said that should be my nickname, so that's how it came to be.

SM: What was the first big break for The Lockers as a dance group?

AQ: We had signed with the ICM Agency and we made an appearance on *The Carol Burnett Show*. Carol was very nice and genuine to us. That was our first big break. From there, we did *Merv Griffin, Johnny Carson*, and other major programs. We also worked with Frank Sinatra and traveled around the world.

SM: It was around this time that The Lockers had a sort of bitter departure from *Soul Train*, right?

AQ: Yes. We went to Don Cornelius and wanted him to manage us. He refused, so we left the show. But later, when we all became world famous, he invited us back to the show as guest stars twice, and in 1981 he invited me to do a dance routine on the show. That was a real honor.

SM: How did you get involved with the TV show *What's Happening*?

AQ: I was told that a TV show loosely based on the movie *Cooley High* was holding auditions for the role of a character similar to the film's character Cochise. The three main characters were supposed to be Roger, Dwayne, and a cool guy who played basketball like Cochise. I auditioned for the role of the cool guy, and I was very close to getting it. I had three callbacks, but the producers changed the role to a fat guy who could dance, so Fred "Rerun" Berry got it. But all of The Lockers appeared on the fourth episode as guest stars.

SM: What are your memories of Fred "Rerun" Berry?

AQ: The rerun was phenomenal. I first met him at the club Summit on the Hill where he was dancing. When I saw him, I was like, "I'm gonna jump on the fat kid." But when I jumped on him, that was a big mistake! [laughs] We became very good friends, and we had made plans to work together again before his death.

SM: When and why did The Lockers break up?

AQ: At this time Fred was doing *What's Happening!* and Toni Basil pursued a recording career. So, I was saddled with the responsibility of keeping The Lockers together since I had organizational skills. Because of this, Greg said I should be recognized as the group's leader. So, one day at a rehearsal in my garage in Anaheim, California, Fluky Luke and Greg said they should have a vote to make me the leader of The Lockers. Don Campbell didn't like it since he said The Lockers is his group, and he told me to go form my own group. So, it was a bitter breakup. Our last show together was on *The Dick Van Dyke Variety Show*. During the rehearsal for that show, we broke up like the group in the movie *The Five Heartbeats*.

SM: What did you do after the breakup of The Lockers?

AQ: I went solo. It was a lot like when Michael Jackson left his brothers to be on his own. At that time, I was doing a lot of dance contests. I was doing this new form of dancing that came out called waacking and fused it with locking. It was also at this time in 1978 and 1979 that I got a call from Kenny Ortega, who was working on a show for Bette

Midler, and I became a part of that show. A producer from NBC TV who was in the audience got in touch with me and said that he was working on a new variety show called *The Big Show*. He needed a dancer on the show who could do the choreography. So, I got Pat Davis, Ana Sanchez, Fluky Luke, and other dancers to be a part of the show and work on the choreography with me.

SM: Speaking of choreography, you also choreographed music videos, notably, Lionel Richie's "All Night Long" and Chaka Khan's "I Feel For You." What were those experiences like?

AQ: Those were excellent experiences. Most people don't know that the footage of Turbo and me in Chaka's video was culled from a video we did called "Street Beat." In it we were modeling clothes by a fashion designer named Norma Kamali, and our dance scenes were simply edited into Chaka's video. The editors did a great job of doing that.

SM: How did you become involved in the movie *Breakin'*?

AQ: I met with the producer and director of *Breakin'*. They suggested I audition for the role of Ozone. What got me the role was the audition for the scene toward the end of the movie where I said, "They're not gonna stop us now. I'm Ozone, Street Dancer!" When I read that line, that got me the role.

SM: *Breakin'* was a phenomenon in the midst of the breakout of the whole hip-hop evolution. As far as hip-hop films are concerned, *Wild Style* started it all.

AQ: Without a doubt. The entire hip-hop dance culture as we know it hinged on the *Breakin'* film. *Wild Style, Breakin,* and *Beat Street* paved the way for the more current dance films like *Step Up* and *You Got Served*. If *Breakin'* hadn't made it, we might not know the hip-hop dance phenomenon as we know it now.

SM: After the equally successful *Breakin' 2: Electric Boogaloo*, you still danced and did choreography, and some years later, you were in the movie *Lambada*. How did that come about?

AQ: I got a call from the director of *Breakin,* and he auditioned me for the role of Ramone. I got it, and I also choreographed the movie.

SM: You, as well as some of the other Lockers, had a chance to work with Michael Jackson in his "Ghosts" video. What was that experience like working with him?

AQ: It was a very interesting encounter. I had actually known him and his family for years. Michael told me, "You are a really good dancer." He was such a special individual. We got to hang out with him on the set, and we dressed in costumes and heavy makeup to do our dance routines.

SM: What else have you been doing in recent years?

AQ: I attended the American Film Institute for screenwriting and directing.

SM: The death of Greg Pope on the night that The Lockers were getting an award in January 2010 was very devastating. What would you like to say about Greg in his memory?

AQ: Greg had a great impact on my life. I love him, I miss him, and I grieve him.

SM: Any final thoughts, advice, or word of wisdom you want to share?

AQ: I always aspired to be something greater. People noticed that about me and would call me names. It's the kind of hatred that was leveled at President Obama. There's a saying that I say during the course of my workshops: knowledge is the new swagger, intelligence is the new cool and the new dope. God gave us all potential, but education helps to unlock that potential. Without an education, without knowledge, you are like a baseball player who has talent but doesn't know how to use it. Talent will get you at bat, but education gets you home.

NOTE: This interview was originally conducted in 2011. A big thanks to the family and Estate of Adolfo "Shabba Doo" Quinones and my deepest condolences to his family.

# William Tyrone Swan

(1973–1976)

William Tyrone Swan was one of *Soul Train*'s "heartthrobs." His looks, style and charisma were eye candy to many female admirers, from his put-together Afro to his stylish outfits. He appeared in several issues of *Right On!* Magazine and received thousands of letters from fans. Indeed, this Soul Train heartthrob had the "it" factor that earned him a place among one of the show's most memorable dancers.

SM: As a child, did you like to dance? What was your passion growing up?

WS: When I was nine or ten years old, I couldn't dance at all. I couldn't quite get the rhythm, and my family would make fun of me because I was a fan of the Beatles. All of my cousins and other family members liked The Temptations and the Miracles, but I was a fan of the Beatles. Then, I started watching *Soul Train*. The dancers looked like they were having such a good time. I just started dancing as I watched the show, and all of a sudden, I thought I could dance.

SM: How did you become a dancer on *Soul Train*?

WS: I guess it was the power of will. When I was twelve, thirteen, and fourteen, I was like, "Wow, it would be so much fun to dance and be on

BACK IN THE DAY

CURRENT PHOTO

TV every week." Then a friend of the family told me that Gary Keyes, who was a regular on *Soul Train*, asked him if he wanted to dance on the show. He said no, but he had a family friend who would love to go on there. Next thing I know, I was connected with Gary Keys. He picked me up and brought me to the show.

SM: What do you remember about your first day on *Soul Train*?

WS: I was terrified! It was like stage fright. When the lights came on, I literally froze. The only thing that kept me from freezing on camera was that I just kept moving, but inside, I was frozen! The very first person I danced with was Patricia Davis. She was so sweet. I didn't expect the dancers to be so nice. Everybody was really nice to me. I was only fifteen. That same weekend, some of the dancers including me, went to a party at the Jacksons home in Encino.

SM: What were your impressions of Don Cornelius when you first saw him in person? Several other dancers felt he was intimidating.

WS: I've never really been intimidated by people, so I can't say I was intimidated by him. But having seen him, he was a figure larger than life. He was so sharp all the time with all the wide-collared suits. When I came to the studio and we were all waiting to get in, he pulled up in a drop-top Corniche convertible. When you pull up in that, everyone knows what time it is!

SM: Who were among your best friends at *Soul Train*?

WS: One of the people who was the nicest to me was Little Joe Chism. He was about seven or eight years older than me, but he was so kind to me. I remember one time when I was sixteen or seventeen, me and my girlfriend were at a club called The Speakeasy. There was a dance contest, and I entered it. I did my little thing, which I thought was something, but Little Joe entered that dance contest, and when he finished, the dance floor was completely shredded. That boy ate that dance floor up! I just thought, 'I'm way out of my league!' Little Joe could dance his ass off! But I really wasn't doing a whole lot of hanging out back then. I was sometimes able to go to

Maverick's Flat when my mother allowed me to have the car.

SM: You were considered a *Soul Train* sex symbol. You did photo spreads for *Right On!* Magazine, and female admirers wrote many letters to you. What was all of that recognition and adulation like?

WS: I didn't really understand it. In hindsight, I wish I could go back and capitalize on that. I remember one time at a photo shoot with six or seven of the dancers, fan mail was given to us. They gave about forty letters to one dancer, then another stack to another dancer, then they gave a small shoebox to another dancer. Little Joe and James Phillips had two shoeboxes of letters. Then when they gave me my mail, it was in two big giant boxes. I was like, "Whoa!" I opened every letter. There were several thousand. Some fans would leave their phone numbers in the letters and tell me to call them collect, which I did. The adoration was cool! I never figured it all out.

SM: Were you ever recognized in public from dancing on *Soul Train*?

WS: One time when I was seventeen, me, my girlfriend, and some other friends went to Disneyland. There was a bus of kids around my age who lost their minds when I walked into Disneyland. Girls were screaming, "Oh my God! It's Tyrone Swan from *Soul Train*!" My buddies started making fun of me and laughing, calling me "Mr. Pretty Boy from *Soul Train*." I didn't really get it. People were really fans of the show. I remember traveling to Texas and girls lost their minds like I was a rock star or something.

SM: Did you ever have an OMG moment when seeing a celebrity?

WS: On the way to my very first interview for *Right On! Magazine*, I was driving up Santa Monica Boulevard, I looked up and I saw Diana Ross with her two little girls in a canary yellow convertible with the top down, driving the other way. I've never been a groupie type or gone crazy over celebrities, but I remember screaming in my car, "Oh my God! It's Diana Ross!" I lost my mind! I thought seeing her was some kind of omen that I was going to be a big star someday.

I remember another time I was walking up LaBrea Avenue, and Marvin Gaye pulled over in a Corniche convertible with his girlfriend, who later became his wife. He gave me a ride since he recognized me from *Soul Train*. He asked me where I was going, and I told him I was just going up to Coliseum. He said, "Hop in, and I'll give you a ride."

SM: Who were some of your favorite artists that you enjoyed watching perform on *Soul Train* as well as memories of those artists on the show?

WS: Gino Vanelli sticks in my mind because everyone said I looked like him. I went home and shaved my mustache so I could look more like him! I enjoyed Al Green and the other artists that came and really put it down on the show. I remember when James Brown came on and showed out. Al Green has so much charisma. He even did the show with a broken arm and tore it up! He brought his band on and did it live. I remember Graham Central Station had this sexy singer named Chocolate, and she wanted to dance on the show, and she asked me to dance with her. Patti Labelle came to the show in this gold lamé suit, and she was so beautiful and so curvaceous. I had a crush on her! I remember she was waiting on the sidelines of the stage, and I asked if I could have her phone number. She looked at me and said, "My phone number? You ain't nothing but a baby." I also got a lot of autographs from the stars. I remember when the Chi-Lites were on, and I got their autographs for my mom. I told them that one time when she was ill, they were on some TV show, and when she saw them, she got better.

SM: Who were your favorite dance partners when you were on *Soul Train*?

WS: Diane Bruner, who was a sweetheart. There was also this pretty, classy girl from Pasadena whom I enjoyed dancing with.

SM: You were also a very sharp dresser on the show.

WS: I can remember being nine and ten years old, and my mother would buy me more clothes than toys. I was always into clothes growing up. On *Soul Train*, you had a whole month to get your outfits together. I had a girlfriend who sewed. There's one outfit in which I had on some knickerbockers and some knee socks and gold metallic shoes, and the knickerbockers had *Soul Train* spelled out in gold studs with gold patches on the knees. My girlfriend at the time made those for me. Another time, my mom and I were on Sunset Boulevard, and we saw this gold lamé suit. She paid ninety-five dollars for that suit, and it became a huge hit on the show. I just had my own natural style.

SM: Did you ever experience jealousy or pettiness from other dancers?

WS: I had a fight on the set with a dancer named Karl Grigsby. It was actually a one-punch fight. I hit him, and he hit the ground. He had been dancing on the show with a girl I had dated in high school named Lisa Baldwin, who was very pretty. I wasn't mad because I wasn't involved with her any longer, but for some reason, he was saying derogatory things to me. I don't know why. I was only sixteen years old, and he was a grown man, about twenty-two years old. At this particular Saturday taping, he just kept on nitpicking at me. So, at the Sunday taping, when we were filming the Soul Train Line, I was coming down the line, and there was a technical difficulty, and the taping stopped for some minutes. They made us start all over. I said out loud, "Aww, shucks! I was just getting started." Karl, who was on the other line, said out loud, "They cut the line because they didn't want two bitches coming down the line together!" Everybody just sort of went, "Ooh!" In the sea of all those dancers, all I saw was Karl Grigsby. I remember parting all the way through the line, hitting that dude dead in the jaw, and knocking him to the ground. I knocked him out cold. Bam! Next thing I knew, Don called me and Karl to the back. I thought for sure we were going to get kicked off the show. Don said, "Man, why do y'all want to f—k up my show?" I told him I didn't want to hit Karl, but that he kept saying derogatory things to me. Don said, "Needless to say, if you weren't who you are..." And then he looked at Karl and said, "And if you weren't who you are, you guys would both be out of here for good. You guys think you can get along on the set?" I said, "I'm fine." Karl

Grigsby treated me with love from that day forward.

SM: When you stopped dancing on *Soul Train*, did you just get tired of it, or did you just want to move on? What was the reason?

WS: It was a bad move for me to stop because I had so much notoriety, but I didn't really know what to do with it. I should have continued on there, because it was free exposure. I could have branched right off into acting. When I turned eighteen, I just stopped dancing on there. I figured I wasn't making any money at it, so I just stopped.

SM: What did you do after leaving *Soul Train*?

WS: I did some college, and then I went to New York and attempted modeling in my late teens and early twenties, which was pretty unsuccessful. I had a few jobs here and there. In my early twenties I did a little art direction and had a calligraphy business. I still do calligraphy and write poetry. But I thought I was too good to work a regular job, and time just kept passing by.

SM: You are now involved in fitness. How did that come about?

WS: I had a major injury in my late twenties, which had a lot to do with me being a vegetarian. I was a vegetarian for twenty-four years. When I stopped being a vegetarian in February 2002, my body started breaking down, and I was skinny. I started having pains for no reason and injuries from nowhere. So, I started eating fish again, but it was difficult. I'm a devout carnivore now. I eat chicken and fish 90 percent of the time. I eat beef at least once a week or two or three times a month. I'm lean and cut and look very athletic, long and lean like a wide receiver. I'm strong, healthy, and fit.

SM: Who do you credit with helping you get to where you are now physically?

WS: I met a young man named Mykel Shannon Jenkins from Texas in 2004. He worked with the Dallas Cowboys and the Louisiana State University track team (LSU). His son Bryce is performing on Broadway. Mykel taught me how to train, how to rehabilitate my body, and how to eat properly. I eat four to five small protein meals a day, drink protein shakes, drink a lot of water, and take my herbs. It was an evolutionary thing for me.

SM: So, now you have your own business as a physical fitness therapist.

WS: Yes. In my late twenties, I became a physical therapist as an apprentice to the program they had me in. Because I had gone through so much with my back, they offered me an accelerated program, and I accepted it. I also learned deep tissue massage, which really heals injuries. I eventually evolved into a healer. I have many letters from clients that have been dealing with injuries for years, and after seeing me for short periods of time, they went into 83 percent recovery. Now, I have my own business called Power Performance. All of my business is done from referrals. I've been doing very well for the last fifteen or sixteen years. I'm also going on commercial auditions and I'm taking voice lessons. God always puts you where you are supposed to be.

SM: How would you describe your overall experience with *Soul Train*?

WS: It was one of the most fun times I ever had in my life.

SM: What would you like to say in memory of Don Cornelius?

WS: His death broke my heart. I'll never forget one time Pam Brown was going to make me leave because my name was not on the list. Don walked up to her and said, "Pam, he can stay."

SM: What word of wisdom do you want to share?

WS: When I see my peers who have let themselves go and become comforted by the fact they are of a certain age and have an excuse to be overweight and not take care of themselves, I say to them, "You have to keep dreaming, keep reaching, keep aspiring, keep striving. To try is to lie, but to strive is to arrive." You have to strive to be better. I have a reason to love myself and take care of myself, and I'm still aspiring. You've got to keep reaching, aspiring, and loving yourself. The best thing you can do is live well and take care of yourself.

# Roderick Dolphin

(1973–1979)

> Ironically, although he was a good dancer, he didn't go on *Soul Train* to dance, but to be a sort of a bodyguard to one of his dear friends on the show who was getting bullied by some of the other dancers. But once he came on, he enjoyed it, particularly hanging out in the bleachers on set talking to the young ladies. This athlete, model, singer, producer and songwriter has quite an interesting story.

**SM**: When did you first go on *Soul Train*?

RD: It was in 1973. My friend Karl Grigsby was already on the show. He said to me, "Man, you can dance and everything. You should be on the show." But that wasn't his purpose for me being on the show. He wanted me to be on the show for his protection because he was getting beat up. At that time, I was a muscular athletic track star and football player. When people would see me with Karl, they thought I was his brother.

SM: Why did people want to beat Karl up?

RD: Karl was comedic. He would get under people's skin, so people wanted to beat him up. That's why I was brought to the show: to alleviate the situation and protect him. Karl and I were from Pasadena. We

CURRENT PHOTO

BACK IN THE DAY

had a little clique, the Pasadena clique. Karl was a skilled comedian, and he would crack on the guys from the rougher parts of Los Angeles.

SM: Aside from going on *Soul Train* to be Karl Grigsby's unofficial bodyguard [laughs] was dancing on *Soul Train* something you always wanted to do?

RD: No. I was always the athlete. But I had a lot of friends in Los Angeles in the entertainment business. My closest friend was Ray Charles Jr. and his little clique. They laughed and said, "You're going on that show?" Karl and his brothers Norman and Joe were the only ones who supported me going on *Soul Train*, but my friends thought it was a "clownsmanship" to go on *Soul Train*. They didn't see it as respectable to go on *Soul Train*.

SM: You personally never got into any fights yourself with anyone on set, did you?

RD: No, because I looked too intimidating! [laughs] I just gave people that look!

SM: Did you have any favorite dance styles?

RD: My favorite dance was the cha-cha, so people would call me Mr. Cha-Cha. I also liked to dress up.

SM: Once you got on the show, did you have to try out?

RD: No. Pam Brown saw me, and she said, "You will do just fine on *Soul Train*."

SM: Aside from Karl Grigsby, who were among your other friends at *Soul Train*?

RD: I was friends with Linda Howard and Thyais Walsh, two dancers from Pasadena, where I grew up. Later on, my hangout crew included Karl, Jeffrey Daniels, and Jody Watley. I really wasn't interested in being on the show, but after I got on the show, oh wow! The lights came on, and it was action time! All my relatives on the East Coast and New England were like, "My cousin's on *Soul Train*!"

SM: What was the recognition like?

RD: Oh, man! When my grandfather, who was a pastor, passed away in 1975, I went back to New Haven, Connecticut. *Soul Train* was so huge there. My relatives were telling people, "My cousin dances on *Soul Train*." People would come to relatives' houses to watch me dance on *Soul Train*. They didn't care about the other dancers like Rerun and Don Campbell; they just wanted to see me.

SM: What are your memories of artists who performed on the show?

RD: There were some artists I wondered how they got on *Soul Train*! [laughs] But in the eight years I was on the show, I really enjoyed and loved the Sylvers. They had that six-part harmony. There was also Marvin Gaye, whom I remember standing out in the middle of the crowd, and all the dancers were just swooning. He is one of my all-time favorite artists. I also enjoyed Sly Stone and the Philly groups who came to the show. But a lot of the artists I met on my own outside of *Soul Train* like Eddie Kendricks and Chaka Khan.

SM: Did you ever go down the Soul Train Line at all?

RD: Yes, I did, once. But it wasn't something I really wanted to do. I wasn't trying to get on the risers or do the Soul Train Line or the Scramble Board. I was suave. I wanted to cha-cha and dress up in Italian suits and designer shoes and hang out in the bleachers, flirting with the women. Then the floor director would yell, "You have to come out on the floor now," and I would be like, "Aww man!" [laughs]

SM: I recall those days when the crew would have to set up the stage for the artists and the dancers would have to wait around.

RD: Oh, man! All day long! The breaks on the bleachers were something I looked forward to, and of course, the Kentucky Fried Chicken! They fed us good!

SM: You were also mistaken for a recording artist sometimes, right?

RD: Right. I used to go to concerts, and women would rush up to me thinking I was Scotty of The Whispers and wanted my autograph! [laughs]

SM: Did you ever interact with Don Cornelius?

RD: Don was so cool! What I appreciated about Don was his hospitality. I would go to his house and I could take my shoes off. He was always Mr. Control, and he was the smartest one in the room when it came to *Soul Train*. He was like a disciplinarian. But at his home, it was clownsmanship. He loved my friend Karl, and he gave him a fifteen-minute slot on the show once.

SM: The other dancers told me about the clubs all of you used to go to.

RD: Oh, yes! The Summit on the Hill and Maverick's Flat were among them,

SM: Were there any other situations that you recall involving Karl getting nearly beat up?

RD: Soul Train dancer Tyrone Swan got into an altercation with Karl on the set. Another time, there was a personal matter involving Karl and Fred "Rerun" Berry when we were all over at Karl's house. Rerun came over and started beating on the door. He kicked the door in and came in the house. Karl and Rerun got in a tussle and rolled down a long flight of stairs. They were rolling and fighting down fifty stair steps! It was a real sight.

SM: How did you get into modeling?

RD: I started making my migration from dancing on *Soul Train* to modeling in 1976. Michael Dorn from *Star Trek* was the wide receiver on my football team in high school, and he helped me get started in modeling.

SM: Karl Grigsby passed away several years ago. Talk to me about Karl's work as a comedian.

RD: As a model, I would do fashion shows, and Karl would supply the comedy at these shows. I would bring a band in to play music and bring food. We would go to different locations to do different productions. Karl was so naturally funny. He would have you crying with laughter so hard that you would want to call 9-1-1. You would lie on the floor laughing! That's how good Karl was.

SM: Karl was on his way to becoming a big comedian in show business.

RD: He became very well known around Los Angeles and in the entertainment community. I would even go with him to the Jackson family's house. We didn't even have to call them. We'd just ring the bell. We were at their house consistently. Aretha Franklin lived not far from them at one time too, right around the corner, and we'd go over to her house.

SM: I heard Aretha made some great dishes!

RD: Man, I remember the first time I met Aretha at her home, she was laying on her couch with her shoes off, and she said, "Don't expect me to make y'all no food. Y'all go in the kitchen and make your own food." [laughs]

SM: [laughs] Aretha didn't play!

RD: Nope! [laughs] Aretha's son, Eddie, was so cool and so down to earth. He would bring Karl and me over to his house and hang out with him and talk to his mom. Karl took me over to Howard Hewitt's house when he was married to Nia Peeples. He had a White baby grand piano and a white bear rug. I even drove Howard to the Grammys since I drove limos at one time.

SM: Wow, Karl was really getting known in entertainment circles.

RD: We would also go to Richard Pryor's house. Richard would say, "Karl's more funny than me Rod! I love this guy. He's gonna be the greatest!" But nothing really happened with Karl like it was supposed to. He was just that funny guy who made you laugh, and he was accepted everywhere.

SM: You were dancing on and off *Soul Train* while you were on the show, but you did a number of other things in the entertainment industry, including working with Redd Foxx. How did this come about?

RD: While I'm grateful to *Soul Train* for the exposure, it wasn't my claim to fame. One time at a fashion show, someone saw me model a mink coat, and I threw it off, and all I had on was my underwear. The audience thought it was swimwear, but it was my underwear. So, when I threw off my mink coat and walked on it everybody went crazy! One of Redd Foxx's people came up to me and asked if I would be interested in interviewing for Redd Foxx Productions. I was like, "Yeah!" So, I was flown out to Saudi Arabia and modeled, danced, and sang with Redd Foxx Productions for two years.

SM: Nice! And you were involved with editing magazines, right?

RD: Right. I became an assistant editor of a magazine—two, actually. One was *Class*, an all-male magazine, and *Style*, a men's and women's magazine out of Beverly Hills.

SM: You actually went to school for modeling at one point, right?

RD: Yes, I went to the Barbizon School for Modeling. I had a friend named Art who I am still friends with. He was six-foot-four and had high cheekbones, and he looked like a model. Me? I'm five-foot-eleven, 180 pounds, and muscular. I was liked for my charm and poise, and I was an athlete. I was supposed to run in the 1980 Olympics, but President Carter stated that the US would boycott the Olympics that were to be held in Moscow that summer.

SM: You are also a great and accomplished singer as well.

RD: Thank you! I am a writer, singer, and producer. I modeled up to 1981. I will never forget that when I lived with the group DeBarge for a year before their *All This Love* album came out, and they asked me if I wanted to sign up with Motown. I told them, "Nope!" I wasn't aspiring to do this back at *Soul Train*. I never went up to Don Cornelius and said, “Hey Don, you know I can sing,” nor was I ever over at the Jacksons or DeBarge’s homes saying, “I can sing!”

SM: In addition to singing, songwriting and producing, you currently scout and manage artists and repertoire (A&R) for TPNG Media.

RD: Yes, and that’s because of my music actually. I was the president of A&R for T REX Radio out of Montreal, Canada, and the reason that was offered to me was because my song, “So Grateful,” went number one in Canada and India internationally and was also #27 on the Slow Jazz charts. I had three number ones back-to-back. I have a song that went number three on the India International chart titled “Why You Want to Treat Me This Way.” I would love to break into the Billboard Top 10, but I will leave that in God’s hand

SM: It’s interesting that in the early seventies no one knew *Soul Train* would last as long as it did, nobody. I remember in an interview Don said he was a little concerned about *Soul Train*’s longevity when disco music was popular and several disco oriented dance shows came on. But *Soul Train* carried on through disco and rap.

RD: I am so grateful to have had the opportunity to be a part of *Soul Train*. A lot of people clowned on me for being on the show but look at me now! They probably look back and wish they were on the show.

SM: What do you want to say in memory of Don Cornelius?

RD: That was a very sad moment when he died. Don was one of the few people who would let me go in his refrigerator in his home and make a sandwich. If it wasn’t for *Soul Train*, I wouldn’t have the exposure or the confidence to do the things I did in the business. *Soul Train* blessed us dancers with so many opportunities, and it gave me an opportunity to model. I was blessed at a young age to have all those opportunities and to be able to do what I’m doing now and help people.

SM: What word of wisdom do you want to share?

RD: God has just been so good to me, and I just stay humble and thankful. I learned from my experiences that no matter what anyone else says or if they are going to support you or not, you have got to keep pushing. I may not make it where I should be, but I am just grateful for what I have, and I try to help people because I am in a position to help people now.

CURRENT PHOTO

BACK IN THE DAY

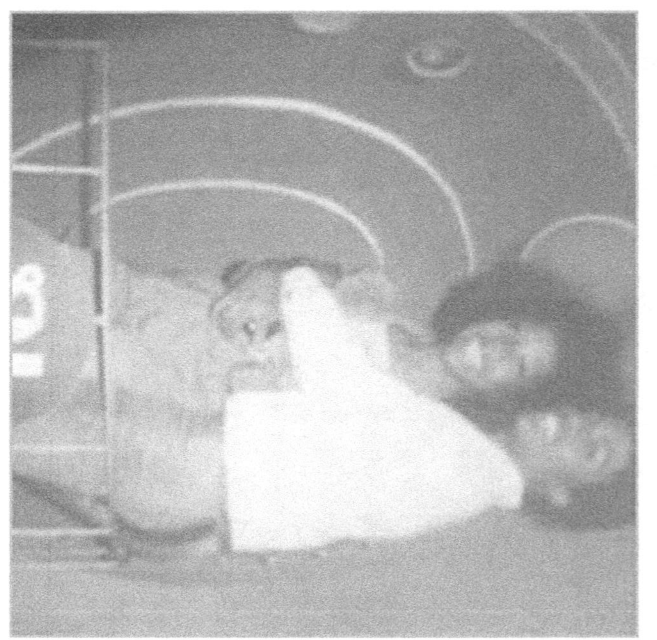

# Benita Hill Johnson

(1973–1977)

This pretty young lady enjoyed her time dancing on *Soul Train* even though she was shy at times. She was also the best of friends with the late and great Natalie Cole, and she, along with another good friend Chaka Khan, helped to guide her daughters into a burgeoning singing career.

**S**M: How did you become a Soul Train dancer?

BJ: Through Pat Davis. She and I used to walk home from high school together. She lived a little further than I did, so once we got to my block, I was like, "Okay, girl, talk to you tomorrow," and then she'd go on. So, we pretty much became friends in school. She was more popular in school than I was. I was more like a nerd. She was already dancing on the show and asked me if I ever wanted to go on the show. So, she set it up for me, and I was on the show.

SM: Great! What do you remember about your first day on the set?

BJ: It was scary. [laughs] Sometimes, I was nervous and didn't want to dance, but then Pam Brown would say, "Come on now, come on!" And after being on there a while, probably after three or four shows, Pam would say, "Now Benita, when you're dancing, you have to look up and smile because the camera is there." I was so shy and petrified, but I took what she said to heart. Once I started doing it, I got lots of camera time and started being placed on the riser. I was never *not* nervous, though!

SM: When you did the Soul Train Scramble Board with Jeffrey Daniel, did you do it in one take or several takes like some other dancers told me?

BJ: Just one take. The interesting thing is that Jeffrey and I had already known each other in third grade. We grew up together in the projects in East Los Angeles. My mom was his den mother in the Cub Scouts. So, when he came to *Soul Train*, it was like a reunion.

SM: Did you get your hair care products and a one-year's subscription of *Essence* magazine?

BJ: I sure did!

SM: What are your favorite memories of recording artists that came on the show during what I like to call the golden era of *Soul Train.*

BJ: One was when the Spinners came on and did "Rubberband Man." In the first take, Phillipe Wynne brought me up on the stage. He had me holding the end of this gigantic rubber band, and I was supposed to dance with it. I didn't know what to do, so I'm kind of twisting the rubber band while some of the dancers were telling me "Benita, do this! Benita, do that!" I couldn't hear a thing they were saying. I was looking into that camera thinking, "Please let this be over!" [laughs] We taped the whole thing, but then they did it over. It never bothered me that they redid it. Other fond memories of artists that came to the show were Labelle when they did "Lady Marmalade," Chaka Khan, whom I already knew before, Donna Summer, Melba Moore, The Whispers, Smokey Robinson, Michael Jackson, Aretha Franklin, Gladys Knight & the Pips, and Billy Preston.

SM: You have an interesting story about Billy Preston.

BJ: Billy Preston did a tour with the Rolling Stones, and I got to be one of the dancers on the stage with Billy Preston and the Rolling Stones along with Damita Jo Freeman, Pat Davis, and Sharon Hill; there were about eight of us. It was so exciting. We were backstage at the Forum. After one of the shows, Diana Ross gave a party at her house. We were all invited, and I was like, "I can't believe I am at Diana Ross's house!" It was just one of those very special moments.

SM: What was the recognition like when your relatives and friends saw you on *Soul Train*?

BJ: It was weird. On my block, they used to call me the star. I was very uncomfortable with that. People would be having family gatherings, and the relatives would be over, and they'd all see me and say, "That's her, that's her!" It was really bizarre.

SM: Did you crave that chicken during those long *Soul Train* tapings? [laughs]

BJ: You'd be so hungry you'd be glad for the two pieces of chicken, the biscuit, and that off-brand can of soda! [laughs]

SM: Did you experience any disappointments or less than pleasant moments at *Soul Train*?

BJ: No, not really. However, there was one girl on the show who was so rude and mean to me. Years later, she told me she was jealous because I was good friends with a mutual friend of hers, but we became friends after she apologized.

SM: Other than the Scramble Board, did you ever interact with Don?

BJ: Oh yes, even outside of *Soul Train*. Years later, I saw him on different occasions when he would have the Soul Train Music Awards and the Soul Train Christmas Starfest specials. I would see him at those events, and he would always acknowledge me and give me a slight peck on the cheek.

SM: You and Natalie Cole were the best of friends, almost like sisters. How did your friendship with her begin?

BJ: I actually met her through Chaka Khan. Natalie and Chaka had met and did some shows in Japan. When Chaka and Rufus were doing a show in West Hollywood, Natalie attended and sat next to me. We were whooping it up like we had known each other forever. When the show was over, she was like, "Okay, Benita, bye!" I was like, "She remembered my name." Sometime after that, there was a big outdoor summer jam concert at the Coliseum, and Chaka Khan and Rufus were performing there. Natalie had flown in from Chicago to attend.

I saw her another time with her husband, Marvin, at this get-together Chaka had where everyone brought a dish. When Chaka needed to go to the store, she told me, "When Nat comes, just show her around and tell her where the pots and pans are." So, Natalie comes in; she had this real funky attitude, and I was trying to be really nice. So, I basically ignored Natalie the rest of the time.

Later, when I was in the middle of the floor just dancing and being a clown, Natalie was leaning up against the doorpost to the kitchen. I was still ignoring her because of what had happened earlier. She started laughing and said, "Girl, you are so silly!" I'm looking at her like, "Huh?" She became a totally different person, and we were okay after that. So, the three of us, me, Chaka, and Natalie started hanging out a lot.

Things changed, and eventually, it was just more of me and Natalie hanging out. Chaka and I were still good friends, but me and Natalie were alike in a lot of ways. That's how Natalie and I initially became real good friends.

SM: What do you want to say in Natalie's memory?

BJ: Natalie and I were close friends for over forty years, and we were together most of that time. We even lived together at one time and traveled together. She was at all the major events in my life, and I was at all the major events in her life. Everything just intertwined with each of our lives. You just don't know how to live without that person being there. It's a struggle. I miss her.

SM: Your daughters are singers, right?

BJ: Yes, they are. They are twenty-eight-year-old twins named Chyna Maria Johnson and Chrystal Brielle Johnson. They started singing professionally over ten years ago. Both Natalie and Chaka taught them a lot. My husband passed away in 2008, and up to then, I had worked and traveled with Natalie. I manage and help my daughters' careers, and I'm always going to be guiding them on their musical goals and career.

SM: What do you want to say in memory of Don Cornelius?

BJ: I can't help but be appreciative of him and his vision and all the effort and diligence he put in to bring his show to fruition. He had to fight for it. I'm not sure if he even knew what it was going to turn into. But he stuck to it, and he blessed, developed, and brought opportunities to so many of us that we wouldn't have had if it weren't for him and his vision.

SM: What word of wisdom do you want to share?

BJ: If you have dreams and goals, don't let other people tell you who you're supposed to be and what you're supposed to be doing. Find a way to stick to it. You may not be able to achieve it right away but stick to it and don't let other people guide and design your life.

BACK IN THE DAY

CURRENT PHOTO

# Gwendolyn Powell

(1974–1976)

> Initially a visitor to the *Soul Train* set, she eventually became a Soul Train dancer and loved making friends with the other dancers and meeting the celebrities. *Soul Train* was also where she first met her future husband Adolfo "Shabba Doo" Quinones of The Lockers. You can call her story a kind of "Soul Train Love Story."

SM: Before you climbed aboard the *Soul Train*, were there any dancers on the show you admired?

GP: Back in the seventies, female dancers like Pat Davis, Damita Jo Freeman, Wanda Robinson, Fawn Quinones, Freddie Maxie, and Thelma Davis were among the dancers I admired. The seventies were the roots.

SM: How did you get on *Soul Train*?

GP: I was so shy, but my father was the one who actually got me on the show. At the time, he was a district manager of a maintenance and security company for several businesses, including KTLA, the studio where *Soul Train* was taped. He knew all the security guards that oversaw and monitored the grounds. He was told that if he had any children and wanted to bring them to a *Soul Train* taping, he should let them know. When my father asked me, "By the way, would you like to come down one weekend and watch a taping of *Soul Train*?" I looked at him like, "Are you kidding me? Of course!" So, he made arrangements with security to put us on *Soul Train*'s guest list. So, that's how I got on the show.

SM: Did you become a regular dancer that weekend?

GP: No, not yet. After that weekend, we were wondering how we could come back to the show again. On the first weekend, we were on the guest list to just sit, watch, and observe the show. After that, we made friends with a couple of people and found out when they were going to hold auditions. So, we went to auditions at Denker Park, and Pam Brown, the dance coordinator, liked us because we were always dressed up, and she added us to the list.

SM: When you were selected to do the Scramble Board, you had on quite an elaborate outfit!

GP: Don clowned me when he was interviewing me and said, "I see Gwendolyn, you didn't come dressed for the occasion." I just chuckled! But my friend Dennis Rich, one of the regulars back then, put that whole outfit together, actually.

SM: It was a very beautiful outfit. If I didn't know that was you, I would have thought they had a famous movie actress doing the Scramble Board. [laughs]

GP: I think that's why Pam and Don chose me that day, because of that outfit. Dennis and I would always go shopping and frequent the Fairfax district and especially Hollywood Boulevard. We saw that dress in Little Boutique on Hollywood Boulevard and I think we went to Frederick's of Hollywood and found the white boa. He found the red platform shoes with fake diamonds that were real glittery. I probably looked like a clown. [laughs]

SM: Did you receive your Afro Sheen and Ultra Sheen products and one-year subscription of *Essence* magazine for solving the Scramble Board? Because quite a few people told me they never received anything.

GP: Yes, I did, and I received a bright yellow eight-track player. I also received a plaque signed by George E. Johnson (Founder of Johnson Hair Care products), and I still have it.

SM: What are some of your favorite memories of artists that came to *Soul Train*?

GP: The three that really stand out for me in my mind are, first of all, Eddie Kendricks. He was one of the guest stars, and I loved me some Eddie Kendricks! [laughs] He was my favorite member of The Temptations. I remember watching him as a child when the Temptations appeared on *Ed Sullivan* on Sunday nights, and also when the Supremes would appear with them. So, when I heard Eddie Kendricks was going to be a guest on that day's taping I was like, "Oh my God!" When he came out on stage and did his numbers, he was so cordial. He gave me a big ole hug and kissed me on the cheek, and I thought I was going to pass out! [laughs] He took a photo with me and put his arm around my little waist. I couldn't believe it!

The second was when Pam Brown asked if I could stand around the piano while Ashford and Simpson performed a love song about being real. My third favorite artist memory was when Sly and the Family Stone appeared on the show. He was walking up to the stage, and I almost got stampeded that day when Sly was there. Those kids went bananas when he showed up! We were in that studio until one or two o'clock in the morning! I got in so much trouble with my parents when I got home because he was late showing up. I was like, "I don't care. I'm just catching heck because I wanted to see Sly and the Family Stone!" [laughs] Before one of his performances, for some reason he spotted me and grabbed my hand and started rubbing it. He told me "You have beautiful hands." He just kept rubbing my hands and then went up on stage. [laughs]

Me: [laughs] You didn't wash your hand for a week, huh?

GP: Are you kidding me? I didn't wash my hand for a month! [laughs]

SM: Did you enjoy the chicken? [laughs]

GP: You took it there! [laughs] For a while, you could deal with it due to the coleslaw and mashed potatoes that went along with it. But the chicken was so doggone soggy and oily that most of the time, we would leave the studio and go to Hamburger Hamlet, Arby's, or even Pioneer Chicken which had crispy chicken. But trust we would crave that box of chicken! Sometimes, the tapings would run into the early evening and midnight, and we'd be hungry, and we couldn't leave, so we would sometimes take some paper towels and wipe some of the oil off the chicken and eat it.

SM: What was it like going down the Soul Train Line?

GP: I was scared to death and nervous as heck! I remember one time coming down that line that the couple that just went down were Eddie Cole and Wanda Robinson, and they always danced their tails off! Me and my partner had to go after them. I was like, "Oh my God! I can't go down the line after them!" We didn't have anything rehearsed. But we did it! [laughs] It got easier. But the first few times I went down the line, I was a nervous wreck! I thought my heart was going to jump out of my mouth.

SM: What was the recognition like for you dancing on the show?

GP: I grew up in Compton, and I became pretty popular in my neighborhood. Some of The Lockers, such as Fred, who we called Penguin back then, would come to our house to eat along with Shab (Shabba Doo), James Phillips, and Karl Grigsby. My girlfriends on the block would be like, "Oh my God! I just saw those guys on *Soul Train* or in *Right On!* Magazine! You're friends with these guys?" That kind of gave me a little clout in the hood. A few times, I would go shopping in the mall and people would take pictures of me and ask, "Don't you dance on *Soul Train*?" Also, one day, when I was a stenographer for the LA Unified School District, my boss asked me into his office and said, "Shut the door." So, I was thinking, I had messed up on something.

When I got in there, he goes "I've got to ask you something." I said, "What's that?" And he says, "Did I see you on *Soul Train*?" I said, "Yes." He said, "I can't believe it! I told my children, 'I think that's my secretary.' I'm gonna ask her Monday when I go to work." [laughs]

SM: Did you experience any jealousy from other dancers or from people in your neighborhood?

GP: Yes. Not from my neighborhood but from the show. There were a couple of haters on there.

SM: What about the memories of the clubs in LA?

GP: Yes. Maverick's Flat, the Citadel, Summit on the Hill, Blueberry Hill, Total Experience. Back in the day, there were so many clubs down on Crenshaw; it was crazy.

SM: You were married to Shabba Doo at one time. How did you two meet?

GP: I used to see him from time to time. He and a couple of The Lockers would pop in on Soul Train and goof around and come down the Soul Train Line and then leave. At the time, he had a girlfriend on the show who was one of the butterfly girls. His sister Fawn and I clicked, and she wanted to introduce me to him. But since he had a girlfriend already, I didn't want to make any waves, so he and I really didn't talk. He used to tell me he would see me when he came to the show. I remember one particular Saturday I had worn this foxtail fur because I liked to dress like the forties and fifties. He commented on the fur I had on, and he said, "I like your outfit." His girlfriend kind of nodded her head; she was not too happy about it.

SM: When did the two of you really get to know each other?

GP: On the *Midnight Special*. There was a tribute to Soul Train on this particular episode and Don was hosting it, so he brought some of the dancers on. The Lockers and Harold Melvin & the Blue Notes were among the guests. Shabba Doo came over and sat with us and asked, "Do you guys have any food?" [laughs] So, we happened to have Golden Bird fried chicken, which we bought before coming out to Burbank, and we shared our dinner with him. That's how we met. He asked me for my phone number, and it took off from there. We were married for six years from 1976 to 1981.

SM: Any fond memories you want to share when you and Shabba Doo were married?

GP: Life with him was so exciting. He was so fun-loving. There were a lot of great moments, but two stand out. When I was giving birth to our son Vashawn, Fawn and Leo were telling Shabba Doo that he needed tell the doctor that he took Lamaze classes. So, they eventually convinced him, and he told the doctors. So, they gave him scrubs to wear and he came into the delivery room. I almost passed out at the time our son was born, but he hung in there and watched our son come into the world.

Another good moment I recall is when he did a tour with Bette Midler, and Luther Vandross was one of Bette's backup singers with the Harlettes. Whenever Luther came to LA, he would make it a point to come to me and Shab's apartment and have dinner. He loved my cooking! His favorite dish was smothered pork chops, rice, gravy, collard greens, and candy yams!

SM: All right now! That's what I'm talking about. *Sooooul* food! [laughs] So, tell me, what was your overall experience with *Soul Train*?

GP: It was a joy and honor to be on the show. It was a special part of Black history.

SM: What would you like to say in memory of Shabba Doo?

GP: He left a street dance legacy, considering he had no formal training. He had a large following, and his legacy will live on forever. My feeling is that the kids now aren't doing anything different under the sun; it's already been done. They're just putting a different kind of flavor to it, but it's basically what our young men from Watts and Compton did and what Shabba Doo did from when he was in Chicago. They laid the groundwork for all these new styles of dancers. It all stems from The Lockers.

SM: What would you like to say in memory of Don Cornelius and his passing?

GP: I couldn't believe it. I was getting ready for work, and I heard an announcement on the news about him. I had to sit down. I was like, "What? This cannot be true." He had a vision. He was a groundbreaker. His show was a success for several decades. A syndicated Black show lasting that many years? Incredible!

SM: What word of wisdom do you want to share?

GP: Don't let anyone tear down your self-confidence. Whatever your dreams are, pursue them, and don't let anyone or anything deter you from them. You're going to be criticized for whatever you want to do. Whether it's being a doctor, a lawyer, a dancer, or a performer, there's going to be somebody or some people who are going to criticize you. Don't let them get in your head to kill your joy and destroy your passion. Just tune them out and do you because if you don't, you will always have that doubt in your mind, the "what ifs" and the "woulda, coulda, shouldas."

BACK IN THE DAY

CURRENT PHOTO

# Leonard Jones

(1974–1977)

> Leonard Jones was one of the standout seventies dancers on *Soul Train* with his wide smile and together dance moves, as well as those sharp and chic suits he wore. Aside from being a Soul Train dancer, Leonard was blessed with musical talent since childhood and in the years since *Soul Train* has become a sought-after musician and producer working with major artists. But it all began when he danced on *Soul Train*.

SM: Before you danced on *Soul Train*, what were your aspirations growing up?

LJ: Basically, what I am doing right now is writing music and producing songs. God gifted me with the ability to recreate whatever I heard. I used to walk to school singing songs, and in church, I played drums and piano, so what I am doing now just kind of grew out of those experiences.

SM: Were there any artists who inspired you or influenced you?

LJ: Yes, Donny Hathaway and Dexter Wansel were two artists that appealed to me.

SM: How did you become a dancer on *Soul Train*?

LJ: I did a martial arts exhibit at Los Angeles Community College (LACC). After it was over, a young lady who was a dancer on *Soul Train* said she liked my moves and asked if I would like to come on the show as her dance partner. I said yes, and the rest, as they say, is history.

SM: What do you remember about that first day on *Soul Train*?

LJ: It was an extremely long day! I had never been in a television studio before, so that was a first for me. Also, I got a box of Kentucky Fried Chicken for lunch! It was great seeing, meeting and fellowshipping with all of the dancers and getting to know everybody. It grew from there into the Soul Train family we have now. To all the dancers who have passed away, including Little Joe Chism and Jermaine Stewart, I pay my respects. When I watch the old shows, it's sad that half of the guys are gone.

SM: Indeed. As I always say, the seventies Soul Train dancers were the roots that influenced the dancers who followed, including myself, definitely. You wore some really together suits and dressed so sharp. Where did you get your suits from?

LJ: Out of a store called Zeidler & Zeidler, which had a large chain of clothing stores. Because I worked at the store, I was able to utilize the store's clothing and would wear it in various issues of *Right On*! magazine. I used to be called the GQ of *Soul Train.*[1]

SM: Wasn't there an incident when you fell in a swimming pool? LJ: Right! I was wearing one of my suits and was trying to impress a girl in the pool area and I wound up falling in the pool! [laughs]

SM: You did the Soul Train Scramble Board several times! Do you have any leftover containers of Ultra Sheen and Afro Sheen products you won as prizes? [laughs]

LJ: [laughs] But you know what's funny? I never received any of the

1 GQ is the abbreviation for *Gentlemen's Quarterly*, a publication featuring culture, politics, and news and men's fashion. The nickname attests to Leonard Jones's sophisticated fashion sense.

Ultra Sheen or Afro Sheen products. I got the eight-track cassette player, but I never got the Ultra Sheen or Afro Sheen products!

SM: I never received anything either after doing the Scramble Board, but at least we got the KFC!

LJ: [laughs] Yeah! I actually did get one or two bottles of Afro Sheen, but not a year's supply of the products as was promised. But those were some really good times.

SM: I know you've seen numerous artists perform on *Soul Train*, but were there any particular artists that stand out from your memory that performed on the show?

LJ: For sure! Labelle, Minnie Riperton, James Brown, and Marvin Gaye. When Nancy Wilson came on the show, she kissed me on the cheek and told me I was cute.

SM: I'll bet you didn't wash your face for a week!

LJ: I had a big crush on her. There were many artists I was able to talk to. They would be in the green room, but for some reason, we were able to strike up conversations with them, which was cool. Marlon Jackson and I were pretty tight back in the day. I lived in Tarzana, and the Jacksons lived in Encino, and I would always run into them. I remember going to the Jacksons' house on Hayvenhurst Avenue and showing Marlon how to do flips. Another group I recall on the show was The Commodores. I was Lionel Richie's favorite dancer. I was able to meet him at Hitsville West, Motown's recording studio in Hollywood, and got a chance to see them rehearse. I also worked with Walter Orange of the Commodores.

SM: Did you have a favorite dance partner while you were on the show?

LJ: Crystal, Keedah, Benita Hill, and a whole bunch of others, but I thoroughly enjoyed those first three I mentioned.

SM: Since I am a Robot dancer, I have to say that I really admired your Robot dancing. I saw one particular show, and you were roboting like Michael Jackson.

LJ: Thanks! Back then, all of the dances you saw that we did on *Soul Train* we were doing at Maverick's Flat on Crenshaw. That was the place! We'd see all kinds of people there, like Richard Pryor, Undisputed Truth, and Lakeside. There was also a Soul Train dancer named Karl Grigsby who performed there as a comedian.

SM: I heard from all of the other dancers that those clubs in Los Angeles were really something, like the Climax and the Citadel.

LJ: Yeah, plus The Summit and Disco 9000. Those clubs were the places to be!

SM: Did you ever interact with Don Cornelius?

LJ: Don was a little standoffish, although he liked the way I dressed, and I was able to get on the risers. I also have to give a shout out to Pam Brown and her cousin and brother who passed. It was just one big happy family on the show.

SM: What was your first professional music job?

LJ: I worked with a local artist first, but the first real big job was working on the soundtrack of Disney's *The Little Mermaid*. Prior to that, I had done Jermaine Jackson's *Don't Take It Personal* tour, and the guy who hired me for Disney was Denzil "Broadway" Miller. I had my own recording studio, and he hired me to do the preproduction for *The Little Mermaid,* and it grew from there. I worked with Ray Charles during the last seven years of his life. I also worked with Earth, Wind & Fire and Phillip Bailey on one of his solo projects. I mixed and mastered Al McKay and the All Stars' *Live in Mount Fuji, Japan.* I also worked with The Whispers, The Commodores, Domino from Ghetto Jam, and many others.

SM: What would you like to say in memory of Don Cornelius?

LJ: Because of his vision, I am able to have a life. Blessings to you, Stephen, for helping to keep the spirit of *Soul Train* alive. There are so many lives that *Soul Train* definitely touched. Many former Soul Train dancers are still working, based upon what we did as kids on *Soul Train*.

SM: What word of wisdom do you want to share?

LJ: Whatever you want to do, do it with passion. Find something that you love to do, and it will make room for itself.

CURRENT PHOTO

BACK IN THE DAY

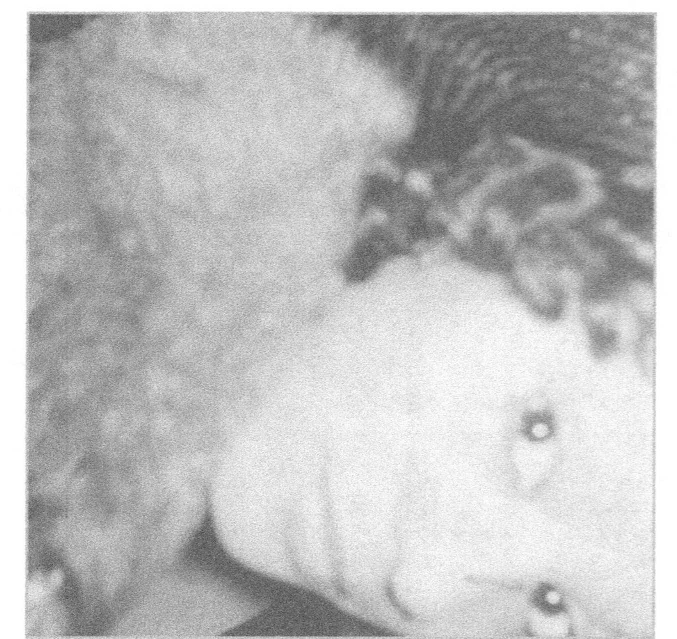

# Denise Weathersby

(1974–1976)

Denise Weathersby was one of the first women to be vice president of a major record label, Warner/Chappell Music, and was responsible for signing artists to the label for publishing deals, including Dru Hill, The Isley Brothers, and many others. Years later, as a former dancer on *Soul Train*, she had a working relationship with the show due to her prominent stature in the recording industry. She booked artists for the show, working directly with the program's creator, Don Cornelius. Here is her story.

SM: When you were growing up, what were your aspirations?

DW: I always had an interest in and love for music. I was a kid who would give my father a list of 45s and albums I wanted. When The Jackson 5's albums came out, I learned all of the lyrics and imitated them. Music and fashion were the industries I had a love for.

SM: How did your journey with *Soul Train* begin?

DW: A close friend of mine, Pam Wilson, and I went down to Metromedia Studios one Saturday to watch a taping of *Soul Train*. When we got there, Pam Brown approached both of us, and we were asked to dance on the show. That was the beginning: Pam took our information down, and for the next three or four years, we got our monthly call to come to the tapings.

SM: What were your impressions of Don Cornelius?

DW: My impression was that he was larger than life. He was somewhat intimidating, not in a negative way, but you knew where your place was!

SM: Did you ever do the Scramble Board?

DW: I did, and of course we knew the answers! [laughs] I got the Afro Sheen and Ultra Sheen kit.

SM: Do you have any special memories of recording artists that came to the show?

DW: Yes! At the time, there was a local club here in Los Angeles called the Total Experience, and a lot of artists like Blue Magic and Harold Melvin & the Blue Notes would appear at that club the same weekend they taped *Soul Train*. When Harold Melvin & the Blue Notes were on in between tapings, the dancers got a chance to talk to them as we did with many of the artists. On this day, I think they were the last artists to finish taping. and Teddy Pendergrass, instead of going to his limo, came with me and my girlfriend Pam to hang out. I had an orange 1974 Vega, and I remember saying, "Oh my God, I have Teddy Pendergrass in my car driving down Highland Avenue!"

SM: Did you have any other buddies on *Soul Train*?

DW: Patricia Davis, Vicki Abercrombie, Kim Jackson, Diana Bruner, and Sharon Hill.

SM: I always ask the dancers this, but Pam Brown was notorious for her gum ritual. Were you a target of her gum ritual?

DW: Oh, yes! Her cup was put in my face several times. [laughs]

SM: What did you do after you left *Soul Train*?

DW: I did a semester at Cal State LA. I followed that path until I got a major opportunity in which someone thought I was perfect for a position at A&M Records, and that was the beginning of my career in the music industry.

SM: What was your position?

DW: I was second secretary to the president of A&M Records, Gil Friesen. By the grace of God, I went through the ranks and earned a pretty prominent position in the music industry.

SM: What did you do after leaving A&M?

DW: After I left A&M Records, I worked for a musician named George Howard for several years, and I traveled the world. It was great! When I started working with him, he had just signed with MCA Records. I was working for the head of A&R, Louis Silas, and at that time, our department solely booked the acts on *Soul Train*. I never really knew Don while dancing on *Soul Train*, but there it was, ten or fifteen years later, when I got a chance to interact with Don on the business side. I got a chance to know him and found out that he and I share the same birthday.

SM: What was it like working with Don in a business capacity?

DW: Don did the booking of MCA's acts himself. Don and my boss Louis had a good rapport. So, he, Don, and myself would be on the phone. If Don would be interested in, let's say, Patti Labelle, Guy, Pebbles, Heavy D & the Boyz—or whoever was on the label—we would always negotiate. If we had a new act, we'd say, "You want the big act, but come on Don, we have this new act," and he would be like, "Uh, no I don't think so." [laughs] We'd be going back and forth. It was very interesting because I got the opportunity to be a part of his iconic show as a dancer and then, years later, work with him as a colleague. It was definitely a full circle moment.

SM: Would you attend *Soul Train* tapings when the label's acts performed on the show?

DW: Absolutely! I would go there with some of the acts throughout my

MCA and EMI Music Publishing days, as well as my Warner/Chappell days. I attended many *Soul Train* tapings with our artists. I also attended every Soul Train Music Awards ceremony until 2003. *Soul Train* was very instrumental in my life.

SM: How did your position as vice president of Warner/Chappell come about?

DW: I was at MCA for a number of years and that parlayed into a stint at EMI Music Publishing. I was the director there. After that, I went to Warner Chappell, starting there as Senior Director and ending as Vice President of Black Music. My position was signing songwriters, artists, and producers to publishing deals. You may not recognize the names of a lot of the songwriters that I signed, but you would certainly know their hits. Some of the artists you would recognize are Johnny Gill, Bone Thugz & Harmony, Dru Hill, Naughty By Nature, and The Isley Brothers. I also signed writers who wrote songs for 2Pac and many others. It was a great time to be in the music industry. A lot of things were happening. I received a lot of gold and platinum plaques for songs I participated in by either the artist or songwriter or both, whether it was 2Pac, Dr. Dre, Janet Jackson, Usher, or others.

SM: Being in the music industry, which is dominated by men as chairs and CEOs, you being a Black woman as vice president must have been a real honor for you. What was that like for you?

DW: I felt that I had accomplished something that I never could have imagined. When I got my first job in the music industry, I thought that it was great just to be a secretary in the industry. I never could have imagined making vice president. In my first four or five years at Warner/ Chappell, I was fortunate enough to work under their first female vice president at the time. When she retired, I was elevated to her position. The recording industry is a male-dominant field; most of the executives in promotion and A&R and managers are men. There are a few of us who are women and fewer of us who are Black women. I enjoyed my position. It was great and fabulous, and I have no regrets.

SM: What are you doing currently?

DW: I officially left the music industry in 2005. I had quite a few independent offers, whether it was starting a publishing company or working exclusively for a few of my artists which was very flattering, but I had lost a lot of the passion. The music industry, as you very well know, has changed dramatically. I had the interest, but I didn't have the passion anymore. By that time, I had met the love of my life, Shelby Middleton, an accountant with William Morris Agency, who became my husband on June 10, 2007. A very good friend of mine, Angela Winbush, was a bridesmaid in my wedding and Johnny Gill and Howard Hewitt sang at my wedding.

SM: What would you like to say in Don's memory?

DW: Don was very instrumental in my youth and in my career. His path, foundation and legacy are phenomenal, and I have nothing but respect and good thoughts for Mr. Cornelius, my fellow Libra.

SM: Do you have a word of wisdom you want to share?

DW: In life, follow your dreams and reach for the moon. You might not make the moon, but you might fall on a star. Keep God first.

CURRENT PHOTO

BACK IN THE DAY

# John August

(1974–1979, 1981–1986)

John August was "discovered" by none other than Jeffrey Daniel dancing at one of the popular clubs in Los Angeles and from there got on *Soul Train* and became a part of the Outrageous Waaack Dancers that performed overseas and is forever thankful to be a part of *Soul Train*'s history.

SM: How did you become a Soul Train dancer?

JA: I'm a native of Baton Rouge, Louisiana. Years later, when I moved to California, Jeffrey Daniel, Tyrone Proctor, and Jody Watley saw me at Maverick's Flat dancing. They asked me if I wanted to come on *Soul Train*, and they got my name on Pam Brown's list. The rest is history.

SM: What do you recall about your first day on *Soul Train*?

JA: I had such an amazing first day at *Soul Train*. I was a little scared, but I already knew Vicki Abercrombie, Tyrone Proctor, and Sharon Hill and Thelma Davis, who lived right down the hill from my first apartment.

SM: Did you enjoy your share of the fried chicken? [laughs]

JA: Yes, but I did quickly tire of the chicken. [laughs] Sometimes, we would go across the street to Denny's and eat, but it was all fun to me; I was just fourteen in my own apartment and working two jobs before

I started college.

SM: Did you ever do the Soul Train Scramble Board or Soul Train Line?

JA: I did many Soul Train Lines but never did the Scramble Board.

SM: Did you ever witness Don Cornelius losing his temper on set?

JA: I never saw him lose his temper although a few times I saw him holler at Tyrone for fooling around! [laughs]

SM: Were you ever recognized in public while you were dancing on the show?

JA: I was greatly recognized, and I did the clubs in Los Angeles with Jeffrey Daniel, Jody Watley, Tyrone Proctor, and Sharon Hill. I was also with the Outrageous Waack Dancers. I was also blessed to be chosen to perform on two *Jerry Lewis Telethons.*

SM: What have you been doing professionally in the years since you were a Soul Train dancer?

JA: I went to Southland Medical Legal School and have been working in the medical field as a medical transcriber.

SM: What would you like to say in memory of Don Cornelius?

JA: I am very thankful to be a part of history. Don was always a perfectionist, and I admired him and thought he was a genius.

SM: What word of wisdom do you want to share?

JA: Always follow your dreams. Never give up on your dreams. Ideas make millionaires every day.

NOTE: John sadly passed away in 2017. His friendship and positivity will never be forgotten.

# Queen Turner

(1974–1978)

> Queen Turner, as she is named, hails from a musical/dance background. The cousin of Ike Turner and a background singer/dancer for Isaac Hayes and others. When she became a part of the Soul Train Gang, she fit right in. Queen Turner shares her memories of *Soul Train* and her work with icons in the music industry.

**S**M: Your name bespeaks royalty. Where did the origin of your name come from in your family?

QT: My mother's father was Jewish, and my grandmother was Black. My grandfather's sister was named Queen, and it was passed down through generations.

SM: Beautiful! Where are you originally from?

QT: I am from North Carolina. but my family and I later moved to the Washington, DC/Baltimore area. When I was fourteen, I moved to Texas.

SM: You are also related to Ike Turner, correct?

QT: Yes. He was my cousin. I used to watch him, Tina, and the Ikettes rehearse many times at his home in Baldwin Hills, California.

SM: What was it like watching Ike, Tina, and the Ikettes rehearse?

CURRENT PHOTO

BACK IN THE DAY

QT: Everyone, from the Ikettes to the band, had to be on point. Whether he said, "hit it" or "quit it," you had to be right on cue.

SM: Ike's abuse of Tina is well known and documented. Did you ever witness him mistreat Tina?

QT: I didn't like the way he treated Tina when he was high and on drugs. But when he wasn't on drugs, he was a different person. He would give you the shirt off his back. Neither he nor his friends were to be messed with. He was good to people as long as he stayed off drugs.

SM: You were a background singer and dancer for a number of acts, chiefly Isaac Hayes a.k.a. Black Moses. How did that come about?

QT: I had an uncle, Vernon Burch, who was with the Bar Kays. He said that Isaac Hayes was looking for some dancers. Although I was fifteen, I was very mature for my age. So, Vernon told Isaac about me, I traveled to Memphis, and the rest is history. I also did backup dancing for Rufus Thomas, The Soul Children, Johnnie Taylor, and The Temprees.

SM: Tell me about meeting a very young Whitney Houston.

QT: I met her because her mom, Cissy Houston, was working with Isaac and Dionne at the time for their *Man & Woman* album and tour. Whitney was about eleven at the time. Cissy had to keep getting on her for misbehaving. She said, "Stop Nippy, stop!" [laughs]

SM: What was it like working with the Isaac Hayes Movement?

QT: Isaac ran a tight ship. He had sixty people in his entourage. He handled the band and the dancers with the utmost professionalism.

SM: Your work with Isaac somehow parlayed into becoming a Soul Train dancer, right?

QT: Yes. During this time, Isaac got the acting bug, so he gave everyone in his entourage their walking papers. He knew I loved dancing, and he knew Don Cornelius. So, he got in touch with him and told him about me, and I was invited to a taping. It was so surreal when I first stepped onto the set.

SM: How was it meeting Don Cornelius?

QT: I actually first met him at the Push Black Expo a year earlier when Isaac and others from the Stax organization had performed there. Don was very cordial.

SM: I know you have many favorite moments from being on the show but was there any special moment that stands out?

QT: I have one funny moment! When I first came to *Soul Train* as a background dancer with Isaac, my head had to be shaved. So, I wore a wig until my hair started growing back. One time, when we were doing the Soul Train Line, something happened. The director yelled cut, and the line had to be retaped about four times. By the fourth time, I was so hot and tired, I snatched my wig off when I came down the Soul Train Line. When this episode aired, that moment was kept in, unedited! [laughs]

SM: What are some of your favorite memories of recording artists that came to the show?

QT: Ike & Tina Turner's appearance was my favorite! Everyone was excited when they came to the show. I also established a good relationship with Michael Jackson when he came to the show. I was studying to be a Jehovah's Witness, and he was already one, so we spoke to one another. I also remember when Barry White, Love Unlimited, and his orchestra came to the show. It took so long for them to get set up. Glodean (Barry's wife at the time) and I became friends from that time on. Both of us had long nails. I also met Minnie Riperton on the set, and we became really good friends.

SM: Did you ever do the Scramble Board?

QT: Yes. My dance partner and I, Chris Benabeade, did the Scramble Board. I won this eight-track tape player. That was surreal at the time. I thought I had it going on!

SM: Did you have any other favorite dance partners?

QT: Besides Chris, my favorite partner was Eddie Franklin (Aretha Franklin's son). He was such a fun, cool, down-to-earth guy. Darnell Williams and Bobby Washington were my other favorites.

SM: Did Pam Brown, the coordinator of the dancers, ever come up to you with that big paper cup asking you to spit out chewing gum?

QT: I fell victim to her gum ritual all the time! She is such a sweet person. I remember that when she was pregnant, I threw her a baby shower.

SM: Did you ever deal with jealousy on the set?

QT: There were haters. A lot of my outfits were specially designed, so some of the girls would make comments or stare. Also, when Don and Dick Griffey were forming the Soul Train Gang recording group, one of the dancers spread an ugly rumor about me and told Don and Dick about it. They both made a big deal about it. They called me into a meeting and gave me the third degree, but I spoke up for myself and told them that the rumor wasn't true and that even if it was, it was my personal business. Because of this situation, I didn't become a part of the Soul Train Gang recording group.

SM: Because of your connections in the entertainment industry, you worked with *Soul Train* for a while in some capacity, correct?

QT: Yes. I did side work for artists that would come to *Soul Train.* If there was an event or party that was going on while they were in town, I would set things up so that they would be able to attend.

SM: What did you do professionally after leaving *Soul Train*?

QT: I became a part of a group called 24 Karat Gold. Natalie Cole's husband, Marvin Yancy, was the manager of the group. We did disco and R&B music. We worked in Canada and Europe. We were really big over there and our music is still being played there. Our music has even been uploaded on YouTube. I was also part of a group called Raw Silk, but it didn't fare very well.

SM: Where did your journey take you after leaving the entertainment industry?

QT: I decided to get out of the music business and became a mortician. I studied mortuary and forensic sciences at Cypress College in Cypress, California. I was a mortician for twenty years.

SM: What have you been doing in recent years?

QT: I am in the process of writing my autobiography entitled *Queen of the Crop*. I've also appeared on a reality show called *Welcome to Sweety Pie's*, which aired on the OWN Network.. I was also part of a show called *Divas Glam*, a spinoff of *Sweety Pie's*. In addition, I am married to my childhood friend, Joseph Gordon, of Maryland.

SM: What was your overall experience with *Soul Train*?

QT: I wouldn't trade it for anything. It was wonderful. I met a lot of good people. God has sent so many good people into my life. Thelma Davis, one of the dancers from the show, played a big part in my life with my kids. She is like a godmother to them.

SM: Sadly, a lot of dancers from the show who were also your friends had passed on. What would you like to say in their memory?

QT: It is so sad. At some of the last Soul Train Gang reunions, I read aloud all the names of the dancers who had died. One of my partners, Chris Benadeade, had so many big plans. Jermaine Stewart and I were good friends. I knew he was sick in later years, but I thought he had it under control. He wanted me to lay down some tracks for some recordings he had done before he died. I lost a lot of friends.

SM: Tell me about your last memory of seeing Don Cornelius.

QT: I had just seen Don and his son Tony at Glodean White's annual party. I saw him yearly at Glodean's parties. When I saw him at the party in 2010, he knew who I was, but when I saw him a year later it took a while for him to recognize me.

SM: What would you like to say in Don's memory?

QT: I am very sad about his death. He was a good, private man. He will be missed.

SM: Do you have a word of wisdom you want to share?

QT: Know who God is because without Him we are nothing.

BACK IN THE DAY

CURRENT PHOTO

# Michael Henderson

(1974–1976)

> An aspiring musician and singer, this young man got his groove on during his years at *Soul Train* before he embarked on a career in acting and music, working with a "who's who" of artists.

**S**M: What were your aspirations growing up?

MH: To be a musician, songwriter, and singing artist

SM: How did you get on *Soul Train*?

MH: Through fellow dancer Darnell Williams. He was a friend of the family.

SM: What were your impressions of the studio and set when you first were able to get inside?

MH: It was smaller than on TV, but still surreal to be there and very cool to be in this environment

SM: Did you ever speak to or interact with host Don Cornelius while you were a dancer?

MH: Not many times at all. Just a hello.

SM: Who were some of your favorite artists that you have seen perform on *Soul Train,* and do you have any special memories of these or other artists who were on the show?

MH: The Brothers Johnson and many others. The memories were all great as I got to be up close and personal with them.

SM: Were you ever caught chewing gum by dance coordinator Pam Brown when she passed around the cup during her "spit out your gum" ritual?

MH: A few times, but I wasn't much of a gum chewer; but I do remember being caught.

SM: Did you have your share of the fried chicken that the show fed the dancers?

MH: Yes! That was all we had, and I didn't have a car to drive anywhere else. I loved the smell and taste of KFC!

SM: Who among the dancers were you friends with?

MH: I had many, such as Vicki Beach, Susie Steiner, Benita Hill, and many more.

SM: Did you ever experience any problems like jealousy on set?

MH: None.

SM: Were you ever recognized in public from being on *Soul Train*, and if so, what was the recognition like?

MH: Yes. It was pretty cool in high school and at clubs throughout Los Angeles. I had lots of people outside of Los Angeles, like family and friends, that would call telling me how I looked and gave many compliments. It was cool to have that recognition.

SM: Did you ever do the Scramble Board? If so, did you receive your gifts?

MH: Yes, I did, but I don't remember getting the gifts. Perhaps the young lady I did the Scramble Board with at the time got them, but I don't recall getting them myself.

SM: How did you keep your Afro so together? You had a really nice fro!

MH: Thanks! I used to braid my hair every night myself. It wasn't easy to keep up!

SM: You were once featured in *Right On*! magazine. What was that experience like for you?

MH: Yes, it was the best! I got fan mail and really got more exposure from all around the country. It was the highlight of it all!

SM: You and fellow Soul Train dancer James Phillips did some acting together, right?

MH: Right. He and I flew to Arizona to work on the movie *Heretic,* which was the sequel to *The Exorcist.* We played Ethiopian kids. I got to sit around and listen to Richard Burton talk about his ex-wife, Elizabeth Taylor.

SM: What was it like for you going down the Soul Train Line?

MH: This was also one of the best highlights, awaiting to get that bigger spotlight. Many times, I didn't make it down as the line was too long. You had to run in order to be among the first ten couples in the line.

SM: Did the long tapings ever get to you?

MH: Yes, a few times when it lasted until midnight; but all in all, it was fine. I was in high school and didn't have much to do, so it was okay.

SM: Was it hard for you to eventually leave *Soul Train*?

MH: No, not at all. I stopped after graduating from high school. I was beginning to play music, so that was my focus.

SM: What are you doing currently professionally?

MH: I've been working in Telecom for more than twenty-nine years, along with being married for twenty-eight years with two sons, ages twenty-six and twenty-one. I've continued playing music as my side enjoyment. After I stopped dancing on *Soul Train*, I started doing extra work. Then I got an agent, and during those years, I booked six national commercials on camera as an actor with McDonald's, Coors Light with actress Ola Ray, Diet Coke with Whitney Houston, Panasonic, and Albertson.

SM: You're also a musician who played with many artists. Who were some of the artists you worked with as well as the experiences?

MH: As a side musician, I played bass guitar throughout Los Angeles. As I improved, I got the chance to work with many acts either as a bass player, songwriter, or background singer on records or demos. Some of the acts were Otis Day & The Knights, Billy Preston live in concert and on *Solid Gold*, and *NBC Features* playing bass. There was also Deniece Williams on *Soul Train*, the *Do The Right Thing* soundtrack, Al Jarreau's song, "Never Explain Love," and on a Cheryl Lynn album. I also had songs I wrote for the R&B group Klique, Syreeta Wright, and a movie starring Corey Feldman called *Round Trip to Heaven*. I produced a single on Roger Mosley from *Magnum PI*. I also sang in small choirs featured on stage with Bill Cosby at the Hollywood Bowl and Hiroshima at the Greek, and I also sang on a Diane Reeves album.

SM: What would you like to say in memory of Don Cornelius?

MH: I am very thankful for his great vision and execution in creating such a great vehicle for us young Black people at that time. We all owe him a debt of gratitude!

SM: What word of wisdom do you want to share?

MH: Something I live by as a professional and that I always keep in mind during our evolving and challenging lives: look back and be thankful, look ahead and be hopeful, and look around and be helpful.

# Epilogue

As I stated near the beginning of this book, the early dancers laid the foundation and roots of what followed in the years to come, not just on *Soul Train* but on the dance culture as a whole that includes the hip-hop dance revolution. The early dancers' stories and histories, like all the dancers in subsequent decades, are truly important to chronicle. Many of these dancers, known and unknown, have passed on without anyone knowing their stories. If it weren't for the dancers, *Soul Train* would not have been as big as it was.

While the artists that appeared on the show were very important, it was the dancers that truly made *Soul Train* the huge iconic program it was. Their popularity in the early days and the years that followed was unprecedented. That is why the early dancers were heavily featured in *Right On!* magazine and other periodicals, as well as being featured in movies. It is also why legendary recording artists and performers wanted to work with them.

Indeed, it was first and foremost the early dancers such as Jan Hunter, Rodney Moss, Patricia Davis, Damita Jo Freeman, Little Joe Chism, Jimmy "Scoo B Doo" Foster, Tyrone Proctor, Sharon Hill, Thelma Davis, James Phillips, Fawn Quinones, Freddie Maxie, The Lockers, and many others who initially contributed a great deal to *Soul Train*'s overall entertainment value.

Look out for *Get On Board Volume 2,* which will spotlight the dancers of the latter seventies, eighties, nineties, and the millennium.

I truly hope you enjoyed the ride with the Soul Train Gang. Until the next journey, in the immortal words of Don Cornelius, I wish you love, peace, and *Sooooul*—and a box of chicken!

www.ingramcontent.com/pod-product-compliance
Lightning Source LLC
LaVergne TN
LVHW020655110826
845149LV00012B/2010

* 9 7 8 1 9 6 9 9 3 5 1 3 8 *